HOW *to* CHEAT
at GARDENING
and
YARD WORK

HOW *to* CHEAT *at* GARDENING *and* YARD WORK

Shameless Tricks for Growing Radically Simple Flowers, Veggies, Lawns, Landscaping, and More

JEFF BREDENBERG

RODALE

© 2009 by Jeff Bredenberg

Rodale books may be purchased for business or promotional use or for special sales. For information, please write to: Special Markets Department, Rodale Inc., 733 Third Avenue, New York, NY 10017

Printed in the United States of America
Rodale Inc. makes every effort to use acid-free ♾, recycled paper ♻.

Book design by Joanna Williams
Illustrations by Michael Gellatly

Library of Congress Cataloging-in-Publication Data

Bredenberg, Jeff.
    How to cheat at gardening and yard work : shameless tricks for growing radically simple flowers, veggies, lawns, landscaping, and more / Jeff Bredenberg.
        p.   cm.
    Includes index.
    ISBN-13 978–1–59486–966–2 hardcover
    ISBN-10 1–59486–966–9 hardcover
    ISBN-13 978–1–59486–959–4 paperback
    ISBN-10 1–59486–959–6 paperback
    1. Gardening.   I. Title.
SB453.B72   2009
635—dc22
                                                                        2008054250

Distributed to the trade by Macmillan
2   4   6   8   10   9   7   5   3   1   hardcover
2   4   6   8   10   9   7   5   3   1   paperback

LIVE YOUR WHOLE LIFE™

We inspire and enable people to improve their lives and the world around them
For more of our products visit **rodalestore.com** or call 800-848-4735

To Stacey Burling
For all the beauty you bring to my world

CONTENTS

ACKNOWLEDGMENTS

The author wishes to thank the following sources for their generous contributions of information for this book:

Edward Adams, horticulturist, Wyndmoor, Pennsylvania

Barbara Arnold, horticultural designer for the Franklin Park Conservatory in Columbus, Ohio

Mel Bartholomew, author of *All New Square Foot Gardening*

Stephanie Bledsoe, technical and training director for Massey Services, an environmentally responsible pest control company in Florida

Doug Boyd, landscape contractor, Greenville, North Carolina

Stewart Clark, a pest control expert who does research and development in St. Louis

Jodie Colón, compost educator for the New York Botanical Garden and the Bronx Green-Up program

Kathleen Cook, landscape designer for the Fort Worth (Texas) Botanical Garden

Nick Covatta, co-owner and general manager of Eastern Shore Nursery in Keller, Virginia

Ellen Covner, landscaper and owner of Custom Gardens in Wynnewood, Pennsylvania

Clea Danaan, author of *Sacred Land: Intuitive Gardening for Personal, Political, and Environmental Change*

Stephanie DeStefano, grounds operations coordinator, American University in Washington, DC

Marvin Duren, owner of Marvin's Organic Gardens in Lebanon, Ohio

Jon Feldman, landscape designer and founder of G. biloba Gardens in Nyack, New York

Tom Flowers, president of Sanctum Design Group in Atlanta and instructor at the Atlanta Botanical Garden

Pam Geisel, based in Davis, California, coordinator of California's Master Gardener Program

Susan Gottlieb, gallery owner, gardener, and conservationist, in Beverly Hills, California

Bill Graham, Master Arborist, of Graham Tree Consulting in Doylestown, Pennsylvania

Katharine Hall, publicist and garden blogger based in Ukiah, California

Robert Hammond, chef and owner of Honeyman Creek Farms in Oregon

Lori Hayes, manager of the Horticultural Center in Philadelphia's Fairmount Park

Leslie Hoffman, executive director of Earth Pledge, a nonprofit environmental advocacy organization in New York City

Sam Jeffries, horticulturist and cohost of radio's "The Garden Guys"

Daron "Farmer D" Joffee, manager of Harvest Lake Farm in Georgia

Dr. Alan Kapuler, Seeds of Change in New Mexico

Heather Kibble, home garden expert for a major seed company in Southern California

Rebecca Kolls, Master Gardener, author, and contributor to TV's *Good Morning America*

John Marshall, a garden products expert in Marysville, Ohio

Michael Mastrota, landscape architect, American University in Washington, DC

John Mollick, lawn care expert for Vigoro

Dr. Kenneth Mulder, director of the campus farm at Green Mountain College in Poultney, Vermont

Charlie Nardozzi, spokesman for the National Gardening Association, based in Burlington, Vermont

Annette Pelliccio, founder of the Happy Gardener, an organic gardening company in Virginia

Trey Rogers, turfgrass professor at Michigan State University, and author of *Lawn Geek*

Felder Rushing, horticulturist, turfgrass expert, and radio show host in Jackson, Mississippi

Peter Sawchuk, home editor for *Consumer Reports* magazine

Emily Shelton, horticulturist at the Chicago Botanic Garden

Sharon Slack, head gardener for City Farmer in Vancouver

Annie Spiegelman, San Francisco-based author and garden columnist for *Organic Style* magazine

Lance Walheim, botanist, researcher, and widely published author based in California

Lin Wellford, artist/author of *Painted Garden Art Anyone Can Do,* Green Forest, Arkansas

The author also is grateful for the contributions of editors Karen Bolesta and Anne Halpin, the designers Joanna Williams and Christina Gaugler, and the rest of the staff at Rodale Inc., as well as agent Linda Konner.

One Incredible Tip, Alone Worth the Price of This Book

"The more we garden, the better we get at knowing what nature wants us to do."
—Garden columnist Charles Fenyvesi, in his book *Trees*

Within the first couple of pages here I am going to give you the full text of a tip that is so ingenious, so laborsaving, so cool, that for many people it's easily worth the price of this book. How can I afford to do that? Gardeners are a caring, thoughtful bunch always ready to lend support, offer a helping hand, and pass along wisdom.

But first, here's a little background. I was talking on the phone the other day with Sam Jeffries, a horticulturist and radio personality. We were about to hang up when Sam dropped a bombshell—one last gardening shortcut. (Yes, this one almost got away from me!)

Consider this scenario: A nursery truck has delivered to your front yard a young tree—a few hundred pounds of wood with burlap-wrapped rootball. You and your garden helpers have dug a planting hole in a carefully selected spot. Together, you wrestle that rootball into the hole. But here comes the quandary. You need to "face" the tree. That is, turn it until its best side is facing forward. This involves a combination of landscape design considerations, including an assessment of branch structure, open spaces, home architecture, surrounding vegetation, and sun exposure. You and your helpers again will have to awkwardly lift hundreds of pounds of wood and dirt, turning the trunk slowly until another person, directing the show, decides that the tree is facing the correct way. (And cover your ears if the director can't make up his or her mind.) Along the way, someone probably will snap off a branch or two in an effort to get a grip on the tree and turn it.

So here's Sam's solution: Before you drop the tree into its planting hole, get your garden hose and fill the hole two-thirds of the way with water. A combination of buoyancy of the rootball and lubrication from the mud will make the tree easy to spin around in its planting hole, so you can quickly "face" the tree any way you wish. Also note that this technique gives the tree a nice start in its new home with a healthy drink of water.

Wow! I felt like I had just picked a gold coin up off the sidewalk. That tidbit has all of the elements of a superb tip—it's easily understood, it speaks to real people living their daily lives, there are no exotic materials involved, and there are no prissy rules to follow.

I hope you have a similar "Wow!" experience hundreds of times as you read this book. I have picked the brains of a horde of gardening and yard maintenance experts, identifying the clever little things they do when working in their own gardens and yards to save time, effort, money, and aggravation. I also asked them about their favorite tools and products and how they use them. (Speaking of products, I should say that it's impossible to give specific advice without occasionally mentioning a brand name. When I mention a brand in this book, it's because I believe in the product—I don't accept any freebies from manufacturers.) And the products recommended in this book are organic, in keeping with Rodale tradition.

So pull on your garden gloves, slap on a broad-brimmed hat, and dive into *How to Cheat at Gardening and Yard Work*. It's jam-packed with ingenious shortcuts, tips, and tricks that are so sneaky that you'll feel like you're cheating. At How to Cheat books, by the way, we use the word *cheat* in a benign sense. There's nothing halfway, slipshod, or disreputable about the advice you will find here. And let me add that if any advice you encounter here makes you uneasy, fret not—I don't want to be your guilty conscience. Just putter along to the next tip without another thought.

Now here's your invitation to join the How to Cheat movement. (Rallying cry: "Simplicity—with *Attitude*.") I'm sure that you have your own collection of clever tips and tricks, too. Feel free to share them by contacting me at www.howtocheatbooks.com or www.jeffbredenberg.com. Maybe I'll name you as a source in a future How to Cheat book!

CHAPTER 1

The
CHEATING FRAME
of MIND

|||||||||||||||||||||||||||||||||||||||||||||||||||||||||||||||||||||||||||||||||||||

Home gardening is the very definition of *complexity*. It boggles the mind when you sit down to calculate the possible combinations of plants, soil conditions, tools, personal tastes, geography, temperature, precipitation, and pests. It's enough to throw a gardener off his or her gourd. Well, How to Cheat enthusiasts carry a banner that reads, "Simplicity—with *Attitude.*" So for all of you who dare to take up hand pruners and step out the back door, your mind swimming with a zillion possibilities, here's a set of simplifying principles, gleaned from the host of experts I have encountered in my research. These observations will help you clarify, reduce, and focus as you garden. These ideas will put you in the right frame of mind to take serious shortcuts, to ignore the things that aren't important, and to set your own priorities—which is to say: to cheat.

Other low-maintenance strategies, which you'll come across in later chapters, are: Grow low-maintenance plants, be frugal, re-use and recycle, and ignore the conventional rules.

1. Gardening Has No End Point

Your garden is an ongoing, perpetually unfinished masterpiece. When you make mistakes, there's always a new season around the corner in which you can apply the lessons learned. This way, your garden gets better and better. Also, there's never a time when you smack the dirt off of your hands and proclaim, "Finally, my garden is done!"

2. It All Starts with the Earth

In just about every gardening pursuit, your success or failure hinges mightily on the quality of the soil that you are working with. This is called the POTS principle (Priority One: The Soil), so named because your author is addicted to shameless acronyms, as you will see.

3. Mother Nature Is More Powerful Than You

As indicated in the quote on page x from the lyrical garden writer Charles Fenyvesi, nature is calling the shots in your garden. You would be well advised to employ the SAIL approach (Stand Aside, Interfere Little) when working with nature. Don't fight natural forces. Instead, use them to accomplish your goals.

4. Feel Free to Make Mistakes—and Learn

Get the best advice you can, try something, and learn from your mistakes. Gardening, like cooking, is not an exact science. Nevertheless, in the kitchen you're accustomed to precise ingredient lists and instructions for your recipes. But gardening is a hundred times more complex than that, with zillions of variables that will affect the success or failure of your garden. Such factors include climate, soil conditions, the materials you buy, the health of your plants, your maintenance habits, and even traditions ("Grandma always did it this way.")

5. Take a Risk and Make Gardening Fun

You got into gardening to express yourself, to learn new things, and to be amazed at what will grow and blossom. So by all means, make your outdoor passion fun. In the hundreds of decisions you will make every day, take some risks, experiment, try a little whimsy, go a little crazy, and do the unexpected.

6. Use Your Garden as a Place of Therapy

Think of your garden as a therapeutic place, not a place of work. In the morning, take the newspaper out to your garden with an espresso. Sip, read, and contemplate. Stop and breathe deeply (and, yes, smell the roses). Later, after a stressful day of work, go out to the garden and pull some weeds—it can be a

Mel's 5 Mind-Blowing Truths about Gardening

Mel Bartholomew is the gardening author who pioneered the revolutionary concept of square foot gardening, a technique recently updated in his new book *All New Square Foot Gardening*. Appalled at the time-wasting, effort-wasting, money-wasting practices he witnessed among home gardeners, Bartholomew applied his engineering skills to devise a simpler, easier way. This makes him a hero to cheat-at-gardening enthusiasts. You will find out more about Square Foot Gardening in Chapter 6, but for now ponder these five truths about gardening that Bartholomew shared with me.

1. **Gardening is not complicated, it is not difficult, and it is not hard work.** You don't need any special expertise. If you manage your garden well, nature does all of the work. All you have to do is provide the proper conditions: the ideal soil (loose, crumbly, and both quick-draining and moisture-holding), correct spacing of plants, and freedom from weeds.

2. **Less is more.** Simplify, simplify, simplify. Also: Reduce, reduce, reduce. Enthusiastic gardeners are prone to making their gardens too big and too complicated—particularly in spring. As summer weeks wear on, row after row of garden plants plead for attention, weeds are having a field day, and watering becomes a dreadful chore. So the discouraged gardeners start neglecting their gardens. Your garden actually requires a small fraction of the space you think it does. If you learn to control the size of your garden, you will be able to maintain it in small spurts of activity and you will have fewer gardening chores all around.

3. **You don't have to plant the entire seed packet at once.** There can be hundreds of seeds in

calming and meditative experience. Breathe deeply and feel the sun on your face. Listen to the songs of birds. Sure, go ahead and talk to your plants. They won't answer—which is therapeutic in a reaffirming way, because you're always right. When you do talk to your plants, your neighbors will stay far away from you, too. Let the garden become a place of comfort and renewal, and you'll look forward to being there as often as possible.

a seed packet. If you tap them all out as you stroll down a garden row, you're going to have to thin out a zillion teensy plants when they start popping up all jammed together. Kind soul that you are, you won't be able to bring yourself to destroy all of the plants that you should. Therefore, your plants will grow up overcrowded, less healthy, and less productive. And you will have worked harder than you would have if you had kept your planting under control.

4. **No, you don't have to turn or till your garden soil every spring.** In Square Foot Gardening, there is no digging. Push your rototiller out to the curb and leave it there. Park your shovel in the back corner of your shed with the other rarely used items.

5. **For a better vegetable garden, add some flowers.** Why is it a good idea to intersperse flowers with your vegetables? Smarty-pants that you are, your mind has probably turned to the concept of "companion gardening," the idea that when certain plants are paired in the garden, they naturally protect each other from pests and disease. That's true, but here's the real reason to plant flowers among your vegetables, says Bartholomew: They're pretty. When you have stopped snickering, consider this: When your garden is pretty, you will go out to it more often to tend it and admire it. When you're more interested in your own garden, you will start getting better feedback from other people who see it. Thus inspired, you will take even better care of your garden, and it will grow better and provide better vegetables and flowers. As if those weren't enough reasons, consider this as well: When you're out there picking salad for lunch, you also get to pick a few flowers for the table.

7. Know Where You Are Going

Having a plan for your landscape lowers the amount of gardening and yard work that you will have to do. This is what's called the HAPS principle (Have A Plan, Stan—known among less polite gardeners as Have a Plan, Stupid).

8. Work Hard to Make Gardening Easy

Here's a sad reality about human nature: The more steps you add to a task, and the more barriers you throw in the way of accomplishing that task, the less likely it is to be accomplished. So consider your gardening practices, your seasonal expectations, and your composting process, for example: Are there any steps that you can eliminate? How about watering? Or mowing? Or leaf raking? Also, review your tool storage, keeping in mind the Accessibility Theorem: "A task will be accomplished on a frequency that is inversely proportional to the distance between the site of the task and the location of materials necessary to perform it." That is, if it's a hassle to get to your tools and other gear, less work gets done.

9. Know When to Call In a Pro

Professionals in the gardening and landscaping business all have sad tales to tell about customers who didn't know when to stop and pick up the telephone. Hundreds of dollars too late, they're weeping into the phone, pleading for help. So keep the HIRE criteria in mind for any project in your garden or landscape: When a task is Hard, Important, Rarely done, and Elaborate, then pick up the phone and HIRE a professional. Gardeners, landscapers, and designers have the training and the equipment to do such jobs properly, safely, and economically.

On the other hand, if the task is a Super-Easy Lightweight Fix (SELF), the job goes to you-know-whom.

10. Award Yourself Two Points for Shortcuts

It's human nature to respond to incentives. So as you go about your gardening duties—pruning, planting, turning the compost, picking bugs off of your flowers—picture a scoreboard in your head. Every time that you cheat—that is, use a sneaky shortcut or save yourself some unexpected time or aggravation—award yourself two points. In this case, TWO stands for Thinking Wins Out.

CHAPTER 2

Soil:
A HEALTHY GARDEN, *from the* GROUND UP

||||||||||||||||||||||||||||||||||||||||||||||||||||||||||||||||||||||||||||||

S oil is the brown stuff embedded in the knees of a youngster's blue jeans. Soil is the rooster-tail splatter on your car's fender. Soil is the grime you wipe off of your sneakers before entering the house, and it's the gray stuff that swirls down the drain when you wash up after yard work.

Oh, yeah—soil also is what you plant your tomatoes and green beans in.

But the truth is that for the most part, we don't hold soil in very high regard. That's probably why many gardeners neglect or abuse their soil—treat it like dirt, so to speak. That's too bad, because the key to successful gardening does not lie in clever trellises, ingenious hand tools, intricate watering systems, and floppy sun hats. The sneakiest, corner-cutting-est, cheating-est, sure-fire way to produce a spectacular garden is to do this: Get the soil right. If you have healthy, well-conditioned soil in your garden, every other thing you do for your garden becomes efficient and easy, says Daron "Farmer D" Joffee, manager of Georgia's Harvest Lake Farm.

Plants that grow in healthy soil are more vigorous and have fewer pest and disease problems than plants in poor soil. That means you'll have to spend less time doctoring sick plants.

How exactly do you go about achieving healthy garden soil? Well, this chapter is packed with simple, anyone-can-do-it tips from experts. But the very best way to get started doesn't require you to even lift a finger—just adjust your perception of what soil is. Creating good garden soil is not like baking a cake—tossing ingredients into a mixing bowl. To garden successfully, think of your soil instead as a living organism, says Clea Danaan, author of *Sacred Land: Intuitive Gardening for Personal, Political, and Environmental Change*. "Soil is really dynamic," she says. Soil isn't particularly demanding, either. All you have to do is supply this living organism with some simple needs: nutrients, organic matter, moisture, air, and a bit of shelter to protect it from the elements.

DIRT: THE INSIDE STORY

Let's take a deeper (ha-ha!) look at what soil is exactly, and how you can supply the needs of this living entity that's supporting garden plants in your yard.

Soil is not just one thing—it's a mixture. There are minerals in soil, inorganic stuff that comes from crumbled rocks. There's organic material, too—stuff that was once alive, such as rotted leaves and wood. And good soil is brimming with living creatures, too, including bacteria, other microscopic critters, earthworms, and bugs. Soil texture often is assessed according to the balance of sand, clay, and silt particles it contains. "Loam" soil is considered to be an ideal balance of the three, while additions of organic matter to your soil may be recommended if you're too heavy on sand or clay. To be honest, organic matter is a great addition to any garden soil, even perfectly balanced ones. The best thing you can do for your garden is to add organic materials to the soil. See Chapter 7 for the dirt on how to make your own compost and read on for more details on handling your soil.

Soil plays a number of roles in respect to your garden. It provides structural support, of course—supplying the base that plants sink their roots into, and allowing stems to grow upright. It provides sustenance, too—the nutrients and water that your plants depend on. It also houses the microorganisms that provide vital support services to the plants growing in their midst. So it's important to understand what kind of soil you're dealing with in your garden. One place to start is to look at the weeds that grow there—some of them can give you clues to your soil type and quality. But to get a better fix, a soil test is an invaluable guide.

Now, I know that testing your garden soil is not at the top of your list of fun backyard activities. It sounds finicky, it sounds like overkill, and worst of all it sounds like extra work. So right away, let me tell you some things that you'll be glad to hear. In some circumstances, you might be able to squeak by without testing your garden soil—particularly if your garden is lush, green, and happy already. On the other hand, testing your soil is actually a very small amount of work, it's easy to do, it's relatively inexpensive, and it requires no special skill or knowledge.

But why should you bother? A soil test will alert you to any severe deficiencies in your soil—the kind of shortcomings that will make your gardening life miserable during the growing season. Along with the test results, you will get specific instructions on what to add to your soil in order to correct any problems, and these additives will be readily available at your local garden supply store or nursery.

If you're just starting up a garden, testing the soil is a great first step before you get immersed in the details of planting and growing. (Some weeds that indicate soil of generally poor quality include broom sedge, dog fennel, red sorrel, sheep sorrel, and yellow toadflax, so if you spot them you'll know you've probably got some soil building to do.) However, if the stretch of land that you want to garden on has had a good sod covering for several years, it's probably pretty rich dirt that's already suitable for gardening, says Dr. Kenneth Mulder, director of the campus farm at Green Mountain College in Poultney, Vermont. As you continue gardening, routinely adding organic matter to your beds (compost in particular) will naturally keep the soil nutrients in balance. Over the years, if mysterious problems emerge in your garden (perhaps your garden plants were once a vibrant green, but now they're yellowed, stunted, and droopy-looking), that would be a good time to test the soil. The solution may be as simple as boosting a depleted nutrient.

For soil conditions, read your weeds before you test. Want a quick indicator of whether your soil is clay or sandy, wet or dry? Just take a look at the weeds that are attracted to it. Similarly, happy weed populations may indicate other flaws in your soil. See the Cheat Sheet on the opposite page for some ways to "read your weeds."

Here's how to test. One of the best ways to get started with testing your soil is to call or visit your local Cooperative Extension office. (Conduct an Internet search using the term "Cooperative Extension," plus your state.) Many Cooperative Extension offices will give you—perhaps even mail to you—a soil testing kit and tell you where to send your soil sample for lab analysis. You'll be instructed to dig up several shovelfuls of dirt from different parts of your garden bed and then to mix the samples thoroughly in a bucket. Dig 6 to 8 inches deep to get your soil sample (but if you hit hardpan, don't continue digging). Put the soil sample in the container provided for mailing. Then fill out a form about your garden, write out a modest check, and pop it all into the mail.

Keep your test dirt clean. Pull on some garden gloves or rubber gloves when you collect soil samples to submit for testing and don't handle the samples with your bare hands. You might not look at it this way, but you can contaminate the soil. Yes, oils from your skin can alter the test results!

Check for soil variation. If you see a marked difference in the color and texture of your soil from one part of the yard to another, consider doing sepa-

Cheat Sheet

Weeds Give Clues about Soil

The weeds growing in your soil offer clues to your soil's texture and quality. Here are some weeds to look for.

HEAVY CLAY OR COMPACTED SOIL

Buttercup, creeping	Plantain	Thistle, Canada
Dock, broad-leaved	Thistle, annual sow	

WATERLOGGED OR POORLY DRAINED SOIL

Coltsfoot	Joe-pye weed	Mosses
Dock, curly (and others)	Knotweed, spotted	Sedges
Goldenrod, Canada	(Lady's thumb)	Sorrel, sheep
Horsetail	Mayapple	

HUMUS-RICH, WELL-DRAINED SOIL

Burdock	Dandelion	Purslane
Chickweed	Lamb's quarters	
Chicory	Pigweed	

SANDY, LIGHT SOIL

Campion, white	Lettuce, arrow-leaved	Thistle, Maltese
Cornflower, wild	wild	Toadflax, yellow
	Sorrel, sheep	

ACID SOIL

Cresses	Hawkweed	Sorrels
Daisy, ox-eye	Knotweed, prostrate	Strawberry, wild
Dandelion	Mosses	Thistle, annual sow
Docks	Plantain	

ALKALINE SOIL

Chamomile	Goosefoot	Spurge, spotted
Chickweed	Mustards	Thistles

rate tests for each part of the yard. The different areas may need to be treated separately.

Respond to the data. When you get the results of your soil test, simply follow the directions for what to add to your garden. Depending on where you live, you may be given organic recommendations—for instance, use of certified organic fertilizer rather than chemical fertilizer. Organic fertilizer will break down more slowly and in the long run will feed your soil better. To buy the organic materials you need, just take your soil test results to a feed store or garden supply store. To supplement your soil, you will need to do some simple math—for instance, to figure out how many pounds of fertilizer to add per square foot of garden (if you have trouble with such numbers, consult a 10-year-old). Even better, skip the math and just follow the directions on the fertilizer bag. Blended organic fertilizers come with application guidelines that'll make your job easy.

Soil test results will typically tell you whether your garden is deficient in the elements nitrogen (N), phosphorus (P), or potassium (K). Nitrogen aids stem and leaf growth, phosphorus helps roots grow and aids in ripening seeds and fruit, and potassium is needed for growth and health as well. Many soil tests (including those performed by USDA Cooperative Extension offices) also indicate the levels of minor nutrients, such as calcium, iron, and magnesium that plants need in smaller amounts. Directions that come with your lab test results will tell you how much of what kind of fertilizer to add to your garden. The truth is, a fertilizer that's balanced among all three elements will probably do nicely, and all you need to do is follow the package directions for how much to add for your size of garden bed. Many organic fertilizers supply important minor nutrients along with the big three—nitrogen, phosphorus, and potassium—so you don't have to worry about deficiencies when you garden organically.

There's one more ingredient of the soil-testing alphabet soup, and that's pH, which is a measure of your soil's acidity or alkalinity. Out of all of your soil test results, getting your soil to the recommended pH level is probably most important, says farm director Dr. Mulder. Soil ranges from a rating of 4.0 (heavily acidic) up to 9.0 (intensely alkaline). The ideal pH for a garden is said to be between 6.0 and 6.5, which is slightly acidic. The pH of your soil is a handy thing to know, because some plants are finicky about the amount of acidity or alkalinity in their soil. Your soil's pH can vary, depending upon where you live. In the United States, for instance, western states tend to have more alkaline soil while eastern states have more acid soil. If you have acid soil, adding ground limestone will raise the pH level (follow the package directions). If you have alkaline soil, adding compost, pine needles, peat moss, oak leaves, sawdust, sulfur, or aluminum sulfate will lower the pH level.

But to save yourself needless time and effort, just know that it's a losing battle to try to change pH by more than a point or so. You can affect a modest change, but don't count on changing it a lot.

Test it yourself. If you would rather not bother with mailing off your soil samples for testing, pick up a do-it-yourself testing kit at your hardware store or garden center. Such kits are reliable and will provide you with the information you need to put your soil into proper balance, says author Danaan. Just follow the directions—it's a little like playing with a kid's chemistry set. Danaan doesn't test her own soil very often, by the way. She knows that her Colorado dirt naturally tends toward alkaline, so she compensates for that.

Consider contaminants. If you have reason to believe that your soil might be contaminated with heavy metals (lead, for instance), spend a little extra on your soil test to screen for that. For example, perhaps your garden plot is near an old house or other building, and it's possible that old lead-based paint flecked off onto the ground. Illegal dumping in the past, a site that

TO CHECK PH, LISTEN TO YOUR DIRT

If you think your soil might be too alkaline, here's a sneaky way to find out for sure: Scoop two or three spoonfuls of dry garden soil into a screw-top glass jar. Then pour in a similar amount of distilled white vinegar (which you'll find in any grocery store), enough to moisten all of the soil. Screw on the lid and shake the jar, then hold the open top to your ear. If you hear a fizzing sound, your soil is very alkaline.

Check Those Fertilizer Labels

Many backyard gardeners have one foot in the burgeoning organic world and another foot still in the past, using nonorganic chemical gardening products. One of the easiest ways to take another step toward organic gardening is to replace your chemical-based fertilizer with a certified organic fertilizer, says Annette Pelliccio, founder of the Happy Gardener, an organic gardening company in Virginia.

It used to be complicated to fertilize organically. Gardeners had to put in individual sources of nutrients—manure or cottonseed meal for nitrogen (N), rock phosphate for phosphorus (P), granite dust or greensand for potassium (K)—but these days there are easy-to-use blended organic fertilizers that contain a balance of the nutrients plants need.

To make sure you're getting an organic fertilizer, simply read the product labels at your garden supply store. But pay attention: Some manufacturers may call their products "organic" because they include some natural, or naturally derived, ingredients—but that doesn't mean that they're truly organic.

Look for products that state they are certified organic by an organization such as the Organic Materials Review Institute (OMRI). Look at the NPK ratings, too. Fertilizers with high NPK numbers (14-14-14, for instance) are probably not organic. A fertilizer with a lower rating, such as 5-3-7, is more likely to be a true organic product.

was once a landfill, or a nearby gas station are other conceivable sources of contamination.

Check your soil's depth. How deep is the rich, loose soil in your garden? This factor could have a big influence on the happiness of the plants you try to grow, says Robert Hammond, chef and owner of Oregon's Honeyman Creek Farms. To check the depth of your topsoil, grab a shovel and dig down into your garden bed until you reach dense, compacted subsoil or even hardpan—a level of tough dirt that's nearly impossible to penetrate without a pickax. Most garden vegetables do best when the loose soil is a foot deep, Hammond says.

If you hit hardpan after digging just a few inches, start out with shallow-rooted vegetables like leaf lettuce or radishes. Then read up on the crops you want to plant to find out what root depth they prefer, and work on building up the soil to meet those requirements.

The best way to build up rich, loose soil, Hammond says (and legions of gardeners agree), is to add compost. Visit your community's distribution center for free compost, use compost from your own backyard operation (see Chapter 7 for info on how to do this), or go to your garden supply store and buy large bags of composted manure, mushroom compost, or leaf compost. (One caution: That manure will add a substantial dose of nitrogen, so if you use it, back off on the nitrogen in your fertilizer so your plants don't overdose.)

How thirsty is your soil? As long as you're using your shovel to check on the health of your garden, add this test to your repertoire of simple diagnostics: Dig down 6 inches into your garden and feel the soil, says Rebecca Kolls, Master Gardener, author, and contributor to TV's *Good Morning America*. If the soil is dry, that's not good. Dry soil even 2 to 3 inches down can be a problem, depending on the root depth of your plants. Dry soil this deep means you are under-watering. Increase the amount or the frequency that you water, then check again in a couple of days.

If your soil drains quickly and is often dry, add compost or other organic matter—don't just water more. Compost acts like a sponge that helps soil hold moisture longer.

Address clay with compost. Having soil that's heavily clay and poorly drained is not the end of the world, says Robert Hammond—in fact, clay provides many of the minerals that your garden plants need. It also holds moisture longer than lighter, sandy soils. You can improve its texture, however, by adding lots of organic material, which will loosen up the soil and make your plants happier. Hammond has clay soil and gets lots of rain, which means that his soil can easily get compacted. The easiest way to cure this problem, he says, is building up the soil in raised beds. (Find out more about that in Chapter 6.)

Improve clay conditions with jiffy gypsum. You can also improve the drainage of heavy clay with gypsum (calcium sulfate) instead of lime, which is another time-honored remedy for clay soil. For fastest results, use pelleted gypsum, which dissolves to a fine powder as soon as it gets wet. Reach for your fertilizer spreader to apply it in record speed—use 20 to 30 pounds per 1,000 square feet of garden. You'll find pelleted gypsum at garden centers and hardware stores.

GOING BEYOND THE BASIC DIRT

Okay, now you're committed to treating your garden soil like a living being. Let's look at some other smart ways to work with soil and get the most out of it.

Convert lawn to garden bed—without digging! Now and then you're going to cast your eyes over your expanse of green lawn and decide to convert several square yards of it into a garden bed. This presents you (or possibly your spouse) with the ugly prospect of an afternoon spent spading up chunks of sod, since you don't want feisty little grass plants having their way with your new garden bed. Which means you will want to know the low-effort, zero-digging *How to Cheat at Gardening and Yard Work* way of converting lawn into a garden bed.

Start the season before you hope to plant—either in spring or even as late as fall for planting the following spring. Go to that mountain of newspapers in your recycling bin. Spread newspaper, at least a dozen sheets thick, over the grass that's occupying your garden-to-be. Then weigh the newspapers down with up to a foot of organic matter—compost, shredded leaves (wet them down so they don't blow away), organic mulch (see below), and such. Now leave your future garden bed alone until the following spring, when it will be ready for planting. The underlying sod will have died back, returning the nutrients from the grass to the soil. The top layer of organic matter also will have compacted. Just poke through the layer with a trowel to do your planting.

Marvin Duren, owner of Marvin's Organic Gardens in Lebanon, Ohio, has a variation on this technique that dispenses with the newspaper. He says just spread a 6-inch layer of compost over the sod that you're converting into garden bed. On top of that, spread 2½ inches of your favorite mulch (many gardeners use shredded bark or pine needles). If you don't have a full 6 inches of compost to devote to the bed, an inch may not kill the sod, but it "will make a world of difference," Duren says.

Coddle your soil with mulch. Mulching is a crucial gardening process, but it's by no means mysterious or difficult. Organic mulches include the stuff you buy in enormous bags from your garden supply store or in bulk from your local nursery and have delivered, such as shredded bark, composted manure, and peat moss. Other organic mulches include hay, shredded newspaper, and lawn clippings. Nonorganic mulches include plastic, fabric, and pebbles. Either way, the function of the mulch is to keep moisture in the soil below it, to prevent weeds from sprouting, to prevent erosion, and to protect plants from temperature fluctuations.

Make sure your new plantings start out life with generous applications of mulch in spring and then add to the mulch layer if it thins out during the growing season. How much organic mulch to use is a judgment call on your part. Generally, small plants do fine with an inch or two (but add more as plants grow—weeds will come up through a scant 1-inch layer of mulch), and larger plants are happy with several inches. Leave some clearance around the stems of your plants—direct contact with mulch could encourage disease.

Poke holes through the covering. At planting time in spring, says Danaan, there's no need to rake your compost-and-mulch covering aside or till it into the soil. Just dig small holes through it and put your seeds or transplants into the soil.

Slip compost under your mulch. In keeping with leave-no-bare-soil advice, author Clea Danaan has a simple fall routine that protects and enhances her garden soil. When she harvests her vegetables and herbs in fall, she snips up all stems and other plant waste right there on the garden bed. Then she covers the bed with hay, and leaves raked up from the lawn. Between fall and spring, she also slides some of her kitchen scraps under this covering to compost them.

Nourish your soil in the off-season by hand-shredding or snipping vegetable and herb stems and leaving them right in the garden bed. Cover the harvested plants with hay and leaves, and add compostable kitchen waste to the bed all winter long.

Welcome worms with compost. Robert Hammond is always overjoyed when he finds earthworms in his soil. They're a good sign—an indication that he has organic material in his dirt. You don't need to physically add earthworms to your soil—they will spontaneously appear when you supplement the soil with organic material, he says. Hammond has had soil that showed no evidence of earthworms. When he added compost, the worms appeared and flourished. Not only do worms feed on compost, they also add to the organic material with the castings they leave behind. Their tunneling aerates the soil as well.

Worms like mulch, too. Mulch is another earthworm magnet. If you use organic mulches on your garden beds and replenish them each year, you'll find that worms will follow . . . and your soil will be all the better for it.

Go easy on the tilling. You might not feel like you're actually gardening unless you have upended a few hundred cubic feet of dirt with a shovel or a power tiller. Well, don't go overboard with tilling your soil, says Hammond. If you till your soil until it is powdered, a crust will form across its surface when the soil is dry (a particular problem with highly clayey soil). That crust will become a barrier, forcing water to run off rather than soaking into the dirt. Eventually, erosion will increase, too.

Deeper down, over-tilling compacts the soil, reducing pores that allow water and air to penetrate—making a difficult environment for the roots of your garden plants. Over-tilling also damages beneficial microorganisms in the soil, such as the mycorrhizae—fungi that help plant roots draw nutrients out of the dirt. If you insist on tilling your garden, don't do it while the soil is wet—that is particularly damaging to the soil, too, Hammond says.

Besides, tillers are large machines that take up a lot of garage or shed space and are probably overkill for the average small home garden, says Heather Kibble, home garden expert for a major southern California seed company. You probably have a hundred better uses for your space—and money.

Marvin Duren, of Marvin's Organic Gardens in Ohio, has quit tilling, plowing, and turning his garden soil by shovel. "I let the earthworms do the incorporating and aerating," he says.

Treat your garden plants to lasagna. Speaking of no-till gardening, lasagna gardening is a low-effort technique that's becoming increasingly popular among cheat-at-gardening enthusiasts. It's named not for what you grow in your garden, but for the technique of layering materials you use to build—and then maintain—your garden soil. To get started, mark the patch of sod or soil on which you want to create your lasagna garden by covering it with corrugated cardboard or several layers of newsprint. Wet this down with your garden hose. Now add the layers to your bed—basically any organic material that you would put into a compost pile. Just alternate the "brown" stuff (say, shredded leaves raked up from the lawn) with the "green" (fresh grass clippings, trimmings from your garden plants, plant-based kitchen scraps). Add the occasional layer of finished compost, topsoil, or peat moss. Within a season or two you will have a bed of loose, crumbly soil that needs no turning. Just plant your bed by troweling straight down.

Then quit tilling for good. Once you have an established garden, just spread compost and organic fertilizers on top of the soil surface once a year and put down a layer of mulch on top. When it's time to plant, just pull the mulch aside and dig with a trowel just deep enough to set in the young plants. As the plants grow, add more mulch (it can be up to 12 inches deep, if the plants are tall). That's it! The organic materials will gradually decompose and nourish the soil. Earthworms will help to aerate the soil from below. And you'll only have to water during prolonged spells of dry weather.

Stick a fork in it. Here's another great alternative to tilling your soil: Just penetrate your garden bed with the tines of a pitchfork. Stick the fork into the soil as far as it will go and rock the handle back and forth a few times. Work your way across the garden bed. This will allow air and moisture into the soil without causing the destruction that tilling or turning the earth can, says Clea Danaan.

Provide some winter cover. Planting a "cover crop" to grow in your garden over winter will also protect and condition your soil. Ryegrass, winter peas, winter greens, turnips, clover, and vetch make good cover crops. Plant them in late summer to early fall, at least 4 weeks before your area's first expected fall frost. In spring, chop down or mow over your cover crop. Leave the chopped

Loosen your soil by rocking a pitchfork back and forth in stages across the garden bed.

Shield Your Soil from Chemical Damage

One of the biggest mistakes that new gardeners make is reacting to problems by using chemical solutions such as pesticides that damage the soil, says Dr. Kenneth Mulder, director of the campus farm at Green Mountain College in Poultney, Vermont. Most of your garden problems can actually be resolved with healthy, living soil. Chemical use is a setback for the biology of your garden, and it can take your garden years to recover. Sure, there's a challenge in chemical-free gardening: Investing in your soil requires a long-term outlook and commitment to such practices as composting, mulching, and growing cover crops. You have to keep in mind that you won't necessarily see an immediate result.

"You don't grow plants—you grow soil, and the rest follows," Dr. Mulder says.

plant material on the garden bed surface. You can till it into the soil (gently, please!) or just cover it over with a layer of compost. Soil that benefits from a winter cover crop will provide much better crops during the regular growing season, says Georgia farm manager Daron Joffee. A cover crop stimulates the biological system of the soil and helps fight off disease.

Use the sun to sterilize your soil. Come spring, there could be some unwelcome bad guys hunkered down in last season's garden bed—namely, seeds left in the soil by last year's weeds, and pathogens that can cause any number of plant diseases. Here's the cheater's technique for sterilizing a garden bed using solar power—and yes, it's free and it's easy. In spring, moisten the garden soil and cover it with clear plastic. Create a tight seal around the perimeter by anchoring the edges, tucking in the ends, and covering the edges with soil. Leave the plastic in place for 4 to 6 weeks. Sunlight will "cook" leftover seeds and microbes in the soil. When you plant, disturb the soil as little as possible; weed seeds deeper than 6 inches may survive solarization and be ready to germinate if you expose them to light.

Protect your pathways with clover. You know the expression "Good fences make good neighbors?" Well, in the same vein, good pathways make good garden beds. This isn't because you need to coddle yourself in the garden with a picturesque place to shuffle your feet. The primary reason for putting paths between your planting beds is to give you a way to reach into your garden without stepping onto the beds and compacting the soil.

Now, leaving the dirt bare on your garden path is not a good idea, says Joffee, because exposure damages the soil. Sun bakes nutrients out of the soil, the soil loses its moisture, nutrients leach out, organic matter and microbial activity disappear, and wind and water erode the dirt. To protect the soil in your garden pathways, Joffee recommends planting clover. His favorite: ladino white clover. It provides a pretty pathway that also feels nice to walk on. Your garden plants will benefit from the nearby clover, since the clover's roots provide a safe haven for beneficial soil microbes and also help to fix nitrogen in the soil.

Joffee recommends leaving a 10-inch-wide pathway between garden beds.

Put in a freebie pathway. Sure, those brick paver or stone pathways look stunning, but they're not always affordable. Try a little earth-friendly recycling for a path that works just as well. Check around the house for any flat, sturdy material that's not being used and could serve as the foundation for a garden path. Open up cardboard boxes and line your pathway, reuse weathered and splintered cedar shakes or clapboard, or lay down lengths of old wood. When you have your recycled path liner material in place, cover it with mulch or straw.

Cast a spell on your garden. What's the best and easiest way to prepare soil for gardening? Master Gardener Rebecca Kolls of *Good Morning America* says all you need are her "three magical ingredients." If you don't already have these magical ingredients on hand, they're available not from wizards or witches, but from your local garden supply store: peat moss, cow manure, and compost. To condition your garden soil, lay a mixture of these ingredients across the top of your soil in both spring and fall, then till it under if you like, or just leave it alone and mix it in the next time you plant. It's that easy.

Feed your soil both ways. Now, we've had recommendations for both adding organic matter to the soil (compost and such) and fertilizing (let's all repeat them together: nitrogen, potassium, and phosphorus). Many backyard gardeners make the mistake of supplying only one or the other, says Annette Pelliccio of the Happy Gardener organic gardening company. You need both the organic matter *and* the fertilizer, she says. One doesn't make the other unnecessary. Luckily, there are lots of organic fertilizer blends on the market that supply the full complement of nutrients and are just as easy to use as synthetic products.

Take care around your trees. When you are amending or mulching the soil around your trees, give them plenty of leeway by ringing them like a donut. Piling too much material in the shape of a volcano on top of tree roots can smother them. Also, piling soil or mulch directly against the trunk of a tree can cause rot. To mulch a tree in less than a minute, use bagged mulch and

Less is more around trees. When mulching near a tree, give the trunk and root flare plenty of clearance so the mulch won't cause rot or smother the surface roots.

A Little Ash Goes a Long Way

Your fireplace wood ashes will add nutrients to your lawn or garden—you just have to be careful not to overdo it. For 1,000 square feet of yard, add no more than a 5-gallon bucket of ashes per year. Ashes raise the pH level of your soil (raising the alkalinity), and if your yard is already testing at a pH of 7.0 (neutral) or higher, the ashes will do more harm than good. So take it easy. If you were paying attention in science class, you know that rising alkalinity means that the acidity of the soil drops. So acid-loving plants (azaleas, rhododendrons, and blueberry bushes, for instance) would not be happy with fireplace ashes in their soil. You also can sprinkle fireplace ashes onto your compost pile—particularly if you have acidic components in the pile such as pine needles or oak leaves.

---

walk in a ring around the tree, letting the mulch fall from the bag. The standard method of dumping the bag in one spot and shoveling it into place around the tree takes three times as long (and often involves bending). See Chapter 10 for more on trees.

Be a mulch doctor. Take the time to cruise your garden beds in winter with a bucket of "911" mulch in hand. If you see exposed roots or plant crowns, administer a little first aid by blanketing the area with a layer of mulch to keep the winter winds and weather from drying out the roots and killing the plants. Saving your plants is easier than replacing them.

Sprouting calls for special soil. There's soil and then there's soil. Just so we don't get confused, let's distinguish between the two kinds of dirt that you will run across in the home gardening biz. The conventional garden soil where you plant your tomatoes in the backyard is lovable stuff, but it's not really suitable for all purposes. For sprouting seedlings indoors and for houseplants, don't just dig up backyard soil. That would expose tender plants to too many potential bugs and diseases. Instead, buy bags of "sterilized" potting mix from your garden supply store. Sterilized soil is free of microorganisms. It usually consists of peat moss and an inactive mineral such as vermiculite. Just be sure to mix in a little compost so the soil will have a healthy population of beneficial microorganisms. It's wonderful to use for container plants as well, since it's lightweight and drains well.

Phone around for free mulch. Call nearby tree-trimming companies and ask if they shred their trimmings and give away the resulting chips. If they do, line the trunk of your car with a tarp (or grab some super-strong trash bags), toss in a shovel, and pay them a visit. If your town has a brush collection program for residents, it may also offer free wood chips. Wood chips make great mulch and can add a distinctive look to paths. If you prefer the look of more expensive, finely ground root mulch, lay down a layer of wood chips first and then cover them with the root mulch.

Shop the neighborhood for soil enhancers. If you have neighbors in town who go all out at Halloween, you may find plenty of free soil builders at curbside—bales of straw, corn stalks (chop just the leaves with a lawn mower), and orange pumpkin-face bags filled with fallen leaves.

Treat your garden to "fish food." When you're changing the water in your home aquarium, take a bucket of the old water out to your garden. Old aquarium water is full of "free" fertilizer, courtesy of your finny friends.

Well, all of this information puts lowly dirt in a new light, doesn't it? So many of the frustrations of gardening will disappear when you start treating dirt like a living being—providing it with water, air, and food, and protecting it by tucking it in with a cozy layer of mulch. Sure, now that your parental instincts are kicking in, pull up a lawn chair at night and read it a bedtime story, too. *Jack and the Beanstalk,* anyone?

Chapter 3

VEGETABLES:
The JUICIEST
SHORTCUTS

I'm not going to lie to you. Growing vegetables can be a demanding—at times tricky—pursuit, with scores of factors just waiting to wreak havoc in your garden. Poor soil, insufficient water, blazing sun, killer temperatures (high *and* low), and bugs and slugs are just a few of the hazards. To be sure, plenty of harried home gardeners are run ragged as they try to coax and coddle their vegetable plants into health and productivity. But that's because they've chosen to garden the hard way.

I consulted a host of vegetable gardening experts and asked them this: What are the big mistakes that most home gardeners make—the kind of goofs that cause them a summer of tedious labor and miserable crops? As it happens, just a few minutes of advance brainwork here and there will spare you many hours of physical labor as you try to set things right in a struggling garden. With the following strategies in place, you will see your backyard trials and tribulations melt away, and you'll discover a wealth of free time for other crucial activities—like test-driving your hammock or practicing your golf swing.

And oh, the rewards awaiting those who do grow their own vegetables! Nothing your supermarket produce department offers can compare with the taste of freshly picked vegetables—and the convenience of your backyard garden can't be beat either.

A grateful garden-trowel salute goes out to Daron "Farmer D" Joffee, manager of Georgia's Harvest Lake Farm; Heather Kibble, home garden expert for a major seed company in southern California; botanist, researcher, and widely published California-based author Lance Walheim; Rebecca Kolls, Master Gardener, author, and television personality on *Good Morning America*; Robert Hammond, chef and owner of Oregon's Honeyman Creek Farms; and Clea Danaan, author of *Sacred Land: Intuitive Gardening for Personal, Political, and Environmental Change*.

DO YOUR HOMEWORK

I know, I know. You're a person of action. You want to turn some soil, toss in some compost, scatter seeds, pop some transplants into the dirt, fertilize now and then, and watch your vegetables spring up from the ground. The idea of doing homework or research sounds like needless delay, something that persnickety literalists do.

Good for you—in the *How to Cheat at Gardening and Yard Work* spirit, you're eager to cut corners wherever you can. But consider this: Just a little advance research about your climate and your soil will save you truckloads of physical labor, time, and aggravation. For instance, when you know how to achieve the ideal nutrient balance in your garden soil, how to select the perfect vegetable varieties for your climate, and how to time planting for best effect, a lot of the gardening hassles that your neighbors wrestle with will just fade away in your own backyard plot. The information we're talking about is easy to come by—finding it is nothing like poring over a college textbook or spending several hours at the public library. And besides, gathering a little information is a breeze compared to the physical side of gardening—there's no lifting, bending over, or even getting your fingernails dirty! Reading this book is a sure sign that you're on the right labor- and money-saving path, too, since you're about to learn the very easiest ways to raise vegetables—advice delivered to you in an easy-to-digest form.

Here are some tips on getting started. First, make sure you have the basics covered.

Take your dirt to a lab. The condition of your soil "is one of the most important aspects of gardening," says Hammond. Soil science, fortunately, is not rocket science. But to get great results from your vegetable garden, you will need to know something about testing your soil, adding organic material, and balancing its content of minerals and micronutrients. (You'll find info on soil testing in Chapter 2.) If that sounds ridiculously fussy to you, then look at it this way: Think of building good soil as your own private crop insurance. When you get your soil properly balanced, a lot of the problems that typically beset gardeners will evaporate. So if you skipped or just skimmed Chapter 2, now's a good time to go back and read it in depth. If you promise to do that, I'll promise not to repeat all of those details here, okay? Just remember the POTS principle (Priority One: The Soil) on page 2: Good dirt makes all the difference.

Study your local climate. Crucial environmental factors that affect the garden, such as length of growing season and amount of rainfall, will vary drastically depending upon where you live. All of your decisions about which varieties of vegetables you grow and how you treat them will be influenced by your knowledge of your local climate. So the more you know about your climate the more successful you will be as a gardener, says Hammond. Your local Cooperative Extension office can provide lots of helpful information about gardening in your climate. You'll learn what to plant, when to plant, how much to water and with what frequency.

Shed light on the best garden spot. How do you know the best part of your yard to devote to a garden? Here are your top criteria.

- **Find good sun exposure.** Make sure that buildings, trees, and any other obstructions will not cast shadows on your garden.

- **Avoid swamps.** Find a spot that's not prone to flooding. After a good rainstorm, go out and walk around your yard and see where the water tends to puddle and pool, and where it stays around longest. Also, avoid planting at the bottom of a slope or in another low spot where water collects, or near the end of a downspout from a rain gutter. And avoid a spot where your garden will be exposed to possible contaminants from road runoff.

- **Look for good soil.** Ensuring that you have good garden soil is a matter of doing a little bit of homework—testing the soil and supplementing it with compost and fertilizer. See Chapter 2 for info on testing your soil.

- **Find a spot you can monitor from the house.** If a groundhog is rampaging among your tomato plants, it helps if you can spot it from a window you look through often. Same goes for rampaging deer, children, and other pests.

- **Consider proximity to a water source.** It's always nice to have easy access to water for your garden. You want to keep the dragging of hoses and hauling of watering cans to a minimum.

- **Locate your garden as close to your kitchen as possible,** so it will be easy to haul your produce inside.

- **Put your garden near an entrance to the home** that will not be ruined by muddy shoes.

Stop inviting strangers to your backyard. Well, the humans you associate with are your business, but in this case we're talking about vegetable strangers. Before you add any variety of vegetable to your home garden, learn as much as you can about its individual needs, says Hammond. Tending to those details will make an enormous impact on the success of your garden. You will want

Squeeze Some Dirt

If you'd like a quick read on the pros and cons of your garden soil, try this layman's test. Scoop up a handful of soil, squeeze it in your fist, and open your hand again. If the ball of soil crumbles before your eyes, it's too sandy. If the soil clings together, even when you touch it, the soil contains too much clay. Ideal gardening soil will have a balance of sand, clay, and organic material. If you are blessed with loam in your garden, the fistful of dirt will stay in a ball when you open your hand, but the ball will fall apart when you touch it.

You can also use this test to tell when your soil is ready to work in spring. Squeeze the soil into a ball and then open your fingers. If it sticks together it's too wet to work; if it crumbles, it's ready.

Understand that while this informal test provides some useful information, it's no substitute for a thorough lab analysis of your garden soil.

---

to know how much sun the plant requires, for instance, how deep to plant it, how far to space it from other plants, and what its water needs are.

To increase your odds of gardening success, pick vegetable varieties that grow particularly well in your locale. For instance, you will want varieties that are partial to your climate, that thrive within the limits of your growing season, and that are resistant to any pests that predominate in your area. How are you supposed to come by that kind of information? Easy—a little schmoozing will take you a long way. Ask your gardening neighbors what varieties work particularly well for them. Keep an eye out for garden catalogs and gardening books that specifically target your region. Talk to the staff at your farmer's market to find out what varieties the nearby farmers are having luck with. And ask the staff at your favorite garden center—"They work there, so they have to talk to you," says Kibble. Also consult any literature that comes with plants you buy from a nursery and review the backs of seed packets.

Imagine the "endgame." Before you load up your garden with young plants, develop a clear vision of what you are going to do with the produce once harvest begins. This will affect how many of each kind of vegetable plant you will want and how much garden space you will devote to each variety. Ask yourself, for instance, whether each vegetable is roundly welcome at the dinner table by all members of the family and how much you will reasonably be able to use. We all know stories of gardeners who have trouble even giving away their bumper crops of zucchini, for instance. With a little clear-eyed planning, you can make sure that the same scenario isn't played out with your string beans and tomatoes, too.

Plan for life after harvest. Just filling up your garden bed with vegetable plants in spring is not the end of your crop planning. Many people fail to factor in the concept of succession crops, says Joffee. This means that after you have completed the harvest of one of your crops, you pull up the spent plants, toss them onto the compost pile, and in their place plant a new (and usually different) crop. Instead of having your garden's production stagger to a halt, you will be extending the harvest season. So read up on the growth cycle of your garden vegetables and chart out your succession plan on paper. This will

Cheat Sheet

How Much Will You Get?

Growing too much of any vegetable is a waste unless you have hungry neighbors or extended family members with a real fondness for zucchini. Save labor (and your potential overflow recipients) by planning your plantings to match your appetite. Look over the following typical harvests you can expect *per plant* from these common garden vegetables, then grow only as many plants as you need. It's easy to see that you won't need a row of plants like cucumbers unless you plan on lots of pickling.

TYPICAL YIELD PER PLANT

Corn: 1 to 3 ears

Cucumbers: 10 to 50

Melons: 1 to 3

Peppers: 2 to 10

Winter squash: 6

Tomatoes: 6 to 24

Cherry tomatoes: Up to 150!

Zucchini: 16 to 36

Cheat Sheet

||||||||||||||||||||||||||||||||||||||||||||||||||||||||||||||||||||||||||||||||||||||||||||||||||||||||||||||||||||||||||||

Succeed with Succession Planting

One easy way to practice succession planting is to plant long- and short-season vegetables together in the same row or bed. You can space the plants more closely together than usual since the short-term crop will be removed by the time the long-term one needs its full complement of growing space. This enables you to fill in some of the nooks and crannies left after certain transplants are set out in the garden or seeds are sown. The first vegetable of the pair is harvested before the second achieves its full growth. Look for early-maturing varieties of the first vegetable in each pair to make sure they'll be out of the ground by the time the second vegetable needs the space.

SHORT- AND LONG-SEASON PAIRINGS

Radishes and cabbage

Early cabbage and tomatoes

Chinese cabbage and eggplant

Lettuce and turnips

Radishes and beans

---

work with most vegetables, Joffee says, but in particular with short-cycle crops such as lettuce, other greens, radishes, and broccoli.

Multiple plantings mean manageable harvests. You can also use succession planting to keep your harvest in line with your needs. By planting crops over several weeks rather than all at once, you'll get a steady supply of produce instead of a one-time bonanza. How much you pick at any one time depends on how much you plant each time. The idea is to get as much as you need for a week or two, plus a little extra if you want to store some vegetables long-term. That way, you'll never be overwhelmed. Succession planting works best with crops that ripen all at once, like salad greens, bush beans, and corn.

To plan on a continuous but not overwhelming harvest, spread out planting times throughout the season. For example, three beds or rows (or pots) of lettuce, each planted 2 weeks apart, will be ready for harvest about 2 weeks apart as well.

Rein in your ambitions. Many inexperienced home gardeners make the mistake of starting out with an enormous plot that quickly gets out of hand. Either tending the garden becomes too much work, or the garden is soon producing much more bounty than the poor gardener knows what to do with, says Kibble. Instead, ease into gardening with a modestly sized plot. For one person just starting out, Kibble recommends a garden bed measuring about 8 feet by 16 feet. For a family of four—with everyone contributing to the garden's upkeep—you could consider a garden twice that size. Plant only what you intend to eat—and what your family will enjoy. With a modestly sized garden, you increase your odds of having a happy growing experience—one that you will want to repeat year after year.

Get the most from your space. A smaller garden means less weeding and less work. To get the most food out of the least amount of space, grow the most space-efficient vegetables: bush beans, pole beans, beets, carrots, leaf lettuce, onions, peppers, radishes, spinach, bush summer squash, tomatoes, and turnips.

Grow up instead of out. Another tactic for saving space is to make use of vertical space. If you love vining and spreading "space hogs" such as indeterminate tomatoes, squash, melons, and cucumbers, try training them to climb a trellis or netting. Support squash and melon fruit by resting them in cloth slings tied to the supporting structure. Old cloth diapers (clean ones, please!) work well, or you can cut up an old sheet to make slings.

Late in the season, try planting a late crop of pole beans next to sunflowers or corn, so the beans can climb their stalks.

Grow the quickest crops. For the fastest payback on your work, grow the vegetables that mature fastest, such as radishes, mesclun greens, leaf lettuce, and spinach. And look for early varieties of your favorites, like Early Girl tomatoes.

Go for less work. If you want to save work, grow veggies that don't need a lot of fussing. Low-maintenance vegetables include arugula, asparagus (once it's established), bush beans, beets, cabbage, carrots, Swiss chard, collards, garden cress, escarole, leaf lettuce, okra, peas, peppers, radishes, and spinach.

Save your seed packets. Some people like to keep a meticulous journal about what varieties they plant in their gardens, planting times, and such. Kibble prefers a much less formal approach to gardening. For instance, if you plant from seed, just saving the seed packets provides an excellent record of what's been growing in your garden. Try putting the empty packets in an index card file box so they're easy to find when you want to refer to them.

Save extra seeds. You might not use all of the seeds from a packet, but you can store the leftovers for a year, or even longer for some vegetables. Keep your seed packets in a cool, dry place. To help keep them dry, store leftover seeds in their packets and those packets in plastic containers or sealable plastic bags. Toss in a couple of silica gel packs, those envelopes of desiccant material that you find packaged with home electronics, sneakers, and other consumer products.

Or just buy fresh seeds every year. Okay, maybe storing your unused garden seeds under ideal conditions is fussier than you want to deal with. Then feel free to use the cheating-est approach of all: Buy fresh seeds every year and toss out the ones you don't use. After all, if your old seeds were to spoil, you're just setting yourself up for failure and disappointment. Why sow seeds of discontent?

SELECTING NURSERY PLANTS

By far, the preferred cheat-at-gardening method for acquiring vegetable plants is buying them from a nursery. At the very least you can rest assured that your seedlings were started by professionals who are a zillion times better trained and equipped to do it than you are. That's not the end of the selection process, however. Not all nurseries are equal, and not all are as meticulous as you might like about the stock that they set out for sale. This matters because making good plant selections—not only the choice of variety, but also the health of each individual plant—has an enormous impact on the future success of your garden. A buggy, diseased, or rootbound plant is just about guaranteed to bring you misery and disappointment in the weeks to come. Such a plant's recovery from a poor start in life is just about impossible. So in the cheatin' tradition of doing everything we can to avoid hassle and grief, let's review how to pick nursery-started plants that have the very best odds of making you look like a gardening genius—with very little effort on your part.

Play plant doctor. Before you buy vegetable plants from a nursery, give them a health checkup first. Don't buy any plants that have insect pests on them. Buy plants that are "stocky" (beyond the tender seedling stage) but not

Cheat Sheet

Sizing Up a Nursery Plant

Out of all the plants on display at the nursery, here are pointers on how to pick one with the greatest odds of success in your garden.

☐	Smaller plants transplant better, so don't buy tomatoes with flowers.
☐	Go for stocky, sturdy plants with good green color.
☐	Plants should be compact, not leggy or stretched.
☐	Avoid large transplants, plants that are pale in color, or with a lot of space between leaves on the stem.
☐	Look for plants that seem small for the size of their container—they won't be rootbound.
☐	Get plants as soon as they arrive in your garden center (see "Spy on your garden center" on page 42).
☐	One or two neglected plants off by themselves indicate that you're looking at the last of a shipment—pass them by.
☐	Some plants are simply best grown from seed because they don't transplant well—peas and beans, for example—so just pass by these plants.

overly mature. Look for good color on the plant, and look for healthy roots that are not pot-bound. To check the roots, turn the container on its side, gently squeeze it, and slide the rootball out. (Don't be shy—if nursery staff should object to this, find another nursery. This inspection is routine and perfectly acceptable as long as you're being gentle with the plant.) The roots should appear succulent and creamy in color. If the roots have filled the entire container and started to swirl around one another, that poor plant will only have a troubled life in your garden. Don't try to tell yourself that you'll be able to untangle those roots—if you try, you'll damage them, which will be even worse news for the unfortunate plant.

If you do end up with a pot-bound plant, all is not lost. When you get the plant out of its pot, lay it down, and with a sharp knife make three vertical slices a few inches up into and equally spaced around the rootball. Then gently spread the rootball apart a bit with your hands before you plant it. Make sure you give the plant plenty of water at planting, and for a couple of weeks afterward, to facilitate the growth of new roots.

Wait for a fresh batch. Make sure you're getting the freshest plants possible from your nursery. Look around you: Are you getting the last two forlorn plants out of a batch that's been sitting around the nursery for several days? Or are you picking plants from a fresh group that was just delivered to the nursery? It helps if you can establish a relationship with the nursery staff. Find out from them when the store gets its new deliveries from growers (often this will be Thursdays or Fridays, so the store will have plants in stock for the busy weekend).

SLEIGHT *of* HAND

Shop with a Partner

When you go shopping for vegetable plants, take a friend or neighbor who gardens and agree to split your newly acquired plants, says Master Gardener Rebecca Kolls. After all, you don't really need six Brussels sprouts plants, do you? This approach allows you to buy a greater variety of plants for less money.

Buy Disease-Fighters

When you're selecting seeds, flip right past any variety that doesn't specify that it's disease resistant. Plants that are bred to fight off the scores of maladies lurking in your yard will increase your odds of gardening success, reduce hassles (like trekking to the garden store with a withering sprig to figure out what's wrong), and reduce your temptation to use pesticides.

On exception to the rule: heirloom varieties. Their superior flavor makes them often worth the trouble. See page 43 for more info.

Avoid the "big" mistake. Many people select vegetable plants at the nursery by grabbing up the largest ones—a big mistake. The largest plants might already be rootbound, which means that their growth has been stalled at a crucial point. Also, these plants won't adjust as well to the garden as smaller plants and will likely suffer transplant shock that will set back their growth for several weeks. Favor the shorter, squat plants with deep, rich green leaves and no signs of pests.

Favor organic growers. When you're selecting garden plants at a nursery, says Joffee, favor the plants that were produced by organic growers. Why? A reputable organic grower puts time and effort into giving garden plants a healthful start in life. Nonorganic growers often pump their seedlings full of synthetic fertilizers that create an induced illusion of health. When you get these plants into your garden, they're unable to keep growing at the same pace and may suffer the setback of transplant shock. Organic plants "won't deceive you" by appearing to be healthier than they really are, Joffee says. To find out if seedlings at your local nursery are from an organic grower, you will probably need to do two things: Ask the nursery staff and read labels carefully. Most nursery plants have the name of the retail nursery on the tag, but not necessarily the name of the grower. It would be natural to assume that nurseries selling organically grown plants would want to promote that fact, but make a point of asking anyway.

Look closely for teensy bugs. Take a magnifying glass along when you go plant shopping (or break out those reading glasses), and examine the plants before you buy them, especially if you're shopping in a greenhouse. In greenhouse conditions, brassica plants (such as cabbage, Brussels sprouts, and broccoli), among others, are susceptible to the tiny life-sucking bugs known as aphids. Aphids are tiny insects that may be white, black, or brown and tend to gather in leaf axils (where leaves join stems). So inspect plants carefully for infestation before you buy, says Joffee. Look in the axils of the leaves and around the neck of the plant for bugs. Leaves may curl if the infestation is severe. If you see signs of aphid infestation, move on to another batch of plants.

To check for whiteflies (also common on greenhouse-grown plants), gently

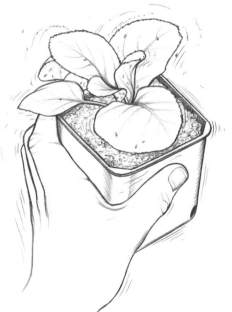

Check nursery plants for whiteflies: Give the plant a gentle shake. A "flurry" of whiteflies is a warning to find another plant. No sense in bringing trouble home with you.

shake the plant; the whiteflies will fly around it like a cloud of tiny snowflakes. Don't buy this one!

Spy on your garden center. Learn to loiter at your garden center. Just hanging out at your garden center and observing will tell you a lot about which plants you want to take home to your garden and which you should leave behind on the shelves, Kibble says. She likes to drop in at her garden center once a week just to watch. Observing as the shipments come and go will help you identify the freshest plants.

Housekeeping counts. The condition of a nursery itself will sometimes tell you as much about the quality of its plants as a direct inspection of the greenery. If the nursery is clean and well organized, you have a better chance of finding healthy, well-cared-for plants for your garden, says Joffee. Also, look at whether plants are well watered; if they are, the soil will be moist, and the pots will feel heavy, not light, when you pick them up.

Pass on the big chains. If you want to be sure that the plants you buy will thrive in your local conditions, stick to stand-alone garden centers and local nurseries rather than the garden department of a "big box" store, says Kolls. Independent garden centers and nurseries will only stock plants that adapt to local conditions. The plant-ordering system for the garden department of a chain "big box" store might not be so precise, she says.

Save container varieties for containers. You may find at your nursery some plants that are varieties developed specifically for container gardening, such as

SHADES OF GREEN ——————————————————————
Adjusting to Drought

If you've been experiencing drought conditions in your region, select vegetable varieties that have a short growing season and plant them as early in the season as possible (see "Grow the quickest crops," on page 36, for some suggestions). Thanks to the shorter growth cycle and cooler temperatures, your garden will require less water. And be sure to mulch, too.

patio tomatoes and bush cucumbers. If you're looking for plants to put into a conventional garden bed, you're probably better off passing by those container varieties. They tend to provide smaller plants and smaller fruit (or vegetables). On the other hand, they might be perfect for your needs if you have a small spot in the garden to fill, says Hammond. But the reverse situation probably will provide awkward results, Hammond says. Conventional garden plants, such as indeterminate (vining) tomato varieties, placed in pots may outgrow their containers and get unruly.

Leave the hard stuff to the farmers. Some much-loved garden vegetables are so labor-intensive that they're not worth the work you put into them, says Kolls. Corn is a prime example. Sure, there's nothing so yummy as fresh-picked corn that's hauled straight to the stovetop and then the dinner table. However, corn takes up an enormous amount of garden space, and it's an infamous water-guzzler. Buy fresh corn at a farmer's market instead. Brussels sprouts are way too much work for a lot of gardeners as well. And you may want to reconsider those famously overproductive staples zucchini and cucumbers—are you really prepared to eat them *every day?*

Order up custom transplants. Are you ever frustrated that your nursery doesn't have in stock precisely the vegetable plants that you want—or that it doesn't have enough of them when you're ready to plant? Joffee has discovered a way around this quandary. The farmer contacts his nursery weeks ahead of time and sends them seeds he would like them to start in flats for him. This way he is guaranteed to get all of the plants he needs at just the right time. A large commercial nursery might not perform a service like this for us ordinary folks. However, Joffee points out that small, organic, mom-and-pop nurseries are popping up all of the time, and they might willingly perform this service for good repeat customers.

Heirlooms: Not for newcomers. When it comes to selecting plants for your garden, the official *How to Cheat at Gardening and Yard Work* approach is to simply choose modern disease- and pest-resistant hybrids that are a good match for your climate and growing conditions. That's the path to an angst-free, hassle-free gardening experience.

Follow Your Nose

When you have identified a plant that you want to buy at your garden store, give it the sniff test. If it smells rancid or sour, that's not good, says Master Gardener Rebecca Kolls. The plant has probably been overwatered, allowing fungus or bacteria to take hold.

Eventually, however, you're going to hear about the wonders of "heirloom" vegetables. No, I'm not talking about tomato seeds that sat in your grandmother's dresser drawer for 30 years. Heirlooms are old-time varieties that enthusiasts enjoy growing for a couple of reasons. For one thing, they produce flavorful food that's way better tasting than what you'll find in a supermarket. Also, since growing heirlooms involves saving seeds from season to season, gardeners who grow them are helping to preserve the genetic diversity of the world's food crops. Growing heirlooms can be a rewarding experience—if you have the time and talent to devote to the process. If you're looking for new gardening challenges and heirloom vegetables pique your interest, one place to learn more is the nonprofit organization Seed Savers Exchange at www.seedsavers.org.

Mix heirlooms with resistant varieties. If you're new to heirloom vegetables and want to give them a try, go for it—but to preserve your sanity, balance your garden with some pest- and disease-resistant hybrids at the same time. Everyone needs some ego-boosting, surefire successes in the garden, Joffee notes. For the uninitiated, heirlooms can't promise that kind of satisfaction.

HASSLES ASIDE, IF YOU STILL WANT TO START FROM SEED

Okay, being a reader of How to Cheat books means that you're an independent sort. Which means that you may have no compunction about ignoring the previous advice about letting professionals start your plants for you. Emotionally, you equate gardening with sticking seeds in the ground, so by golly that's going to be part of your experience. That's okay—I'm going to help you anyway. Besides, some vegetables grow better from seed—peas and beans, for instance.

Plain ol' dirt won't do. When you plant seeds indoors in a flat or a pot, put them in a good seed-starting mix from your garden store. Look for a mix that contains peat or perlite (or maybe both) to lighten the texture. And choose a mix that does not contain fertilizer—it's better to add your own, so you can use a mild liquid seaweed or fish-based fertilizer, or compost tea. Don't sow your seeds in dirt from your garden or in regular potting soil—they're too heavy. Pack the mix firmly enough into the container you're going to use so that there are no air pockets below the surface. Moisten the mix, but don't let it get sloppy wet. The ideal is to have it as damp as a wrung-out sponge, wet but not dripping. Most seeds will want to lie in darkness in order to germinate, though a few sprout better with light. Read the planting directions on the seed packet.

Once seedlings emerge above the soil, they have entered a critical stage when they need lots of light, says Joffee. Take them to a sunny window in your home or put them under a grow light or a bank of fluorescents. (A two-tube workshop fixture will work just fine; use one "cool" white and one "warm" white tube, and position the lights so the seedlings are just 4 to 6 inches below them.)

Start with the hearty. If you're hankering to start your own vegetable plants from seed, pick vegetables that are famous for being hearty and withstanding a certain amount of abuse. Kibble's candidates: squash, pumpkins, leafy crops such as lettuce, root vegetables such as carrots, and beans, which all start more easily from seed than other vegetables.

Run the figures first. If you're going to start your own vegetable plants from seed, says Kolls, get your timing right by doing some simple math. Buy your seeds in mid-winter so you'll have an early start on the project. Read the backs of the seed packets so you'll know how long it takes your seeds to germinate and when they can be planted in the ground outdoors (you'll need to know the last frost date for your area—get it from your closest Cooperative

Cheat Sheet

When to Start Vegetable Seeds

To plan the best time to start seedlings indoors in spring, you need to know the approximate date of the average last spring frost in your area. Count back from that date the number of weeks indicated below to determine the appropriate starting date for various crops. An asterisk (*) indicates a cold-hardy plant that can be set out 4 to 6 weeks before the last frost.

- **12 to 14 weeks:** Onions*, leeks*, chives*
- **8 to 12 weeks:** Peppers, lettuce*, cabbage-family crops*
- **6 to 8 weeks:** Eggplants, tomatoes
- **2 to 4 weeks:** Cucumbers, melons, okra, pumpkins, squash

Try the towel trick. There are many and varied techniques for germinating seeds. Here's Joffee's approach, which he says works particularly well with squash, winter squash, cucumbers, and pumpkins.

1. Dampen a paper towel, fold the seeds up in it, and place it in a lidded plastic container. Slide the container into a drawer or find some other dark spot to store it.

2. Mist the paper towel once a day—don't allow it to dry out.

3. Check the back of the seed packet to find out how long the seeds usually take to germinate, and check them when the time is up. If your seeds have sprouted, gently peel back the paper towel and transfer the sprouts into your prepared garden bed (which you have raked fine and moistened). Place the root pointing down, about 1 inch under the surface of the soil (check the seed packet for the best planting depth).

4. Lightly water. Cover the planting areas with a light layer of straw mulch or shredded leaves.

An alternative: Instead of planting the sprouts in your garden bed, plant them in 4-inch pots filled with a good organic potting mix. Or make your own mix from equal parts of peat, compost, and perlite or sharp (builder's, not beach) sand. Park your pots in a greenhouse, a cold frame, or by the kitchen window.

Extension office). Get a calendar with space to write notes for each day and use it to calculate when you need to start the germination process in order to have the seedlings ready for planting day. Write the starting and planting-out dates for each vegetable right on the calendar.

Check viability of stored seeds. If you saved seeds from last year, you're probably not sure if the little guys are still any good. Here's an easy way to check their viability: Drop the seeds in question into a glass of room-temperature water and wait. Seeds that float to the top are probably not good anymore. Throw them out and plant the seeds that sink to the bottom of the glass.

Get the depth right. Before you plant vegetable seeds—whether into a flat indoors or directly into the garden—check the seed packet for the right depth to place the seeds. If you can't find such information, here's a rule of thumb: In general, plant seeds 2 to 3 times as deep as the diameter of the seed.

Sterilize your containers. All containers that you use for starting seeds must be sterilized first so diseases are not passed along to your young plants, says Kolls. The procedure is simple: In your sink or a large bowl, mix 9 parts water with 1 part liquid chlorine bleach. Wearing rubber gloves, dunk each seedling container in the solution, rinse well with clear water, and wipe it dry with a clean cloth.

Keep moisture in the mix. For newly planted vegetable seeds, keep the soil

ZERO-MAINTENANCE MARVELS
Let Your Seeds Water Themselves

Master Gardener Rebecca Kolls loves to germinate her seeds using convenient self-watering seed-starting kits. Such systems use a wicking mat to draw water from a reservoir into little containers where you plant your seeds. (You fill the containers with your favorite seed-starting mixture.) Look for such systems at garden supply stores or on the Internet.

MYTH-BUSTERS
Seeds of Frustration

Have you been thinking that you'll save a lot of money on the cost of vegetable plants by starting your own from seed? You're dreaming, says Rebecca Kolls, Master Gardener, author, and *Good Morning America* garden expert. Growing from seed is a full-time job, she says, calling it "total babysitting." If you're fairly new to gardening, let the experienced professionals start your plants for you. You'll spare yourself a host of mistakes and pitfalls that are common to amateurs. If you insist on starting your own plants from seed, there's nothing wrong with that—just enter into it with the proper expectation: You're choosing the more labor-intensive path.

• • • • • • • • • • • • • • • • • • •

consistently soft and moist, Joffee says. This applies to indoor flats as well as outdoor garden soil. Water the soil lightly two or three times a day until the new plants establish their roots and the first leaves appear. The goal is to keep the soil evenly moist but not sopping wet.

Give sprouts a warm welcome. When you start certain vegetables from seed, they will need a warm place to germinate, says Kibble. In particular: tomatoes, peppers, and eggplant. In the past, Kibble has used the top of her refrigerator as a warm spot for a flat of vegetable seeds. (That worked splendidly until she bought a more energy-efficient refrigerator that doesn't give off as much heat.) Now she likes to place her seed flat on an electronic warming mat designed just for that purpose. You can buy such warming mats for relatively little money in garden catalogs, garden centers, home stores, and online.

Meet your babies' new needs. Once your seeds have sprouted, your baby plants have new needs: light and food, says Kolls. Give them 12 to 14 hours of light a day. Placing them in a sunny south-facing window in your home will do. Or suspend an artificial light over the seed flat as close to the container as possible, raising the light as your plants get taller.

Once your plants have developed four to six leaves, you can feed them. (The seed-starting mix you may have bought at the garden store has no nutrients.) Fish emulsion or a liquid fish and seaweed fertilizer will do nicely—but whichever you choose, dilute it to 50 percent of the recommended strength.

Feed the seedlings every 10 to 14 days. As your plants continue to grow, transfer them to larger containers as needed.

Give crowded flats a trim. If you were a little over exuberant when you planted seeds in an indoor flat, you might find them crowding each other once they're a few inches high. If that's the case, you need to thin them out. But don't just yank some seedlings out of the soil mix—that could harm some of the neighboring plants that you had intended to save. Instead, take a pair of small, sharp scissors (manicure scissors work great) and snip off the unnecessary plants at ground level. Use the same procedure if your seedlings are crowding each other in an outdoor bed. A bonus if you're thinning salad greens or spinach: You can use the thinnings (if they're big enough) in salads, solving your crowding problems and eating as well—the very definition of cheating! Just sprinkle your trimmings straight into the salad bowl.

Introduce seedlings gradually to the outdoors. Plants that you have started indoors from seed will be very sensitive to outdoor conditions, says Walheim. So you need to "harden off" such plants—that is, introduce them to the outdoors gradually. During the day, take your young plants outside in their flats and set them in the shade in a spot where they're protected from wind. Start out giving them an hour outside on the first day, and gradually increase their daily exposure over the next couple of weeks. Also, gradually increase their exposure to direct sun. On nights that are going to be cool, be sure to take them inside again.

Be nice to your back. If you're planting seeds in the garden, give your back and knees a break. Here's how to plant your seeds without kneeling or digging: First, determine how deep your seeds need to be planted. Now take a garden rake or hoe, turn it upside down, and use the end of the handle to poke holes into the soil. Mark the desired depth for planting holes on the handle with a bit of masking tape, twine, or a rubber band.

Now find a section of narrow pipe (copper or PVC will do) that's about 4 feet long. Set the lower end of the pipe in the spot where you want to plant a seed, drop the seed into the top opening of the pipe, and let the seed land home. Withdraw the pipe and gently brush your shoe over the seed to cover it.

Egging On Your Little Seedlings

You probably already know that egg cartons make excellent containers for starting seeds. But unbiodegradable plastic or foam cartons, which aren't quite suitable for this use, have crept into many supermarkets, leaving us longing for the good old-fashioned cardboard type. So here's the trick for securing old-fashioned cardboard egg containers. Just switch to buying organic eggs, which often come in cardboard containers.

Here's a refresher course in how to use them for seed starting in early spring: Poke holes in the bottom of each of a carton's compartments, then fill those compartments with soilless seed-starting mix from your garden supply store, or your own mix of peat moss and compost. Plant two or three seeds in each compartment. Set the egg carton in a pan or some other container that will catch drips when you water. When your young plants are ready for transfer to the garden, use shears or a utility knife to cut the carton up into individual containers. Set these mini-containers straight into the soil, where the cardboard will rot.

You'll wonder why folks call gardening backbreaking work!

Weed well before sowing. Planting your vegetable seeds directly into the garden bed can make later weeding tricky, because it's difficult to weed around delicate seedlings without damaging them. So if you're going to direct-seed, says Joffee, be sure to prepare the soil well first by removing all weeds and old roots from the dirt.

PLANTING IN THE GREAT OUTDOORS

Up to now, you've had a lot of behind-the-scenes gardening activity and very little to show for it. This is where the rubber meets the road—or should we say where the roots meet the row? Finally, you will have bona fide vegetable plants poking up out of your lovingly prepared garden soil (and for organic gardeners, using the words *compost, manure,* and *loving* in the same context is entirely permissible). As nature would have it, there's more to planting than just poking holes in the ground. But as the cheatin' life would have it, the fine points of planting are easy. Here's a bumper crop of planting tips that will make sure your garden "gets off the ground" without a hitch.

Welcome them with water. Water your garden bed the day before you plan to bring new plants home from the nursery. Putting your new arrivals into the ground the day that you bring them home is ideal, says Kolls. If you have already watered the bed, the soil will still be moist by the time you plant. Water again when you put the plants in the ground, to settle the soil around the roots.

Don't let plants dally in the heat. When you buy plants at the nursery, says Kibble, don't leave them in the car all day—the heat will destroy them in short order. Instead, get them home as soon as possible. Place them in partial sun, in the shade—or even in the garage. Water them right away and crowd them together for protection. Don't set your new plants down on hot asphalt or concrete. Also, don't plant them first thing in the morning. Rather, wait until late in the day, when the afternoon heat subsides, so plants have time to adjust before they sit through their first hot spell.

Handle with care. Those young plants you buy from the nursery to transplant into your garden are in the midst of a strong momentum of growth.

SLEIGHT *of* HAND

How to Handle a Seedling

Little seedlings are delicate, and rough handling can damage roots or even break the growing tip of the stem. At the very least, rough treatment will set back the plants' growth. At worst, it can stunt or even kill them. Here's how to handle young seedlings during transplanting.

Pick up the seedling by two of its leaves, not by its stem—if you break the stem, you lose the plant. But if the plant is intact, it will grow new leaves. It's also a good idea to give support under the little rootball with your hand, a spoon, a piece of cardboard, a garden knife, or a ruler.

Rough handling can stall that momentum, which will mean disaster for a plant's future, says Hammond. So make sure you don't neglect watering, damage the plant's roots, or bruise its stem during the transplanting process.

Get the depth right. Put your transplants into the ground on a shady, late afternoon. Water your plants in their containers several hours before you make the transfer. For each plant, dig a hole in your garden bed that's wider and just a little deeper than the rootball. Place the rootball into the hole, fill in with more soil, and press down firmly around the roots.

Try this tomato trick. Handle the transplant of tomatoes a little differently, Hammond says. Plant a tomato's rootball deeply enough so that the plant's lowest leaves are at ground level—meaning you're burying some of the plant's stem. Alternatively, dig a trench and lay the tomato's rootball in it with the stem lying horizontally. Then gently bend the top several inches of stem upward and fill in soil over the rootball and rest of the stem. Either way, you will get better development of the tomato plant's root system.

Conserve water. If your soil tends to drain quickly, and your summer weather is often hot and dry, make a basin to catch and hold water for your plants. Make a saucerlike depression around the base of each plant's stem when you plant. An easy way to do this is to build up a small mound of soil in a ring around the plant, a few inches out from the stem. Water from rain or irrigation will collect in the depression and soak slowly into the soil, with less runoff.

Douse them in fishy fertilizer. Water your newly transplanted vegetables liberally. This also is the ideal time to feed your new plants seaweed or kelp, providing nutrients and microbes they need to get rooted well. An alternative: Add 1 tablespoon of fish emulsion and one tablespoon of liquid seaweed to one gallon of water. (Ask about these fertilizer products at your nursery.) Water each new transplant with one 1 of this starter solution.

Anchor your plants firmly. Many home gardeners fail to anchor their transplanted vegetables firmly enough, says Joffee. Start by making sure that your plant is deep enough in the ground. Joffee places the "neck" of the plant—the spot where it branches out with leaves—at ground level. Then he presses down

Watch the Calendar

One of the most common mistakes that home gardeners make is planting their vegetables at the wrong time, says Daron Joffee, manager of Georgia's Harvest Lake Farm. Timing is "the make it or break it factor," he says. For example, if you plant lettuce too late in spring, it will leaf out when the weather is too hot. Your lettuce will bolt (go to seed) and the leaves will turn bitter. Many crops actually do well in cool spring weather, including lettuce, carrots, spinach, parsley, and peas.

Just how are you supposed to come by this crucial when-to-plant information? Rely on sources of information that are specific to your region and climate. Seed catalogs often have excellent planting charts, but look for a catalog that is geared to your region. Your bookstore may also carry garden guides that are specific to your area. Also speak with your local Cooperative Extension agent, the staff at your garden center, and local farmers for good timing information. Or use the "Cheat Sheet" on page 54 on "Best Weather for Vegetables."

lightly on the surrounding ground to anchor the plant further. Without such anchoring, wind or rain could knock your plant over.

Place your stakes early. At planting time, you already know which vegetable plants are going to need support during the growing season—peas, beans, tomatoes, and other tall growers. So install all of your support devices (cages, stakes, and trellises) early. Trying to retrofit a cage or trellis to a mature plant is much harder than having your plants grow up with their support already in place. Spend the money on high-quality garden stakes, says Kolls—they're worth the investment.

Improvise your cages. If you're growing tomatoes, get the biggest, best support cage you can, says Kolls. She likes to make her own using ½- or ¼-inch PVC pipe, plus several elbow and T joints. She arranges the main support posts around the plant in a square about 18 inches per side. These posts are about 6 feet tall, with 1 foot sunk into the soil and 5 feet rising above it.

Cheat Sheet

Best Weather for Vegetables

Some vegetables thrive in hot weather; others like it cool. Here's a guide to which veggies like which conditions.

COOL-WEATHER VEGETABLES

These veggies can take cold temperatures and the occasional frost.

Broccoli	Kohlrabi	Radishes
Cabbage	Leeks	Spinach
Collards	Mustard greens	Turnips
Garlic	Onions	
Kale	Peas	

These veggies also like it cool and can take some light frost, but prolonged frosty weather will hurt them.

Beets	Cauliflower	Endive
Cabbage, Chinese	Celery	Lettuce
Carrots	Chard, Swiss	Potatoes

WARM-WEATHER VEGETABLES

Plant this group shortly after your last frost date. Their leaves may be damaged by frost, but they can tolerate cool temperatures.

Beans (snap and shell beans, bush and pole types)	Corn
	Tomatoes

These veggies like it hot and need temperatures of at least 70°F to grow well. Don't plant them until a few weeks after your last frost.

Lima beans	Peppers (hot and sweet)
Cucumbers	Pumpkins
Eggplant	Squash (summer and winter)
Melons	Sweet potatoes
Okra	

She connects the main support posts with three tiers of cross braces that give support to the plant as it grows (see below).

Kibble also is not impressed by commercially made tomato cages. Her favorite approach: Take three 5-foot stakes, stand them on end, and tie them at the top to create a tepee shape. Then use twine to create cross supports 6 inches apart running between the stakes. Plant a tomato plant inside each tepee.

Reuse, recycle. Gardening author Clea Danaan is a big believer in reusing everything in her garden. She saves the straight sticks (suckers) that she prunes off of a box elder and binds them together with twine to make plant supports—a tepee for beans, for instance, and a trellis for peas. You can also use pruned branches to build rustic fences, gates, and arbors if you're feeling ambitious.

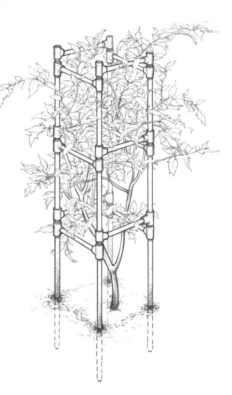

Grow up instead of out. Save space in a small garden by training vining crops to climb netting, strings, or a trellis. You can support fruit of squash and melons (which can get heavy) with cloth slings. Tie the sling to the support, and rest a fruit in each one.

Upgrade beans and peas to flower trellises. Kibble also is picky about support devices for her beans and peas. Rather than "official" supports for these plants (that is to say, gizmos designed and marketed specifically for this purpose), she uses taller flower trellises. Which sounds a lot like cheating to me!

Master Gardener Rebecca Kolls uses narrow PVC pipe, including T joints and elbow joints, to improvise tall and sturdy tomato cages.

Brighten up your vegetable garden. When botanist and author Lance Walheim is finished planting his vegetable garden, he likes to liven things up by adding flowers—sometimes as a border and sometimes just intermingled with his veggies. This touch makes his garden an even nicer place to visit frequently, Walheim says, and makes it an inviting spot for other people, too. (Plus the flowers make the garden attractive to pollinating insects as well.) And why not go a step further? Place such amenities as a table and bench nearby, making the garden a nice place to hang out, a place to read and drink coffee, and a pleasant spot for contemplating nature.

Plant in quadrants—and rotate them. If you have a large garden, divide it into quadrants and group all of your plants from the same family in the same quadrant, says Kolls. For instance, all members of the nightshade family—such as tomatoes, eggplant, and peppers—can have their own section. This way, if disease strikes it will be confined to one quadrant of your garden. In subsequent years, rotate each plant family to a new quadrant, so that a plant family will not return to the same quadrant for the next 3 years. This old-time farmer's trick prevents the spread of disease and avoids soil depletion, since each plant family makes different nutrient demands on the soil.

Other families include legumes (peas and beans); the mustard family (cabbage, broccoli, Brussels sprouts, and radishes); the gourd family (cucumbers, squash, pumpkins, and melons); the onion family (onions, leeks, and garlic); the goosefoot family (beets, chard, and spinach); and the carrot family (carrots, parsnips, and celery).

Take it easy—try raised beds. If you have a small garden, planting in raised beds will make garden maintenance easier in a number of ways, says Kolls. With raised beds, you mix your own soil in a mound above the original grade of your garden (see details in Chapter 6). This soil will drain more quickly and warm up more quickly in spring as well. Because pathways typically surround your raised beds, the plots are easy to reach into, and you needn't step onto the soil (so you avoid compacting it). This arrangement makes gardening easier if you have physical limitations. It's also harder for destructive critters such as groundhogs, squirrels, and rabbits to hide on a raised bed.

Cheat Sheet

||||||||||||||||||||||||||||||||||||||||||||||||||||||||||||||||||||||||||||||||||||||||||||||||||||||||||||||||

The Simplest Crop Rotation

Another easy way to rotate vegetables around the garden lets you equalize the drain of soil nutrients without depleting them in any one part of the garden. Divide the vegetables you grow into three categories according to the amount of nutrients they use. You can group them into Heavy Feeders (the ones that use the most nutrients), Light Feeders, and Soil Builders (crops that actually add nitrogen to the soil), as identified below. To rotate the crops, follow a heavy feeder with a light feeder and then a soil builder. The next season, plant a heavy feeder again.

HEAVY FEEDERS

Beets	Cucumbers	Pumpkins
Broccoli	Eggplant	Radishes
Cabbage	Endive	Spinach
Cauliflower	Kale	Squash
Celery	Lettuce	Tomatoes
Collard greens	Okra	
Corn	Parsley	

LIGHT FEEDERS

Carrots	Mustard greens	Sweet potatoes
Chard, Swiss	Onions	Turnips
Garlic	Peppers	
Leeks	Potatoes	

SOIL BUILDERS

Alfalfa (winter cover crop)	Clover (winter cover crop)	Peas
Beans	Peanuts	Soybeans

Don't plant in single rows. Instead of old-fashioned single rows, with lines of plants running down the garden with loads of empty space between them, make better use of your space. Plant in wide rows, using the same spacing recommended on the seed packet for spacing between plants *and* between rows, too. Just stagger the plants from one row to the next, and plant two or three rows of the same kind of plant like this. Then leave a wider space before the next row of a different type of vegetable.

Plant in small stages. Don't plant your entire garden bed all at once, says Kolls. Instead, plant just a portion of your garden, then 2 weeks later plant more, and 2 weeks after that plant still more. With your garden plants at different stages of growth, your maintenance duties will be staggered and therefore easier to deal with.

PROTECTING YOUR PLANTS

An unfortunate aspect of outdoor gardening is that all of nature is out there with you—more than happy to share your bounty. Chapter 13 is jam-packed with ways to coexist peacefully with Mother Nature. But until you get there, here are some ways to build veggie protection into your garden as you prepare for planting—some labor- and angst-saving tips from the Ounce of Prevention Department.

Entice good bugs into your garden. Add to your vegetable garden, or the nearby vicinity, the kind of plants that attract bees and other beneficial insects, says Hammond. His top choices for good bug attractors include borage, cosmos, parsley, fennel, dill, rockcress, bishop's flower (*Ammi majus*), rudbeckia or black-eyed Susan, asters, sunflowers, and gaillardia or blanket flower.

Exactly what kind of bugs are we attracting with such plants? For one thing, pollinating insects such as honeybees, bumblebees, and butterflies. These plants also entice predatory insects (such as green lacewings, ladybugs, syrphid flies, and praying mantises) that kill harmful bugs. You'll also attract

Cheat Sheet

Plants to Attract Beneficial Insects

Angelica

Anise

Asters

Astrantia

Bishop's flower

Bishop's weed

Black-eyed Susan

Blanket flower

Blue lace flower

Borage

Caraway

Coriander

Cosmos daisy

Dill

Fennel

Lovage

Parsley (if you let it bloom in its second year)

Rockcress

Sea holly (*Eryngium*)

Sedum

Sunflower

to your garden parasitic insects—such as tachinid flies and trichogramma wasps—that lay their eggs in the larvae of harmful bugs.

"The idea is not to totally eradicate the harmful bugs, but to keep them down to a level where they don't do much harm to your garden plants—a nice, natural equilibrium," says Hammond. "If you use pesticides, you'll kill all of the bugs, beneficial and harmful. Much better to establish a balanced ecology surrounding your garden—a peaceful coexistence."

Marigolds make an excellent border plant for a vegetable garden, since they're known to repel some harmful insects. They are reputed to be particularly good at repelling nematodes, which are teeny little worms in the soil. French marigolds (the smaller kind) work best.

Give your plants a head start with plastic mulch. When you think of mulch, your mind probably turns first to the shredded stuff you buy in huge bags at the garden store. But plastic sheeting that you spread over your garden soil can protect early crops of veggies from the cold by helping the soil to warm up faster. The plastic can also help to conserve moisture in the ground, suppress weeds, and keep your vegetables cleaner (preventing mud splatters). In some cases plastic mulch does a better job than the natural stuff. One caveat: Depending on where you live, you may need to remove plastic mulches when the weather warms up, or the intense summer sun could heat the soil underneath them so much that it could actually hurt your plants.

Try colored mulch for higher yields. Hammond says that use of black plastic mulch will increase your yield of peppers, squash, and pumpkins. Green plastic mulch boosts the yield of watermelons, cantaloupes, cucumbers, and sweet and hot peppers. And red plastic mulch does wonders for tomatoes. Blue mulch appears to promote growth for melons, and silver mulch discourages aphids from feeding on pumpkins.

What difference could the color of the plastic mulch possibly make? Scientists say plants have light sensors that can modify their growth patterns, depending upon what kind of light the sensors pick up. For instance, if the sensors are picking up green light reflected from plastic mulch, a plant might interpret that green to be the leaves of an encroaching competitor plant—inspiring the plant to grow taller. If you want to try other colored mulches and they aren't available in your local store, check for sources in garden catalogs and on the Internet.

Some notes on using plastic mulch: Plastic mulch works particularly well on raised garden beds. Make sure the soil has been thoroughly prepared before you install the plastic mulch. Hammond likes to lay down a soaker hose on the garden bed first, 4 to 5 inches from the center of the bed or 2 to 3 inches from the vegetable plants themselves. Then lay plastic mulch over the soil, anchoring the edges of the plastic. Poke holes in the plastic to allow water to pass through. When you're ready to plant, cut an X in the plastic at each spot where you want to put a transplant. When it's time to fertilize, you'll have to apply liquid nutrients through your soaker hose—applying dry fertilizer won't work with the plastic in your way. A range of water-soluble fertilizers is available for drip systems. One brand of seaweed/fish fertilizer is Neptune's Harvest.

Distract Pests with a Sacrificial Crop

Are your vegetables plagued by flea beetles? Distract them with a yummy alternative crop, says Robert Hammond, chef and owner of Oregon's Honeyman Creek Farms. Flea beetles are small bugs that love to munch holes in the leaves of young plants. When you disturb them, they tend to leap into the air like a flea—thus their name. When Hammond finds these jumpy little critters on his brassica vegetables (such as cabbage, Brussels sprouts, and broccoli) he likes to plant arugula in the same garden—away from the vegetables he wants to protect. The fickle little flea beetles will jump ship and head for the arugula. If flea beetles are often a problem for you, plant arugula in another part of the garden to attract them over there.

It's pretty widely available, but one source is the Drip Store online: www.dripirrigation.com. Black plastic mulch is generally less expensive than other colors of plastic mulch. You probably can find it at your garden center.

Or tuck in your veggies with landscape fabric. The use of landscape fabric in your vegetable garden is a sneaky way to pare wheelbarrow loads of maintenance work off of your gardening duties list. Landscape fabric will hold moisture in your garden soil, prevent weed growth, prevent erosion, and keep the temperature of your soil stable. The material is tough but porous, meaning that water is allowed to seep through to reach the soil. So you get a lot of value for a modest cost and a small amount of up-front work, says Kibble.

Here's what you will want to know about using landscape fabric in your vegetable garden.

- **First, prepare the soil.** Before installing landscape fabric, strip out any vegetation that lies in the way, till the soil, and make all of the additions of compost and fertilizer that your soil requires.
- **Buy the right stuff.** Buy a strong landscape fabric that is difficult to tear with your hands. Good landscape fabric will have some stiffness to it—it

won't be limp like conventional cloth. You can buy it in large rolls from your garden supply store. It should last several years before it breaks down and needs to be replaced.

■ **Lay out the fabric.** Measure the garden space to be covered and roll out the fabric. You can purchase securing pins to hold the fabric in place, but that's probably not necessary, since you're going to be anchoring it down with mulch anyway. In spots where overlap is needed, overlap at least 3 inches

Cheat Sheet

Spacing Distance for Vegetables

Here's how far apart to plant your vegetables.

Beans, lima—9 inches

Beans, snap—6 inches

Beets—6 inches

Broccoli—18 inches

Cabbage—18 inches

Cabbage, Chinese—12 inches

Carrots—3 inches

Cauliflower—18 inches

Celery—9 inches

Chard, Swiss—12 inches

Collard greens—15 inches

Corn—18 inches (best planted in a square rather than a row)

Cucumbers—18 inches

Eggplant—24 inches

Endive—18 inches

Garlic—6 inches

Kale—18 inches

Leeks—6 inches

Lettuce, head—12 inches

Lettuce, leaf—9 inches

Mustard greens—9 inches

Okra—18 inches

Onions—6 inches

Parsley—6 inches

Peas—6 inches

Peppers—15 inches

Potatoes—12 inches

Potatoes, sweet—12 inches

Pumpkins—36 inches

Radishes—3 inches

Spinach—6 inches

Squash, summer (zucchini)—24 inches

Squash, winter—36 inches

Tomatoes—24 inches

Turnips—6 inches

to make sure weeds don't have an opportunity to wriggle through to the sunlight. Look up the diameters that your intended garden plants will be when fully grown, or use the Cheat Sheet on the opposite page to find the best spacing distance between plants. On the fabric, mark circles for positioning these plants. At the center of each circle, use a knife to cut an X that's just large enough to accommodate the stem of the plant when it's mature.

- **Top it with mulch.** Cover your landscape fabric with 3 or 4 inches of mulch after planting. Not only does the mulch help to hold moisture in the soil below, but it also protects the landscape fabric from direct sunlight, which will shorten its life.

- **Watch for weeds anyway.** Yes, you have dealt a formidable blow to the weed kingdom with your landscape fabric. However, be aware that weed seeds that settle into your mulch covering can still germinate. If they do, they can send their roots down through the landscape fabric and into the soil below—so you still need to keep vigilant about these interlopers.

Try cost-free mulch. Kolls has a couple of other sneaky ways of obliterating weeds—both employing cost-free materials. One is to save a pile of old newspapers over the winter. In early spring, place the newspapers—four to six layers thick—over spots in your garden bed where you want to discourage weeds. Dampen the newspapers and cover with shredded mulch.

The other technique is to save your grass clippings in a pile. By early spring, you should be able to pull up the grass in matted layers. Spread these layers of clippings over your garden soil as a barrier to weed germination.

Set sail with floating row covers. Hammond loves to protect his young garden plants with floating row covers—spans of lightweight, spun polyester fabric that shield young garden plants from wind, sun, and bugs, while letting in a healthy amount of light and air. The covers also help to preserve moisture in the soil.

Floating row cover fabric is sold in rolls in a variety of sizes, and you just cut them to fit the size you require. Some types specialize in frost prevention and others emphasize bug control, so make sure you buy a kind that matches your needs. Since they're made of light fabric, they can "float" above your young plants without damaging them. You will want to anchor the edges of your floating row covers, either with stones, soil, or special plastic or metal "staples" you can buy for this purpose. You can also use the U-shaped metal pins that landscapers use to fasten down irrigation lines—they're widely available and cheap.

Row covers appeal to cheat-at-gardening enthusiasts because they're so much faster and easier to use than cloches or other devices that cover individual plants. You can also just leave the covers in place as long as you need them, because they let in light, air, and moisture. Glass and plastic plant covers can get really hot on sunny days and need to be vented or removed. Milk cartons and jugs block light and also need to be removed during the day. Row covers can just stay there—the only time you need to remove them is when fruiting plants like zucchini and tomatoes are blooming, so bees can get in to pollinate the flowers. Row covers are a cheater's dream come true!

Improvise a plant shield. In a pinch, Hammond says, you can achieve

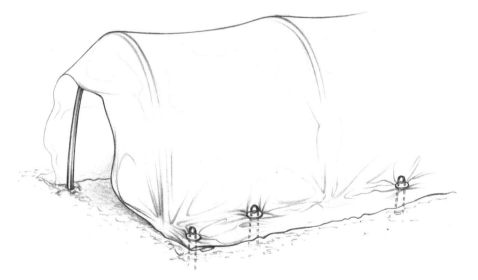

Secure the edges of your floating row cover with soil, stones, or special anchoring staples.

Won't Touch It? Why Eat It?

Here's how Master Gardener Rebecca Kolls explains her reluctance to use pesticides and other nonorganic garden products: When an acquaintance is considering using a pesticide, Koll asks, "Would you rub this same stuff on your skin?" The inevitable answer is "Of course not!" To which Koll replies, "Then why would you put it onto your food and into the soil in which it grows?"

some of the same effect of a floating row cover by folding a large piece of cardboard and propping it over some of your plants like a tent. Just remember to remove it as soon as the weather permits—cardboard won't let sunlight or rain reach the plants.

You also can give your young seedlings a measure of protective cover by using the plastic mesh baskets in which you buy cherry tomatoes or berries at the supermarket. Invert one of these little baskets over each vulnerable seedling during its first week in the garden bed. Weight the basket down with a rock or stake it in place with a couple of twigs. The basket will provide your seedling with some protection from direct sun and wind.

GROWING SEASON MAINTENANCE

Once you have carefully prepared your garden soil, carefully chosen your vegetable plants, and carefully planted them in the ground, you may feel like raising your fists into the air and letting loose a victory "Hurrah!" (cue the *Rocky* theme song). But don't hang up your gardening gloves just yet. The duties may shift now, but there's still plenty of work to do during the growing season. Gardens take work, but there are ways to make the maintenance chores easier and quicker. The following expert-recommended habits will make your vegetable garden the envy of the neighborhood.

■ **Constant observation.** Be ever on the lookout for bugs and weeds. Remove both by hand promptly. The keys to success for us garden cheaters is to catch these problems when they're just getting started. A few bugs are easier to get rid of than a major infestation. Small weeds that you identify and remove early are much easier to deal with than weeds that have had their way with your garden bed for a few weeks before you attack them. Light-and-easy hoeing will vanquish young weeds (buy a scuffle, or action, hoe that has three sharp, flat, narrow blades in a triangle-shaped head—great for weeding), or you can just pull them up by hand.

■ **Keep fertilizing.** Side-dressing is a way to add compost or fertilizer a time or two during a plant's growing cycle. Typically, you dig a shallow ring around each plant several inches from its stem, put the fertilizer into the trench, and cover it with soil. Alternatively, you might dig one long trench along an entire row of plants, add the fertilizer, and cover it over. Topdressing—spreading the fertilizer right on top of the soil—is even easier. Just scratch it in lightly with the tip of your hoe. If you're top-dressing with compost, just leave it on top of the soil.

■ **Be hygienic.** Keep your garden tools clean. Don't introduce to your garden any buggy or diseased plants. Wipe tools with a clean cloth after using them. If you did need to work around—or remove—plants infested with pests or disease, dip the tool you used into a solution of one part liquid chlorine bleach to nine parts water to disinfect the tool before you use it on or around other plants.

■ **Don't leave any soil bare.** Cover any bare patches of soil with mulch or plant a cover crop for the purpose of protecting the soil. Otherwise, the sun will bake the nutrients out of the soil, the soil will dry out, nutrients will leach out, and your soil will lose microbial activity and organic matter. What's more, wind and water can erode soil that's left bare.

■ **Keep your garden organic.** While use of nonorganic products in your garden might provide a bit of temporary convenience, they become a long-term setback for the biology of your garden overall, says Joffee. Strong chemical products can damage microbial life, drive away earthworms, and generally throw off the balance of the garden's ecosystem. You can end up with more pests than before, because beneficial insects are killed off along with pests. Chemical fertilizers are far more concentrated than organics, and what doesn't get absorbed by plants runs off, finding its way into groundwater and eventually into drinking water. It can take your garden years to recover from the use of such chemicals.

Water steadily—with a drip, drip, drip. No matter what type of mulching system you're using—plastic, fabric, shredded bark or root, or anything else—a drip-type watering system is ideal for vegetable gardening. "Most vegetables prefer to have their feet wet, not their heads," says Hammond. So a soaker hose is more efficient than overhead watering. A soaker hose puts the water right where you need it—at the roots of your plants, rather than on the leaves. Besides, with conventional sprinkling, as much as 50 percent of the water can evaporate before it ever gets to the plant. Of course, a drip system also saves

THE *MOST* LIKELY PROBLEM
Take a "Rain" Check with Your Shovel

Is your garden looking a little droopy and under the weather? Here's how to check whether your garden plants are getting enough water. Dig down with a shovel 3 to 6 inches, says Master Gardener Rebecca Kolls. If the soil is dry that far down, that's not good. Water a little longer, a little more often, and check again. Watering your garden consistently is crucial during spells of dry weather.

Bear in mind, though, that vegetable plants will often look a little limp at high noon under a hot sun, even when the soil is moist. They'll perk up again later in the day. So don't rush out and water them at lunchtime or you might actually overwater. If the plants still look limp closer to dusk, or first thing in the morning, by all means get them some water right away.

Ⓜ️YTH-BUSTERS
Sprinkling Warning Is All Wet

Some people like to argue against the use of lawn sprinklers for watering the garden, saying that getting water on vegetable foliage creates a "magnifying glass" effect that burns leaves. That particular explanation is balderdash, says master gardener Rebecca Kolls. Don't run the sprinklers between 10 a.m. and 2 p.m., when the sun is at its peak; in the morning or late afternoon your plants won't be at risk of sunburn. Nevertheless, soaker hoses are still a superior way of watering your veggies because they deliver moisture straight to the roots, and they use water more efficiently than overhead sprinklers.

● ● ● ● ● ● ● ● ● ● ● ● ● ● ● ● ● ● ● ●

you the work of lugging a watering can or hose around the garden.

You can pick up soaker hoses at your garden supply store or home improvement store. These are basically lengths of hose with tiny holes in their sides that let water seep into the ground (some types are made from recycled tires). If you keep the water pressure in the hose low, the water will merely drip, drip, drip. Under higher pressure, such hoses will send up a fine spray—which is potentially more wasteful. Also buy a timer for your garden-watering system. Timers vary in complexity, but basically are valves that are affixed to your outdoor spigot and then to your garden hose. The timer shuts off the water after a specific amount of time—which is quite handy if you're the forgetful type. Some models also have a rain gauge, which means that they will shut off the hose when nature herself has provided sufficient water without driving up your water bill.

Water like clockwork. Inconsistent watering can spell disaster for your vegetable garden, so get serious about it. If you are leaving town on vacation for a week, arrange for a neighbor to tend to the watering for you. (It will be much easier to persuade a neighbor to do this, by the way, if you have a modestly sized garden rather than a plot on the "south forty" scale.)

Don't waste time on water wasters. Poor watering techniques not only waste tremendous quantities of water, but they also waste your time and water. It may be time to give up your sprinklers altogether. They're inefficient at delivering water to plant roots since much of the water that's shot into the air evaporates as it falls to the ground; wind also sends water in unwanted directions. To reduce evaporation, choose sprinklers that create large water droplets that fall more quickly. And you may want to try watering in early morning instead of during the heat of the day to reduce evaporation.

Make sure you water your plants deeply, instead of just until the ground looks wet. Watering a thirsty plant just until the soil looks damp creates more problems than it solves. Plants watered this way need more frequent watering and develop shallow roots. Try watering less often, but water deeply each time so you soak the entire root zone. This encourages plant roots to grow deep into the soil, making them more drought-resistant. After a watering session, jab your finger into the ground to see how deeply you've watered. You'll be amazed at how dry soil can be under a surface that looks soaking wet.

Provide custom feedings. Fertilizing requirements will vary from one plant type to another, so study up on the feeding requirements of each plant in your garden. Some need frequent feedings—cabbage, for instance—and others get by with a couple of feedings during their growing season.

Help your tomatoes pollinate. When your tomato plants are in bloom, give the plants a gentle shake now and then, says Kolls. Such movement causes the flowers to release pollen, so you're ensuring that your tomato plants are pollinated and productive. Call yourself a busy little bee, if you wish.

Pick before they crack up. Do the skins of your tomatoes tend to crack on the vine? Start picking them a few days earlier—when they're starting to turn red rather than when they're fully ripe. Take them inside and find a warm and dark spot where they can finish ripening. Now that they're no longer drawing in more water, your tomatoes won't crack before they ripen.

Don't waste those nutritious liquids. You may be routinely pouring out liquids that your garden plants would love. When you change the water in your aquarium, drain the old stuff into a bucket and pour the nutrient-rich water onto your garden soil. Do the same with leftover coffee—just make sure it has cooled first, and dilute it 50-50 with tap water.

Organize your plants by thirst. Cluster your vegetable plants in the garden according to their water needs. Put the plants that need lots of water together and cluster the plants that do well in drier conditions in a separate part of the garden. This will shave time and effort off of your watering duties and will allow you to conserve water as well.

Keep on picking. When your vegetable plants start producing their crop, go ahead and pick them—and keep picking. "Most plants will produce more the more you pick," says Kibble. What's more, they will quit producing if you *don't* pick them.

Let kids get their hands dirty. Involve your kids in working in your garden. Children can be a big help with such regular duties as watering, weeding, and pulling bugs off of your plants. Not only will your children learn about nature, but you also might be surprised to find them developing a taste for vegetables that they've never willingly eaten before, says botanist Lance Walheim.

Green manures improve veggie soil. If you have some empty space and you're not ready to plant a food crop, sow warm-weather green manures like buckwheat, cowpeas, or soybeans to fill the vacancies. These are plant 'em and forget 'em crops. You can chop down these crops when you need to reclaim your planting space and work the plant debris into the soil. (Don't let these crops get too big, though. If you're not ready to plant a veggie crop, cut down the green manure plants before they get 8 inches tall or go to seed.) Just plant another round of green manure to keep the soil improvement process moving along until you need the space.

Wait two or three days to plant new summer vegetables after chopping down a green manure crop. The chopped material will shrivel and start to disappear in warm weather in about two days. If you can't wait (cheaters can be impatient!), simply rake the green manure onto a pathway. Once it dries, rake it back onto the bed as mulch. This humus-rich blanket will keep the top of the soil from drying out and will give your newly planted summer or fall seedlings a wonderful nutrient boost.

Give your garden some winter cover. When your vegetable garden is done producing yummy food for the season, it's a good idea to plant one more crop in fall—except that this time it will put no produce on your dinner table. The purpose of a winter cover crop is purely to protect your soil from weeds and erosion, and to add organic matter to the earth. Sow the garden with a cover crop such as clover, vetch, alfalfa, or winter rye. Several weeks before the start of the new spring planting season, use a shovel or tiller to turn the cover plants into the soil.

As it turns out, the sharpest vegetable-gardening tool is not a trowel, a hoe, or pruning shears—it's information. (And that's a tool that won't cause blisters no matter how often you use it!) With good background on the vegetables that you want to grow, the condition of your soil, and the peculiarities of your local climate, you will be able to avoid the time-consuming mistakes that 95 percent of your neighbors are making in their gardens. If you feel guilty about that, take your neighbors a few of your luscious tomatoes now and then—show them how generous a "cheater" can be.

CHAPTER 4

The Sweet 16:
EXPERTS' FAVORITE CAN'T-MISS VEGGIE VARIETIES

||||||||||||||||||||||||||||||||||||||||||||||||||||||||||||||||||||||||||||||||||||||||

Some vegetable varieties are an outright nuisance in the garden, while others just about care for themselves until maturity and then jump onto the dinner plate fully prepared. Not wanting to invite any troublemakers into my garden beds, I put this question to several gardening experts: What are your favorite varieties of the most popular garden vegetables? Naturally, I'm looking for superb taste. But I also asked them to take into account such cheat-at-gardening issues as hardiness, productivity, and the lowest maintenance. Here are their responses, with some tips and notes on growing and using each. Where I list a "recommended variety," that gives you an example that one expert takes great pleasure in and finds to be a great performer in the garden. Explore other varieties on your own, too. There are sure to be several alternatives that offer many of the advantages mentioned. Besides, one of the joys of gardening is discovering amazing varieties you've never heard of.

ARUGULA

Arugula leaves are known for their spicy taste (often described as peppery). This salad green has a nutty quality, too, and is kind of uniquely aromatic— you either love it or hate it. The leaves often are mixed with other salad greens for flavor balance. Common in Mediterranean cuisine, arugula is low in calories and rich in vitamins A and C. Arugula is so easy to grow that it's almost impossible to fail.

Recommended variety: 'Astro'. While arugula is known to bolt (go to seed) early and produce bitter leaves, 'Astro' is a slow-bolting, flavorful variety. 'Astro' is known as a hardy, bushy, quick-growing plant with a high yield.

Growing: Sow arugula seeds right in the garden. The seeds are tiny and hard to handle; try mixing them with some dry sand to make planting easier. Space your plantings a few weeks apart so that more arugula becomes available into fall. Arugula grows to less than 3 feet tall and resembles a long-leafed lettuce. It thrives in direct sun, although in hot and dry summer months, partial shade will help.

Using: Pick the young, lobed leaves off your arugula plant when they're 2 to 3 inches long. The older leaves will be less tender and more bitter. If your plants start to bolt into bloom, the small flowers are a tasty addition to your salads as well. If your plants do bolt, let some go and they will self-sow for a new generation of plants later in the season (depending on when they flower) or the next spring. Eat arugula within 2 days of harvesting. Rinse the leaves in cool water and pat dry with a towel. Store them in a zip-closing plastic bag. Arugula also can be made into pesto or sautéed lightly in olive oil.

POLE BEANS

Pole beans are a cheat-at-gardening favorite. Not only are they easy to grow, but they also grow vertically—which means you get more produce from less space, as well as easier access to your plants. You'll find pole beans in two categories: fresh and dry. Fresh beans (also called snap or string beans) include green, yellow, and purple varieties, as well as green shell beans such as limas and cranberry beans. Snap beans are picked before the beans inside the pods begin to swell and are eaten pod and all. Green shell beans are left on the plant until the beans inside the pods plump up, but are picked while the pods are still green. Dry beans (hard beans such as black beans and kidney beans) are allowed to mature completely on the vine and are stored in dry form. All kinds of beans provide fiber, protein, and vitamins A and C.

Recommended variety: 'Mountaineer White Half Runner'. While half runner beans generally won't climb up a trellis as high as conventional pole beans, this one will give you a vine 5 to 8 feet long. Despite the name, it's a pole bean. Gardeners rave about the taste of this variety's tender white seeds as well as its long, slender pods. 'Mountaineer White Half Runner' is an heirloom German variety that was introduced to America by early settlers. If you can't find this variety, try the more conventional 'Blue Lake' or 'Kentucky Wonder' green snap beans.

Growing: Pole beans are easy to grow and aren't picky about climate, but they grow best in loose, well-draining soil that has plenty of organic content. Don't plant them too early—bean plants will rot in cool, moist earth. As their name implies, pole beans need some kind of support, such as trellises, nylon netting, or, yes, poles. Remember to water your bean plants consistently. They may be a warm-season vegetable, but stress from lack of water will damage their productivity. Over-watering, however, will cause rot. If you need to weed or otherwise disturb the soil near your bean plants, proceed cautiously—your plant's root system is shallow and easily damaged.

Try a bean tower. To save space in a snap, use a bean tower to support your pole beans. Bean towers are available in garden supply and seed catalogs.

They're easy to put together once you get used to them, and gardeners say they get more beans per square foot than with other vertical support systems. The tower looks like a string trellis in a tepee shape, with the pointed top cut off. Because the top is smaller than the bottom, the strings—and the bean vines—slant, so the beans hang down inside the tower where they're easy to see. Allow a space 3 feet square for each tower.

Using: If you keep up with your picking, pole beans will keep producing until fall's frost kills them—particularly if you staggered your planting to ensure a long harvest season. (To do this, plant every 2 to 4 weeks until mid-summer.) If you're expecting a long growing season, feed your bean plants a side-dressing of compost halfway through the season. Bean picking requires ongoing judgment calls—make sure you catch them young, before they toughen up. Beans are ready to pick when they snap easily and the seeds inside aren't fully mature. Pick them by pulling each individual bean away from the vine, or by snapping it off next to the vine. And pick gently, since bean plant stems and branches are fragile.

If you have picked more beans than your family can eat immediately, store them dry in zip-closing bags in the crisper of your refrigerator, where they'll be good for up to 3 days. Don't wash your beans until you're ready to cook them, as the moisture will damage them in storage.

BROCCOLI

Some nutrition experts call broccoli the perfect food—it's that packed with nutrients, particularly vitamin C and beta carotene. And even if the broccoli florets are your favorite part, don't neglect the stem—that's high in fiber.

Recommended variety: 'Packman'. This flavorful variety is known for good production of side shoots after you have harvested the main central head of the broccoli (more on harvesting in a moment). 'Packman' grows vigorously and is known to develop heads as large as 10 inches across. 'Packman' adapts easily to varied climates and soil conditions. For a broccoli plant, 'Packman' is also fairly tolerant of heat, which could give you some flexibility in your planting schedule.

Growing: This member of the cabbage family grows best during the cooler parts of the gardening season. In many climates you can get two separate crops—an early summer harvest and a fall harvest—by avoiding the hottest days of summer. So get sneaky: Give your broccoli plants a head start by using transplants from the nursery rather than starting from seed, and plant in early spring and late summer. Also, keep your eyes open for the newer heat-tolerant varieties, such as 'Green Comet' and 'Green Goliath'—they may help you sidestep the killer heat of summer, too. Your broccoli should weather a cold snap nicely unless the temperatures drop below 20°F. In that case, coddle your plants with floating row covers or other protection.

Keep out cabbage worms and avoid weeds. Hide your broccoli under floating row covers (see page 63 for info) and you'll never have to pick off little green cabbage looper worms. The covers keep the adult moths from laying eggs on your plants. And to save yourself the work of pulling back the covers to weed the broccoli every week, mulch the broccoli plants with 2 inches of straw or other organic mulch after you plant, then install the row covers.

Using: Those large green broccoli heads are actually composed of zillions of unopened flowers. To harvest, cut off the central lobe along with several inches of the stem—before those flowers get around to blooming and before the lobe starts to separate itself naturally from the rest of the plant. This first harvest will encourage more rapid development of smaller side shoots, keeping you supplied with the veggie for weeks to come. Try not to store your broccoli in the refrigerator any longer than a few days. The longer you store it, the more taste and nutritional value it loses. Don't wash your broccoli until you're ready to consume it.

CANTALOUPE

Think of cantaloupe as a warm-weather friend. Also known as muskmelon, it tastes best when harvested in summery weather. Cantaloupe is high in vitamins

A and C. It's a sure crowd pleaser any way you serve it—simply sliced at breakfast, adding a splash of orange color to a fruit salad at lunch, or capping off dinner as a fruit smoothie for dessert (in a blender or food processor, combine melon chunks, fruit juice, ice, and honey).

Recommended variety: 'Pride of Wisconsin'. Juicy and highly productive, 'Pride of Wisconsin' is known as a great crop for home gardeners. It gets rave reviews for flavor.

Growing: Cantaloupe plants love warm weather. Don't attempt early planting if that will expose them to cool weather—your cantaloupes will just fail. They won't tolerate root disruption either. If you're starting them from seed indoors, plant only one per container to make transplanting simpler. The best way to start from seed, if you don't live where the growing season is long enough to plant seeds right in the ground, is to plant in peat pots, thinning to one seedling per pot. Then just sink the biodegradable pot and all into the garden—it makes for the least root disturbance. Include plenty of composted manure in the garden bed. Floating row covers and black plastic mulch (see Chapter 3) work well for cantaloupe. Drip irrigation is a good idea, too, since cantaloupes like consistent (but not frequent) watering. Give them the same amount of water on a regular schedule, but let the soil dry somewhat between waterings. Watering is particularly important during vine and melon growth, but ripening melons do better in drier soil. When your vine produces runners, give your plant a side-dressing of organic nitrogen fertilizer. Be careful not to disturb your cantaloupes' roots when you weed or otherwise work the soil.

Cantaloupes like elbow room in the garden. If you don't have a lot of space to devote to your cantaloupe plants, use your engineering skills to go vertical. Train the vines up a fence, trellis, or cage. Once you have fruit growing to 2 or 3 inches in diameter, make slings to support the fruit until maturity and to take stress off of the vine. You can make slings from the plastic mesh bags that you buy oranges in, or whip out your holey-est pair of panty hose. Inspect your slings as the cantaloupes grow to see if they need additional support.

Cantaloupes lying against the soil are susceptible to rot, particularly in damp weather. Go to your recycling bin and find a can or other container that will support your fruit up off the ground. Mice and moles may be attracted to your cantaloupes as well. Raising the fruit on a can or board may help keep it out of trouble. Set a few traps, too, if rodents are a problem.

Get the sweetest cantaloupes. For the sweetest melons, quit watering 8 to 10 days before you expect to harvest—dry soil means sweeter flavor, because the fruits can develop the sugars that give them that flavor.

If you get rain during that time, try to harvest your 'lopes within a day or two. If you wait 3 or 4 days, the quality of the melons will decline.

Using: Pick cantaloupes when the stem looks dried up and the fruit separates easily from the vine. The background color on the rind will have turned to beige or yellow, rather than green. Smell the stem end, too—cantaloupe smells sweet when it's ripe.

An upended tin can will hold your cantaloupe above the fray—that is, away from pests and ground rot.

CARROTS

Carrots are packed with disease-fighting beta carotene (hmm, I wonder where the word *carotene* comes from?). Light cooking makes carrots even sweeter than they taste when they are raw. And unlike many vegetables, cooked carrots tend to hold onto their nutrients.

Recommended variety: 'Little Finger'. This "baby" variety produces sweet, crunchy, 3½-inch carrots. The cylindrical miniature carrots are great raw or cooked. And because they're small, they'll be ready for harvest quicker than longer-rooted varieties.

Growing: Carrots grow best as a cool-season crop, so plant them in early spring. The roots need to penetrate straight down, so good soil is important. For most varieties of carrot, you will need loose, clump-free, stone-free soil as deep as 9 inches—even deeper for some of those monster varieties with really long roots (sandy soil is recommended in such cases). Carrot seeds take their time germinating, so mark their location carefully—a few weeks later, you'll have forgotten where they are. (Some gardeners add to the row some radish seeds, which sprout quickly, marking the carrot area.) Young carrot seedlings are delicate and need your protection, so weed thoroughly but carefully around them. If you have a late planting maturing in fall, generous use of straw mulch may extend your harvest into winter. You can leave your carrots "in storage" right in the ground well after the tops have died off.

Keep out carrot rust fly maggots. To keep carrot worms (the larvae of the carrot rust fly) from attacking your crop, cover your carrots with floating row covers so the adult flies cannot lay their eggs near your carrots. Be sure to bury the edges of the row covers so the flies can't sneak in underneath them. An alternative tactic is to plant later. If you wait until early summer to plant your carrots, you'll miss the flies' egg-laying season.

Using: Most carrots can be pulled or dug up once they have reached a half-inch in diameter, although some varieties call for three-fourths of an inch. Depending on when you plant them, 'Little Finger' carrots are ready for harvest in late summer or early fall. Carrots that grow to an inch or more in diameter start to lose their taste and get tough and woody. If you like, you can harvest some of your carrots early, at the tender "baby" stage, and let others mature. To store carrots in the refrigerator, trim off all but an inch of the tops (otherwise, they'll pull moisture and nutrients out of the root). Put the carrots in a perforated plastic bag. They'll last several weeks in the crisper drawer.

SWEET CORN

Corn is so popular with gardeners because no supermarket offerings can compete with that fresh-picked taste. You'll find sweet corn in various color schemes, including white, yellow, and bi-colored. Maturity dates vary from one variety to another, so pay attention to your calendar and your dinner plans when you make a selection. Corn is up to its ears (ha-ha!) in vitamins, minerals, and fiber. If you want to get a head start on the growing season, protect these cold-sensitive plants with plastic mulch or row covers while the days are cool.

Recommended variety: 'Kandy Korn'. This variety gets raves for its sweet taste, its texture, and the large ears it produces. Growers say it holds onto its sweetness for as long as a week after picking (but who can wait that long?). The creamy kernels are yellow, while the tall stalks are a striking burgundy.

Growing: Make sure your sweet corn gets 8 hours of sun each day. Plant it on the north side of your garden, unless you need it to provide shade for other plants. Yes, sweet corn is a warm-weather crop. Nevertheless, water your corn plants consistently, because a dry spell can seriously affect growth and quality. When your corn plants reach 1 to 1½ feet in height, give them a side-dressing of nitrogen fertilizer. Give them another dose of nitrogen upon silking. Expect each stalk to produce at least one ear, sometimes two—the second one takes longer to develop.

Corn plants depend on pollination, and when pollination doesn't happen, gaps appear on the ear where kernels failed to develop. That's why gardeners are advised to group corn plants of the same variety in close proximity in the garden; plant them in blocks, not with plants strung out along a row. Pollen from the male tassels must spread by wind to the female silks. So help nature along with some careful positioning.

Plant clover for weed control. Corn has a lot of shallow surface roots that can make weeding a challenge. But you can plant clover around your corn plants to control weeds without digging, hoeing, or pulling. After you harvest the corn, till the clover into the soil to add organic matter and nutrients for next year's crop.

Using: Sweet corn has a 1-week window for ideal harvesting, when the kernels produce a milky liquid when punctured with a fingernail. This will come about 3 weeks after the appearance of silk. You'll notice the silk turning brown and drying out. The kernels on the tips of the ears will be full, and the ears will feel firm inside their husks. The whole point of growing your own corn is to achieve that fresh-picked taste, right? So pay attention to the timing of the harvest and check your corn frequently. When you see these signs, tell someone to boil a pot of water while you start picking—peak freshness is that fleeting.

You probably already know how to shuck corn. (Pull the husk leaves from the tip of the ear down to the bottom. When you have gathered all of the leaves, grab them in your fist and snap off the stem.) However, those corn silks are a tad more annoying, unless you know this trick: Hold the bare ear in the kitchen sink under cold running water. Brush away the corn silk by scrubbing lightly with a vegetable brush using a circular motion.

KALE

A member of the cabbage family, kale is highly nutritious and rich in vitamins A and C, as well as B vitamins, calcium, and iron. Since it's hard to find fresh in the supermarket, that's all the more incentive to grow your own. Kale comes in a broad range of colors and frilly leaf shapes, making it a favorite of creative salad makers and cooks.

Recommended variety: 'Winterbor'. This is a hardy variety that produces well. Like all kale varieties, it stands up to frosty weather, so you can plant a second crop in midsummer for late fall or even winter harvest. Known for vigorous growth, it produces thick, blue-green leaves with frilly, curled edges.

Growing: Plant kale in full sun and in soil that drains well. Kale grows vigorously from seeds planted directly in the garden, so you can pretty well forgo looking for transplants. It thrives in slightly acidic soil with plenty of organic matter. Kale plants typically grow 1 or 2 feet high. The flavor turns bitter in hot weather and sweeter in cold weather, especially after a light frost. So the leaves that mature before the full heat of summer, or in the frosty days of fall, will taste best. Since mature kale can withstand the coldest temperatures of many climates (kale will grow in any region where there is frost), try leaving it in your garden and harvest it throughout the winter. Where winters are not too severe, and if it is well-protected with mulch, kale can last all winter. (It's a sure bet that the buggy pests of summer won't hang around, so there's another maintenance duty you'll be able to cross off your to-do list.) Kale matures quickly—within 2 months. Providing plenty of water and mulch will keep your kale sweet and tender. Harvest kale leaves as soon as they grow to full size. Kale can have shallow roots that spread laterally, so take care whenever you are weeding or otherwise turning soil near one of your plants.

Using: Pick the youngest center leaves to add to salads. The older, outer leaves can be used as cooking greens, much like collards and Swiss chard. If members of your family turn up their noses at kale, introduce it gradually by adding just a few leaves at a time to salads. But it's really best when cooked—try it topped with butter or a cream sauce.

LEAF LETTUCE

Leaf lettuce is popular with home gardeners because you don't have to do much more than plant it and come back at harvest time (though it's a good idea to weed it also—lettuce can't compete with weeds). Leaves grow quickly and loosely on the stem, rather than compacted into heads (like the iceberg or Boston lettuce you find in supermarkets). Among the kinds of leaf lettuce, you will find plenty of color, shape, and texture variations to keep you entertained.

Recommended variety: 'Amish Deer Tongue'. This hardy heirloom variety is known as a bountiful producer that can tolerate heat (unlike most leaf lettuces). 'Amish Deer Tongue' is a distinctive plant with a compact body. That charming name comes from the unusual triangular leaves. Gardeners rave about their pleasant texture and sharp taste. If you can't find 'Amish Deer Tongue', try 'Oak Leaf' as an alternative—it's heat tolerant, widely available, and easy to grow.

Growing: Growing lettuce is about as easy as gardening gets. While most varieties are a cool-weather crop, some types tolerate heat and are slow-bolting—which will help you extend the growing season. Look for 'Tropicana', 'Summer Crisp' (there are several varieties), 'Red Sails', 'Royal Oak Leaf', 'Simpson Elite', or 'Lovina'. Plan ahead so your lettuce will mature in late spring to early summer, or in fall. If you want a summer crop, locate your lettuce where the plants will have partial shade during summer heat.

If you plant your lettuce in wide rows or bands 18 to 24 inches across, instead of in single rows, the plants will form their own mulch—the leaves will form a canopy that will shade out weeds.

Lettuce likes soil that's fertile, contains plenty of organic matter, and retains moisture well. Give young lettuce plants protection from the wind, since they can dry out easily. Also protect your plants with careful weeding, because lettuce doesn't stand up well to competition with interlopers. If you are planting your lettuce from seed and have clay soil, cover the seeds with potting soil rather than garden soil. This will prevent crusting on the bed's surface, which will interfere with the sprouting lettuce. On the other hand, using transplants is a good idea if that gives you a head start on the growing season and you can harvest before the extreme heat of summer hits.

Grow three crops in one-third the space. Triple your harvest when you grow three vegetables in the space it used to take to grow just lettuce with the

"LRB" method. "LRB" stands for lettuce, radishes, and broccoli and is the brainchild of Dr. Alan Kapuler, former director of research for Seeds of Change, a national organic seed company in Santa Fe, New Mexico.

Plant all three crops sparsely in the same row. The radishes come up quickly and are the first to be harvested. Removing the radishes leaves extra room for the lettuce, which is harvested soon afterward. Then the slower-growing broccoli has the run of the row, and it will produce main heads and later side shoots for the remainder of the growing season.

Using: Leaf lettuce can be harvested once your plants reach 5 or 6 inches in height. Pick individual leaves, starting with the larger outer leaves, or cut off the entire plant where leaves meet stem. Store excess lettuce leaves dry in a plastic bag in the crisper drawer of your refrigerator.

Try the "LRB" method: Plant lettuce, radishes, and broccoli in a row and stagger your harvest as the vegetables mature.

HOT PEPPERS

Is it any surprise that such a fiery plant would be a bit temperamental? But if you love spicy food, you've got to have hot peppers in your garden. Before you commit yourself to any particular variety of hot pepper, do a background check first. Some don't perform well outside of a hot, arid climate, and others will tolerate cooler regions—if you baby them a bit. If you get rainy summers, grow a hot pepper variety that's resistant to bacterial leaf spot, such as 'El Rey', 'Super Cayenne II', or 'X3R Hot Spot'. Also, consider how you'll use your peppers. Some varieties are better for drying, others are better used fresh, and still others are better pickled.

Recommended variety: 'Mucho Nacho Jalapeno'. This large-size variety produces 4-inch-long peppers that are longer, thicker, and spicier than your everyday jalapeno. 'Mucho Nacho' is a vigorous, high-yielding plant.

Growing: Hot peppers, wouldn't you know, thrive in hot weather and abhor frost. So if you live in a cold climate, coddle your hot pepper plants by pulling out your entire repertoire of warmth-giving devices—floating row covers, plastic mulch, and such. Hot peppers grow well in raised beds and like full sun, soil that drains well, and loads of compost. For an extra boost, water the plants when they are setting fruit with a solution of 1 teaspoon Epsom salts to 1 quart of water.

The limbs of a pepper plant can be fragile and, on a heavily laden plant, in danger of breaking. In such cases, use a stake or a tomato cage to protect the plant. Most garden pests are not as fond of spicy food as you are, although you may need to defend your peppers from the occasional aphid or caterpillar.

Pinch plants for more peppers. It's a good idea to pinch off the tips of your pepper plants when they're young, to encourage bushier growth that leads to more peppers. Wear gloves to pinch your plants, to avoid unpleasant encounters with hot pepper oil. Better yet, snip off the plant tips with scissors, so you don't have to touch the plants at all.

Using: For harvesting, you just need to know the final color of the variety of hot pepper you have grown. Colors vary widely: commonly green, yellow, or red. To get the most peppers from each plant, pick them green until late in the season, then let the last peppers ripen (if you let peppers ripen early on, it slows down the plant's production). When the peppers have reached the target color, they're mature. Use shears to clip them from the stems. Wear rubber gloves when you're handling hot peppers and do not touch your hands to your face. The chemicals that cause that fiery taste also can scald your skin and your eyes. Rubbing alcohol will remove those chemicals from pepper-burned skin, and hemorrhoid ointment will relieve the pain.

Wash your harvested hot peppers, dry them off, and store them in the refrigerator, where they'll last a couple of weeks. For longer storage, freeze them, dry them, or can them.

Just before your first frost, pull up the entire pepper plant (roots and all) and hang it upside down in your garage, your basement, or some other dry place with good air circulation. The peppers remaining on your plant will mature, and you will have saved them from a destructive cold snap. Alternatively, you can severely prune down your pepper plant late in the growing season, pot it and take it inside for winter, then move it outside again next spring.

POTATOES

Not only are potatoes fat-free, but they provide a healthful dose of fiber, vitamin C, and other nutrients. Although many of us have been long taught that potatoes are a starchy food, they have fewer calories and are denser in nutrients than rice, pasta, and bread. They do have a high glycemic index, though, and make blood sugar rise pretty quickly like starchy foods do.

Recommended variety: 'Yukon Gold'. Unlike the most common, white-fleshed potatoes, 'Yukon Gold' has a tasty yellow flesh—so moist that you'll reduce the amount of butter you slather on. Sometimes you can find 'Yukon Gold' in the supermarket—if you do, there's your chance to "test-drive" this variety before you commit to an entire crop.

Growing: Potatoes like growing in relatively cool climates and can even stand up to a bit of frost. Some of the best potato-growing areas are places where summers are fairly cool, such as Maine, New York's Long Island, and Idaho. Moisture in the soil must be consistent for proper formation of the tubers. On-again-off-again water will result in knobby, deformed growth or cracking. Potatoes like light, loose, slightly acidic soil. A layer of organic mulch will help preserve moisture in the soil, discourage weeds, and keep the ground cool, too. Potatoes are grown from seed pieces—that is, tiny potatoes or chunks of potato. Each piece needs at least one eye that can produce a sprout. Make sure that the seed pieces you buy are certified—which means they won't be carrying diseases into your garden bed. Supermarket potatoes aren't certified disease-free, and most are treated to inhibit sprouting, so don't try using them to start your garden crop.

Gardeners use a technique called hilling to encourage the development of the tubers (a potato is actually an expanded section of stem, not a swollen root). Place the seed piece in the planting hole or trench 4 or 5 inches deep. Cover it with 3 or 4 inches of soil. When sprouts emerge, add another few inches of soil. At least twice more during the growing season, add soil halfway up the height of the potato plant. Your actual potatoes will develop between the soil surface and the original seed piece. The point is to keep light from reaching and damaging the developing spuds. Add to your hill whenever it appears that your potatoes are going to shoulder their way through the soil.

You might find it easier to use straw or peat moss to do your hilling, rather than soil. At harvest time, reaching your potatoes through those loose materials will be simpler than digging your potatoes out of dirt and possibly damaging them.

Grow in containers to avoid disease. If blight and other diseases are problems in your garden, grow your potatoes in bushel baskets or 5-gallon pails with holes punched in the bottom. Fill the container halfway with compost and set one seed potato on top in a 5-gallon bucket, two or three seed potatoes in a bushel basket. Add more compost to completely cover the seed potatoes. As the stem and leaves come up, add more compost so the tubers always stay buried. When the plants grow above the top of their container, fill it three-quarters full with compost.

Harvest is easy, too. For "new" small potatoes, when the plants stop blooming, just reach in and pull out what you need. Or in fall, when the leaves start to turn brown, tip over the containers, spill out the contents, and pick out the spuds.

Using: You can harvest your potatoes during the growing season while they're still small or "new." As mentioned above, when the plants finish flowering, poke around in the soil to see if any small tubers have formed. When they do, you can harvest new potatoes. Cook them up right away, as they lose moisture quickly through their thin skins. Alternatively, wait until the plants begin to turn brown or die off at the end of the growing season and pull up your mature spuds. Store mature potatoes in a cool, humid area where light cannot reach them.

RADISHES

Radishes are considered a great crop for small garden beds and even for containers. They grow quickly and easily (ready to harvest just 4 or 5 weeks after planting) and don't take up much space. Such quick results make them an excellent vegetable for beginners and children to grow. Not only do radishes add a zingy taste to the dinner plate (salads and salsas in particular), they're also rich in vitamins and minerals.

Recommended variety: 'French Breakfast'. Many varieties of radish thrive in the cool of spring, but 'French Breakfast' can handle the summer heat, too. 'French Breakfast' produces delicately flavored radishes. The 3- to 4-inch roots have an exotic appearance—oblong and mostly scarlet with a white tip.

Growing: Radishes grow from seed quickly and with little trouble. All you have to do is provide good soil and moisture for the 3 or 4 weeks of growth. Radishes like rich, loose soil that's free of rocks and other obstacles. Make several sowings a couple of weeks apart to extend your harvest. Also, switch between cool season and warm season varieties as appropriate. If you time things right, you'll still be pulling up radishes in winter. When your radish seeds sprout, treat them to some mulch to preserve moisture, to keep the soil cool, and to discourage weeds. Speaking of weeds—keep after them. Radishes don't compete well for nutrients and moisture. Unless you have a heat-tolerant variety of radish, plant them near taller plants that will shade them in the heat of summer.

Using: Radishes are ready to harvest when they're about 1 inch in diameter. If they're left too long in the soil, radishes turn squishy and bitter. To harvest them, just grasp the base of the stem and pull up gently. To store your radishes, cut off their tops, put them in a plastic bag, and place the bag in the vegetable crisper of your refrigerator. If you find that a radish is too peppery for your taste (or that of a family member) whittle at its skin with a vegetable peeler—most of that taste lies on the surface.

SWISS CHARD

Fans hail Swiss chard as one of the easiest vegetables to grow. It grows aggressively, stands up to cold, and is even forgiving of a little neglect. It's a good source of vitamins (A and C), calcium, iron, and fiber. While Swiss chard is a member of the beet family, don't go looking for a bulb below ground—there isn't one. Swiss chard makes an excellent substitute for spinach in both the garden and the kitchen.

Recommended variety: 'Bright Lights'. This variety wows everyone with the red, orange, and yellow colors of its stems. Some gardeners even grow 'Bright Lights' in ornamental beds. The plants also do well in containers.

Growing: Like kale, Swiss chard loves sun and soil that drains well and has plenty of organic matter. Also like kale, Swiss chard leaves are the tastiest when they're picked in cool weather rather than hot, though the plants can take a great deal of heat without bolting. Swiss chard does best with an inch or two of water a week. Inconsistent watering can make the leaves tough, stunt their growth, and detract from their taste. Use mulch to preserve moisture and to keep weeds under control. Young Swiss chard plants are not street fighters and don't do well when competing with weeds. Start harvesting leaves, cutting them off at the base of the stem, when the plant reaches 8 inches in height.

Using: Harvest the outer Swiss chard leaves first, cutting them off near the base, as low as 2 inches above the soil. The leaves actually make fine eating at any stage of growth, from young leaves to full-size leaves. Swiss chard can be eaten raw in a salad, cooked like spinach, or used as a wrap for other foods. It's delicious stir-fried or sautéed: If you're cooking mature leaves, separate the leaves from the stems, chop the stems, and sauté or steam them for a few minutes before adding the leaves to the pan.

TOMATOES

There's a clear advantage to growing your own tomatoes. The varieties you find in the supermarket have been bred to protect the fruit from the rigors of shipping, toughening them to the point that they have the texture and taste of rubber balls. They just can't compete with the juicy, tasty homegrown version. Not only do tomatoes provide vitamins A and C, but they're also a good source of lycopene, which reduces risk of prostate cancer (are you paying attention, guys?).

Recommended variety: 'Early Girl'. As the name implies, 'Early Girl' is a variety that provides an earlier-than-usual harvest, as soon as 45 days after transplanting. But there's a bonus: It's known to keep producing through the summer. 'Early Girl' grows tall (requiring support), produces tasty fruit, and gets high marks for disease resistance. It does well in many different kinds of climate. The fruit are classic salad tomatoes in the standard tennis ball size.

Growing: There are a zillion varieties of tomato available—choose one that perfectly fits your circumstances. Start by looking for resistance to diseases and pests. If you have a cooler climate, select an early-producing variety. Then settle on a variety that's suited to your favored use—some are ideal for slicing onto salads, others are ideal for cooking in sauces or canning. You will find varieties marked either as determinate or indeterminate. Determinate tomato varieties top out at a particular height—say, 2 or 3 feet—and are easier to control, but produce their crop over a shorter period of time. They're a good choice for small gardens and northern gardens where the growing season is short. Indeterminate tomatoes can grow taller (as high as 6 feet), bushier, and may produce rather late. (Jack had a beanstalk like that.) But they will keep on producing fruit until the first fall frost shuts them down.

Give your tomatoes a location in full sun. Pay careful attention to the spacing requirements of the variety you have chosen. This can vary from 1 foot to several feet. A cluster of aggressively growing, entwined tomato plants is not a pretty sight. If you provide support to your tomato plants (stakes or cages), lash them to the support only loosely with twine. A tight loop can restrict growth of the stem or even damage the plant. Tomatoes like soil that drains

Accelerate the ripening of a tomato by enclosing it in a plastic bag with a piece of fruit that gives off ethylene gas.

well, has a good dose of organic matter, and is lightly fertilized. Look for an organic fertilizer that provides phosphorus, which will help your tomato plants with root growth (go easy on the nitrogen, which will just give you a lot of leaves). If you plant early in the season, provide your tomato plants with protective cover anytime a late frost sneaks up on you.

Using: You can pick tomatoes before they're fully ripe, and that's a particularly good idea if the temperature is 90°F or more. Such heat degrades the quality of your tomatoes. Picking fruit encourages production of more tomatoes and relieves the plant of weight that could damage plant stems. If your tomatoes have more ripening to do, leave them out at room temperature on the kitchen counter, or put them in a brown paper bag out of direct sun. Don't put them in the fridge or in a window. Refrigeration slows ripening, kills a tomato's taste, and turns the texture mushy. Another good method is to put the not-quite-ripe tomatoes in a plastic bag with a banana, orange, or apple. The fruit gives off ethylene gas, which hastens ripening. If you have to pick all the remaining tomatoes on your plants to keep them from freezing in fall, try wrapping them individually in newspaper and storing them in a cool, dry place. All the fruit that has started to turn a lighter shade of green while still on the plant will ripen indoors.

When cutting tomatoes, make sure you have a very sharp knife so it doesn't crush the fruit as you try to cut it. (Or start the cut first by nicking the skin.) To keep more juice in your tomato slices (for use in sandwiches, for instance), cut lengthwise, from the stem end to the base.

CHERRY TOMATOES

Cherry tomatoes are generally hardier and easier to grow than their larger brethren. The mini-fruits are also less afflicted by the cracking and rot that sometimes trouble larger varieties. They will produce fruit more quickly, too, and keep producing into early fall.

Recommended variety: 'Sun Gold'. 'Sun Gold' cherry tomatoes are golden orange, have outstanding sweet flavor, and are easy to grow. They adapt equally well to warm or cool climates. Their fruit produces few seeds.

Growing: Purchase seedlings from your nursery and plant after the last frost date for your region. If you're planting more than one cherry tomato, stagger the timing of your planting so one will be producing in its prime while the other is petering out. One or two cherry tomato plants should be sufficient for a family. Pick a sunny spot for your cherry tomato plant—at least 6 hours of direct exposure a day. Protection from wind is a good idea. Place a garden stake next to the plant and secure it loosely.

When you select a variety of cherry tomato, check what size the plant will reach in maturity. If the size is listed as "indeterminate" (that's the case with 'Sun Gold'), your plant could grow several feet tall. However, they are easily pruned for height, forcing the bush into more lateral growth.

Using: Expect to harvest 'Sun Gold' cherry tomatoes twice a week. Pick the fully orange fruits, taking stem with each one, and store at room temperature (refrigeration will weaken their flavor).

Cherry tomatoes are wonderful in salads. They also make a healthful (not to mention sweet and delicious!) finger food on a veggie-and-dip tray. Because cherry tomatoes needn't be sliced, they can be tossed in a salad without creating a sloppy mess. Cherry tomatoes come in a wide variety of colors (red, orange, yellow, and green), sizes, and shapes—a lovely opportunity for experimentation. If your children are reluctant to eat regular tomatoes, cherry tomatoes are a great way to get them started. Hard-working gardeners who pluck a few for a midday snack are hereby forgiven.

TURNIPS

Turnips are easy to grow and taste best when they grow quickly—so pay attention to the instructions that are specific to your variety. Not only does the root of the turnip plant provide crunch and flavor, but you also benefit from loads of fiber, vitamins A and C, plus iron. Both the root and its green tops are nutritious. You needn't look for a variety that specializes in production of greens—the tops of any variety will do nicely.

Recommended variety: 'Hakurei'. 'Hakurei' produces beautiful white spherical turnips. One of my advisors calls them "sweet, tender, and phenomenal." Sometimes referred to as a "salad turnip," 'Hakurei' roots can be eaten raw or cooked. The green tops are ready for your salad straight out of the garden. To catch 'Hakurei' roots at their yummiest, harvest them at a diameter of 2 inches.

Growing: Turnips are a cool-weather crop, making them best-suited for colder climates and higher elevations. Plant them from seed in a sunny spot with soil that drains well and includes plenty of organic matter. To prolong your harvest season, plant more turnip seeds every 4 weeks. Turnips are most tender and tasty when harvested at a diameter of 2 or 3 inches. When they get larger, turnips develop a stronger taste and a woodier texture. They also taste better when harvested before the extreme heat of summer. If you want to extend a late harvest into early winter, provide your turnip plants with the protection of straw or fabric mulch. Turnips require an inch or two of water a week, depending on your soil type. Water consistently—fluctuations can lead to root problems.

Using: The leafy tops of your turnip plants can be cooked as greens. Snip off young and tender leaves and cook them as you would spinach. When you pull up the turnip root, snip the tops, wash the root, and store the root in the refrigerator for as long as 3 weeks.

ZUCCHINI

Zucchini plants are famous for high production. So much so that a family probably doesn't need more than one plant. Otherwise, you might turn into one of those pathetic souls who leaves grocery bags full of zucchini on a neighbor's front porch in the dead of night. This summer squash won't store long either, so make sure your family is receptive to zucchini before you plant it.

Recommended variety: 'Costata Romanesca'. This Italian heirloom variety is beautifully striped and known for its excellent, nutty flavor. Because the fruit are ribbed, cross-section slices have a charming scalloped look. This variety is pretty easy to find, but if you'd rather grow a more contemporary zucchini, try 'Raven' or 'Tigress.'

Growing: Zucchini will do well in just about any kind of soil, particularly if it drains well. If your soil is particularly poor, or last year's harvest was disappointing, they'll benefit from compost in the soil and fertilizer during the growing season. How much space should you leave between zucchini plants? Don't be silly—you don't need more than one. However, you can count on your single plant taking up a space about 3 feet in diameter.

Zucchini grows quickly, especially when the weather is hot, and can be ready to pick less than a week after flowering. Inspect your plants every day to stay on top of their production. If allowed to grow too large, zucchini will get tough—pretty much fit for the compost pile or for pummeling burglars. Pick zucchini when they're a tender 4 to 6 inches long. Early picking also will prompt greater productivity (if you can stand it). Zucchini plants don't hold up well to frost, so don't count on an early or late growing season. Keep up with your watering; otherwise the fruit will fall off prematurely.

Seal out those squash borers. Squash vine borers are little white caterpillars that love to make a meal of the very object they find themselves on when they hatch from their eggs. Unfortunately, that's often the stem of your zucchini plant. The small black-and-red adult moth lays her eggs in late spring along the base of the zucchini stem (or some other plant in the squash family). The hatching caterpillar digs straight into the stem, damaging the plant. There are a few preventive tricks you can use to combat such borers.

Floating row covers (described in Chapter 3) will keep the mother moth at bay (just have them in place from the day you set your zucchini plants out in the garden). The drawback to this method is that you'll have to pollinate the plants yourself, by touching a dry artist's paintbrush to the male flowers and then to the female flowers (which have a small swelling at the base that will become the fruit). Alternatively, cut some strips of row cover fabric and use them to wrap around the base of your zucchini stems. From Day 1 of planting, make sure each wrap extends under the soil. (If you prefer, use old panty hose for your wrapping material.) As the stem grows, just extend the wrap higher. Another remedy: Once a week, wipe the stem of your zucchini plant with a moist cloth that's saturated with insecticidal soap or the organic pest control BTK (you'll find both in most garden centers).

Using: Store zucchini dry in a plastic bag in the crisper of your refrigerator for no more than 2 or 3 days. Handle them carefully. Because they're harvested when they're young and tender (if you've been paying attention), their skin is easily damaged. Don't wash your zucchini until they're ready for use. And don't peel them—they carry most of their nutrition in their skin. Zucchini are great stir-fried, steamed, or sautéed. To grill them, slice them ¾-inch thick, marinate them in Italian salad dressing, and grill them until the slices are not quite limp. Or coat slices in batter, much as you would prepare onion rings, and fry them in oil on the stovetop.

CHAPTER 5

SNEAKY GARDEN and YARD DESIGN

||||||||||||||||||||||||||||||||||||||||||||||||||||||||||||||||||||||||||||||||||||||

I t's those snap judgments that get us into trouble. While the term *design* may carry connotations of an artsy and mystical process that's beyond us normal folk, it actually involves little more than thinking things out in advance. So if you have been intimidated by the prospect of designing the grounds surrounding your home, allow me to introduce some attitude-adjusting observations. None of these costs you any money, by the way— *ignoring* them is what's expensive.

■ Having a plan for your landscape in itself lowers the amount of garden and yard maintenance that you have to do, says Tom Flowers, president of Sanctum Design Group in Atlanta and an instructor in low-maintenance landscaping at the Atlanta Botanical Garden. This is what's called the HAPS principle. What's HAPS? It stands for Have A Plan, Stan (also known in less genteel circles as Have A Plan, Stupid), as mentioned in Chapter 1. See page 105 for a Cheat Sheet that will help you shortcut the design process.

- Sweat the details. Put careful thought into the individual choices you make about what will be part of your landscape, says Flowers. Having nothing planted in a particular spot is better than having the wrong plant there. Similarly, having no patio is better than having a dysfunctional patio. This concept is more complex than the old chestnut "Any job worth doing is worth doing well." A poorly done patio will not resonate with your family, will see little use, and will therefore not be a good value.

- When you invest in your landscape, at a minimum you want the improvements to create a lifestyle change, says Flowers. That's the bottom line. Does the new landscape feature fulfill your family's need for, say, outdoor dining, entertaining, respite, or play?

- Having a garden and yard is a matter of give and take. Lawns have to be mowed, flowerbeds weeded and deadheaded. Maintenance really depends on what you plant. But this chapter will show you some ways to cut down on maintenance chores in the landscape. However, way too many people are oblivious to the fact that plants are living, breathing, growing beings, says Jon Feldman, landscape designer and founder of G. biloba Gardens in Nyack, New York. This means that some level of care is necessary.

There you have the Zen of landscape design. Now that your attitude is properly adjusted, let's look at a nuts-and-bolts approach to achieving the kind of landscape you can be proud of—without having to work too hard for it.

MOVING TOWARD A MASTER PLAN

Any homeowner can do a reasonably good job of designing and implementing a residential landscape plan once they've got one. But don't reach for your pencil and paper just yet. First give a lot of thought to crucial questions that your plan will have to be founded upon, says landscape designer Feldman.

1. **What are the physical limitations of my yard?** This will include such factors as sun exposure and availability of water—considerations that will limit which plants you can successfully grow.

   Make the most of a tiny yard. If your yard is tiny, create a series of terraced raised beds to gain more growing room and create an illusion of more, and deeper, space.

   Save time with shady gardens. If you don't have much time for gardening, plant in shady areas rather than sunny ones. Shady gardens generally have fewer weeds, fewer pests, and don't need watering as often as sunny ones. Where do you think the expression "made in the shade" comes from?

2. **What do I want out of my plantings?** For instance, do you want to add color to the yard? Do you need to screen parts of the yard for privacy? Every time you establish such a goal, you narrow down your possible plant choices—which is not a bad thing. If you're sticking to your plan and only buying plants that meet specific criteria, your decision-making becomes easier and the selections you make become more and more reliable. Also, if you stick to low-maintenance varieties every time you choose a plant, you are easily cutting the range of plant possibilities in half, says Feldman. Cheat-at-gardening enthusiasts don't view that as a problem—it's a wonderful leap forward in the planning and decision-making process.

There are a couple of ways to think about low-maintenance plants. Some groups of plants, such as ferns and ornamental grasses, and unpruned broadleaved evergreens, are naturally low in maintenance. So are regional native plants—they're naturally adapted to the climate and growing conditions in your area. But within most plant categories, some plants require less maintenance than others. If you want to grow roses, for instance, steer clear of persnickety hybrid teas and opt instead for shrub and landscape roses, such as Knockout and Meidiland varieties. See the Cheat Sheet on page 102 for a list of good bets.

(continued on page 104)

Cheat Sheet

Low-Maintenance Plants

Here are some generally low-maintenance plants to put on your radar when you're making choices for your garden.

TREES AND SHRUBS

Arborvitae

Barberry

Bayberry

Beautybush

River birch

Blue-mist shrub

Lemon bottlebrush

Bottlebrush buckeye

Burning bush

Butterfly bush

Cedar

Cotoneaster

Leyland cypress

Forsythia

Fringe tree

Gold-dust plant

Hackberry

Hawthorn

Holly

Thornless honey locust

Hornbeam

Juniper

Amur maple

Hedge maple

Ninebark

Oak

Redbud

Serviceberry

Sourwood

Spiraea

Sumac

Viburnum

Witch hazel

Japanese zelkova

ROSES

Fairy (a polyantha variety called 'The Fairy')

Floribundas

Flower carpet

Knockout

Meidiland

Rugosas

PERENNIALS

Agapanthus

Amsonia (bluestar)

Artemisia

Aster

Baby's-breath

Balloonflower

Black-eyed Susan

Blanket flower

Fringed bleeding heart

Bugbane

Bugleweed

Siberian bugloss

Butterfly weed

Columbine

Purple coneflower

Coral bells

Coreopsis

Montauk daisy

Daylily

Euphorbia

Hardy geranium

Gayfeather

Globe thistle

Goatsbeard

Green-and-gold

Hellebore

Hosta

False indigo

Siberian iris

Liatris

Golden marguerite

Meadow rue

Monkshood

Obedient plant

Peony

Rockcress

Russian sage

Salvia

Sea holly

Sea thrift

Sedum

Snakeroot

Spiderwort

Sundrops

Turtlehead

Vinca

Yucca

ANNUALS

Ageratum

Alternanthera

Sweet alyssum

Wax begonia

Calibrachoa (million bells)

Celosia

Coleus

Cosmos

African daisy

Dusty miller

Impatiens

Johnny jump-up

Larkspur

Nicotiana

Polka-dot plant

California poppy

Portulaca

Salvia

Sunflower

Sand verbena

VEGETABLES AND HERBS

Arugula

Beans

Beets

Carrots

Chives

Cress

Leaf lettuce

Onions

Oregano

Parsley

Peas

Radishes

Sage

Tarragon

Thyme

Sketching Out a Master Plan

With those two questions answered, now you're ready to put pencil to paper. Here's the simple five-step process for sketching out your landscape plan, recommended by Kathleen Cook, landscape designer for the Fort Worth Botanical Garden.

1. Inventory and Analyze Your Entire Yard

Make a drawing of your property, showing all of the current features (see the Cheat Sheet on Landscape Design, on the opposite page, for help). If possible, make the drawing to scale. You can use conventional drawing paper, but graph paper will help. For a small yard, you might have a quarter-inch on your drawing equal a foot of land. For a large yard, try 1 inch on the drawing equaling 10 or 20 feet of land. When you bought your property, you might have received a plat that can get you started with this drawing.

Include in your drawing not only the house, but also the exterior features of the house, such as doors, windows, porches, and spigots. Indicate the property lines on all sides, the street, and overhead wires (power, phone, and cable). Make note of environmental factors, too, such as prevailing wind, sun exposure and shade, slopes, low spots, drainage, and perpetually damp areas. And indicate all existing features in the landscape, such as walls, driveway, shed, paths, garden beds, patio, trees, and hedges. Make your drawing bold enough to show through tracing paper. If you're not confident in your drawing abilities (and may not later recognize that squiggle as the tree it was meant to be), drop by an art supply store and buy one of those plastic templates that designers use to draw landscape features such as trees, shrubs, pathways, and more.

Once you have completed the drawing of the existing yard to your satisfaction, it will serve as your base for mapping out landscape changes. Don't

Cheat Sheet

Landscape Design

Here's a simple, shortcut way to work through the design process.

Step 1: Get some enlarged photocopies of your property survey, with the house (and usually the driveway) already indicated.

Step 2: Draw (with pencil!) locations of "hardscape" and constructed areas—decks, patios, sidewalks, and the driveway if necessary.

Step 3: Indicate where you have or will want to have paths and walkways to get from one place to another (house to garage, driveway to side door, deck to play area, kitchen door to trash cans). Build the landscape around the travel routes you take through your yard in the course of daily living.

Step 4: Draw locations and shapes for garden beds (rectangular or geometric if you want a formal look; curved, kidney-shaped, or freeform for an informal look).

Step 5: Draw planting areas within the garden beds—rows or raised beds for veggies and herbs; clumps or drifts for perennials; hedges for privacy, screening, or marking property boundaries; trees for shade or ornamental value; groups of shrubs.

Step 6: Decide which plants go where.

---

mark your new ideas directly onto this base map. Overlay it with tracing paper and sketch out new concepts on that. You can buy rolls of tracing paper at art stores.

2. Decide What You Want

Brainstorm a list of your goals, desires, and needs in the new landscape. Start with broad ideas. (Do you intend to entertain? Do you want a patio? A vegetable garden? Do you want lots of flowers?) Consider all members of the household and ask them what their priorities are. If you have pets or children, what do they need? And don't forget the physical details of everyday life. (Will you need a shed, a potting table, or a cold frame? Where will the trash cans and the woodpile go? Do you like to grill, or snooze in a hammock? Where will you park the basketball hoop?)

When you have a fix on what kinds of amenities you want in your landscape, take it a step further and make a list of what you will need in order to reach your landscaping goals. For example, if you want space to entertain, you'll need, first of all, a deck or patio. Then you'll need one or more outdoor electrical outlets, tables and seating, an umbrella or other source of shade for daytime use, lighting for nighttime use, a barbecue grill or maybe a complete outdoor kitchen, and probably some storage space, too.

3. Sketch Out an Informal Plan That Meets Those Needs

With tracing paper laid over your base map, informally mark circles for areas of the yard that will satisfy the list of goals you developed in step 2. For instance, you might indicate a patio, a shady sitting area, a vegetable garden, a kids' play area, and other features. Don't worry—this is rough drawing without details. As you rethink it or consider alternatives, you can make several versions.

Sketch in your compost pile. Position your garden and your compost pile so that they're near each other. Since you'll be perpetually taking garden trimmings to the compost pile and also shoveling compost into your garden, having the two close to one another will save you a lot of walking back and forth. To make things super convenient, why not design your compost pile right into the garden? Put it either smack in the middle of the garden or in one corner, says Joffee, manager of Georgia's Harvest Lake Farm. Remember, it also helps to have your compost pile near your back door, so hauling out your kitchen trimmings is not a big hassle. But don't overdo it. If your compost pile were to attract any pests, you wouldn't want them getting comfortable too close to your house.

4. Narrow Down Your Plan

On a new sheet of tracing paper, start filling in the specifics. Use whatever drawing implements you're comfortable with—pencils, pens, markers, or crayons. Indicate a size and shape for your patio and garden, for instance, and a specific location for that shade tree and bench. Make notations about what materials you want to use for each feature. The more detail you establish, the closer you are to your final plan.

You don't have to be an accomplished artist to pull this off—just get scribbling like an elementary school kid. Edward Adams, a horticulturist in Wyndmoor, Pennsylvania, fondly remembers the first sketch of his own backyard. He and his family were in a spaghetti restaurant where he scooped up the paper and crayons that were meant for entertaining kids and started scribbling the drawing that became his master plan.

5. Implement Your Plan

Break down your landscape plan into separate projects. Not trying to implement the entire plan at once has two major advantages. You will stay sane and

Easy Choices for "Hardscape"

One sure way to reduce landscape maintenance is to pick materials for the "hardscape" features in your yard that will last for years and will need very little care or upkeep. For hard walking surfaces, concrete is as low-maintenance as they come, says Kathleen Cook, landscape designer for the Fort Worth Botanical Garden. Sure, pouring concrete for a sidewalk or patio is best left to professionals. But once it's in, concrete requires no care other than, perhaps, some sealer every several years. And it might just outlast Stonehenge. A beautiful alternative to concrete: interlocking pavers. While pavers are simpler than concrete to install, you will need to pay careful attention to the manufacturer's directions for preparing the underlying surface on which they are set. Pavers are expensive, so if you can't afford to install your project all at once, implement it in stages.

Remember that pavers or bricks that are set in sand will allow water to penetrate the soil below, rather than causing runoff as solid concrete will do. This is good for the soil, but unfortunately, it also means weeds can grow in the tiny gaps between pavers—and eventually they will. You may have to pull weeds between your pavers from time to time.

For decking and fencing, says Cook, choose a durable wood such as cedar (which has a 10- to 15-year lifespan) or the rot- and insect-resistant tropical wood *ipe* (which can last as long as 50 years, but be sure to check that the wood was sustainably harvested). The newer composite (plastic and wood pulp) deck materials are more expensive but long-lasting and very low-maintenance as well. Look for benches and other yard fixtures made from recycled plastic, too.

you also will spread out the costs over time, making your budgeting easier. Decide which of these projects you want to accomplish yourself and which are the trickier projects that hired contractors should handle. In some cases, a contractor might be willing to divide the work with you.

Give first priority to installing the "hardscape" features. These elements are the permanent, inanimate aspects of your landscape, such as a deck, patio, fencing, buildings, walls, walkways, an irrigation system, plumbing for a new spigot, water features, electrical lines (for exterior lighting or a fountain pump), and underground pipes if your yard needs drainage help. It's especially important to plan for large-scale features such as a patio, sidewalk, shed, or walls. If any features require excavation, hold off all planting in that vicinity until the earth-moving and building are done. Otherwise, construction folks may be oblivious to the sensitivity of your garden beds, trampling new plantings and compacting the soil. When there's soil upheaval, you may need to work with the earth to get it garden-ready again.

GATHERING SOME EXPERT INPUT

You don't have to make all of the landscape design decisions on your own. Even the handiest homeowners can benefit from expert input now and then. Focusing your efforts instead of browsing aimlessly through Web sites, books, and magazines will save you plenty of time and trouble. Here are some great ways to gather valuable information about what will work in your yard, says landscape designer Jon Feldman.

- Hire a landscape designer to visit for just an hour or two to review your options and help you solidify your plans. (More on design consultants in a moment.)
- Drop by the library and pick up a book on basic landscape design, or research the subject on the Internet. Brushing up on the lingo that landscapers use will help a lot in developing and implementing your plan. Research the plants that you might want to use in your yard. Drive around the surrounding neighborhoods and study other yards. Visit garden centers and ask the staff questions. Flip through books that specialize in plants that thrive your region. Make a list of plants you like as potential candidates for your garden.

Cheat Sheet

‖‖

Before You Hire That Landscaper

☐	Be clear in your mind about what you want to accomplish.
☐	Ask to see a portfolio of their work, then go look at some of the properties.
☐	If you can, get a few names and talk to some past customers and ask if they were happy with the company's work.
☐	Get a written estimate for the work and an outline of what the company will do. While many companies provide free estimates, don't waste their time by requesting one unless you are really serious about their proposal.
☐	If you want plants guaranteed, seek out a company willing to do that (and be prepared to pay extra).

▪ Or skip the pros and learn to do it all yourself. Take a course in landscape design at a nearby community college or botanical garden.

Let's consider the first two of these ways in more detail.

Pick a professional's brain. For a relatively modest investment, you could have a professional landscape designer consult with you about your plans for your yard and garden, Feldman says. An hour or an hour and a half of talking-and-walking with a consultant will help you hone your ideas about what you want to accomplish in the yard and will help you develop a realistic idea of how much your plans will cost to implement. Also, a professional's fresh eyes studying your property will point up factors that you have become blind to over the years—perhaps a tree that's growing inadvisably close to the house, steps that aren't functional, a deteriorating sidewalk, other safety consider-ations, or shrubs that are terribly overgrown. You might pay $150 to $300 for such a consultation, Feldman says, but the insight you gain could prevent thousands of dollars' worth of landscaping errors in the near future.

A landscape consultant will help you view your design plan as one unified project—even if implementing the entire plan at once is impractical. If you have budgetary restrictions, a landscape consultant can help you split your plan into separate projects that can be fulfilled over multiple years. Such a consultant also will help you estimate what each stage of the plan would cost, in what order your projects should be accomplished, and what logistics and timing would be involved.

Before you invite a landscape consultant over to the house, do a little homework, says Feldman. Write out a list of questions to ask. Also, gather up some home-and-garden magazines and rip out photographs that represent the kind of look you would like to achieve. Pictures will help the communication process immeasurably, while mere words can easily fall short.

When your consultation is over, the next steps are up to you. You may feel confident that you can fine-tune and implement your own landscape plan from that point on, or you might decide to hire the consultant to develop an overall plan or provide sketches. Don't feel pressured—the consultant's role is not to sell you on further services.

Sharpen your communication skills. If you've decided to hand over big bucks to have a landscape contractor implement your design plan, you naturally will expect a result that's exquisitely done and meets your expectations to the letter. Unfortunately, not all professionally done landscape projects turn out that way. Here's the key to working successfully with a landscape contractor, says Feldman: communication. First, make sure you have a clear idea in your own mind of how you want your yard to turn out. Finding vivid and specific ways of communicating those ideas—like ripping pages out of magazines, as I mentioned earlier—will help demonstrate what you're looking for. Get the contractor to repeat back to you in his or her own terms how the project will turn out. That way you can make sure that your goals and desires are thoroughly understood. Also ask the contractor to sketch out how the finished job will look. Before any building or installation is done, ask the contractor to show you samples of any stone, gravel, mulch, or other materials that will be used so you can be sure in advance that they fit your vision.

The Real Secret to Finding the Right Landscape Contractor

If you have decided to hire a landscaping contractor, at some point you will have a candidate drop by the house for an initial discussion. You might expect me to list 18 penetrating interview questions for you to ask at this juncture. Relax. There's really only one interview question that you need to ask, says Tom Flowers, president of Sanctum Design Group in Atlanta and an instructor in low-maintenance landscaping at the Atlanta Botanical Garden: "How many times have you done a job just like this, for a person just like me, under conditions just like these?" Here's how to interpret a contractor's response.

If the answer is zero to 5 times: You have a C-grade contractor. This person definitely will be less expensive to hire. Say, for a job that would typically cost you $5,000, you may only have to pay $1,200. However, this contractor will make many more mistakes during the project, and the job will require much more personal involvement on your part.

If the answer is 10 to 50 times: You are talking to a more knowledgeable, B-grade contractor. There will be some, but fewer, mistakes made during the project, and it will require less involvement on your part. Your final bill will be more like $4,000 for this hypothetical job.

If the answer is 50 times or more: You have a highly experienced contractor who will bill you the full $5,000 for the job. However, his or her work will probably be the best value in terms of quality of work, fewer mistakes and hassles, and low involvement on your part.

Ask around for possible contractors. Finding a landscape contractor by word of mouth may feel like an informal approach, but it's actually a great way to ensure success with the project, says Feldman. Ask your friends and neighbors which landscape contractors they have worked with successfully. Drive around town and when you see a landscape you like, ask who the contractor was (many landscape companies place signs in newly completed landscapes for a time). Also ask the staff at your garden center to recommend some contractors. Invite at least three contractors to drop by your house to discuss what you have in mind. Remember this, says Feldman: The chemistry between you and your contractor is very important. There has to be a level of comfort between you and the contractor, or the project will not come together smoothly. Before hiring, check any candidate's reputation with the Better Business Bureau.

Talk about the sketches. To get the best results out of a landscape contractor, you need to understand one of his or her greatest challenges—that's drawing out of *you* a clear idea of what you want in your yard. Without good communication about what your expectations are, a landscaping project will turn into a frustrating experience of missteps and expensive errors for both of you. If a landscape contractor supplies sketches of a yard design for your home, don't freeze up. Such sketches are not a hard-and-fast plan that your contractor is stuck on. On the contrary, finding out what you *don't* like in the sketches is all part of the process. Think of sketches as a tool for getting your response. Remember, a landscape contractor's job is not to impose his or her will upon you.

CORNER-CUTTING DESIGN TIPS

When you're designing your home's landscape, you're making decisions that you and your family are going to live with for years or decades to come. Here are some ways to plot out and implement a landscape design that you will adore because it will suit your lifestyle and it will be a snap to maintain.

View your yard from outer space. When starting out with a landscape design, many homeowners are tempted to start listing features they want in the yard—a deck here, a trellis there, a hedge here, and a fireplace over there. Whoa—you're getting way ahead of yourself, says landscape designer Flowers. Early in the process, start with a broad overview of your entire yard, what Flowers calls an "up in the space shuttle" perspective. First, establish which directions are north, south, east, and west. Unfortunately, many homeowners leap into landscape design without considering the points of the compass. But identifying your yard's southern exposure is vital to a good landscape plan. Note which parts of the yard get the most sun. Consider other exposures, too—for instance, which parts of the yard are exposed to the neighbors, and which are exposed to the street and passersby. Also include in your earliest plan a notation about which parts of the yard tend to collect water.

Consider public vs. private. When you're designating functions for the different parts of your yard, it helps to consider whether each area falls into the category of public or private, says horticulturist Edward Adams. Public and private areas are treated quite differently. Public areas are those spots that passersby can see easily and a casual visitor has easy access to—the driveway, front sidewalk, front stoop, and a side yard, for instance. Most often, public areas are in the front yard, and curb appeal—a pleasant design as viewed from the front sidewalk or street—is a primary concern. The front yard landscape also needs to complement the architecture of the house. Private areas might be a children's garden or an outdoor dining spot—roles most often reserved for the backyard. To preserve the privacy of these areas, walk the periphery of your yard and beyond, taking note of all of the views from the outside. This would include not only views from the street or front yard, but also from neighbors' yards and houses. Strategically placed fencing, shrubs, and trees will screen such views and enhance your privacy.

Design with people in mind. Plant hedges and position screens (also fences and walls meant for privacy) to be high enough that you can't see over the top

SHADES OF GREEN ————————————————————

Sidestep Airborne Contaminants

When plotting out what will go where in your landscape, avoid positioning a vegetable garden near a busy road, says Hammond, chef and owner of Oregon's Honeyman Creek Farms. Toxins in the exhaust from the passing traffic, including lead, can contaminate your vegetables. Leafy vegetables are particularly vulnerable to such contamination. If you have no choice other than to put your garden near a roadway, then plant a hedge between the street and your garden. The hedge will serve as a filter that will trap pollutants.

of them when standing. Place stepping stones in a path far enough apart that you can step comfortably from one to another. When you pick out a bench, sit on it first to see if it's a comfortable height.

Vary the vistas. When you stand in many typical yards, you can take in the entire space in one glance—there's no mystery and nothing to explore. However, an engaging landscape will offer various views as you walk through a yard, Adams says. When he sketched out his own backyard, for instance, he plotted a zigzag pathway that offers the stroller new vistas at every turn. His garden starts at the end of his driveway (a public area for the trash cans, the air conditioner housing, and some stored landscape materials). Then the pathway angles behind the house to the right, crosses a dry riverbed he has built, and continues several feet past a stand of trees. Next, the path crooks left toward the back of the yard, offering a full view of a tree that provides great fall color (a nice highlight for a color-starved season). Elsewhere, strategic plantings provide more seasonal color to draw the eye as well.

The sensory treat doesn't stop there. Adams also likes to incorporate fragrance into his landscape. A viburnum and a lilac occupy an "extremely fragrant" back corner of his backyard.

Out front, keep it clean and simple. Many homeowners take a haphazard approach to designing the front yard—a little bed under a tree in one spot and another bed surrounding a statue in another. That's a mistake, says designer Kathleen Cook. What's really needed in the front yard is a focused design that puts emphasis on the front door, rather than distracting the eye away from it to five or six different parts of the front yard. This focused approach creates that desirable curb appeal, she says.

Careful with those "room" additions. If you read about landscape design just a little while, you will quickly run into the concept of "rooms" out in your yard. No, leave the lamps and sofa inside. This is a process of establishing specific purposes for certain sections of your yard. This is not only done with the use of physical features (such as plantings, borders, and a bench) but also conceptually—an entertaining area, a meditative area, and a kids' recreation area, for instance.

Dividing a small yard into multiple garden rooms has the advantage of making the property feel bigger. However this is a trend that can lead to trouble, says landscape designer Flowers. Don't add rooms to your yard willy-nilly. A homeowner who goes overboard with this trend is just inviting extra maintenance chores. That's because each room that you add to your yard will include features that require ongoing upkeep—for instance, mowing for that small patch of lawn, hand-clipping under the bench, cleaning that fountain, and trimming that little hedge that delineates one "wall" of a room.

The low-maintenance approach, says Flowers: Create a multipurpose space that incorporates many different functions rather than separate rooms for each function. One single spot, for instance, might accommodate quiet rest, recreation, and grilling as well. To keep maintenance to a minimum, try to compress these functions into as small an area as is comfortable. Also, situate such an area as near to the house as possible—the harder it is to get to, the harder it is to maintain. And we're all looking for more time in the hammock, right?

Assign plantings by function. When you're sketching out a plan for your landscape, you're going to be tempted to pencil in a few of your all-time favorite plants. Stop that. By playing favorites, you're probably forcing some inappropriate elements into your design. Instead, indicate the plantings in your plan according to function—for instance, a hedge to screen a private part of the yard, or a bed that will provide a splash of color. Only when you start to implement your plan will you need to decide which plants best fill those purposes. Who knows, one or two of your favorites might fit the bill after all!

Install the "hard" stuff first. Oh boy! You have done your homework, enduring the research, planning, and sketching stages of your landscaping project. But don't start digging holes and throwing plants into them just yet. You would be well advised to first install what designers call the "hardscape" elements of your new yard—the constructed parts of your landscape, such as a deck, patio, fencing, buildings, walls, walkways, an irrigation system, plumbing for a new spigot, water features, electrical lines (for exterior lighting or a fountain pump), and underground pipes if your yard needs drainage help. You want to have these items in place first because they often will influence the precise location of your plantings. Also, someone involved in a construction-type project (you or hired help) will have less awareness of plants in the vicinity and could easily stomp on a new shrub, whack a young tree with a 2-by-4, or stack a ton of pavers on a freshly seeded garden bed.

Consider the existing architecture. Select hardscape features for your yard that naturally complement the architecture of your house, says landscape designer Flowers. He often sees such gaffes as an all-brick home with an elaborate stone patio out back. The two materials clash with each other visually, creating an expensive eyesore.

Think inside out. What's going on *inside* the house should influence your landscape design as well. If the kids have designated areas in the yard, make sure those spots are easily seen from the rooms you frequent—through the kitchen window, for instance. A kids' area should have easy access to your mudroom, too. Also consider the view from the inside when you're positioning trees, shrubbery, flowerbeds, fountains, and other picturesque features in your landscape. Look out of your windows and think about where you'd like to have something green or colorful to see.

Beware scattershot buying. Many homeowners start off a landscaping project with a trip to the nursery in which they make many and varied plant purchases—three of this, five of that, four of those, and two of those thingies over there. That's getting off on the wrong foot from a design standpoint, Flowers says. For one thing, you're going to get the plants home and then you will have to figure out where to put them—jamming them into the landscape without regard for an overall design. Also, heaping more and more varied plants into your landscape creates a scattered and unfocused look. Simplicity—that is, fewer varieties of plants—is easier to work with in creating a smooth and harmonious design. Follow Mother Nature's lead: Broad swaths of repeated plants work out beautifully.

Landscape designer Kathleen Cook concurs. In a small-scale garden, five to seven varieties of plants will do nicely. Learn the art of strategic repetition of the same plant, she says. Your landscape will look better and be easier to care for when your plants need similar kinds of care and maintenance.

For security or drama, add light. If you want to add lighting to your landscape, either for dramatic effect or for security, explore the low-voltage systems available at home improvement centers. Low-voltage lighting can accomplish just about any goals you may have for exterior illumination, and installing it requires little in the way of technical know-how. First, make sure you have an exterior electrical outlet to power your lights, or ask an electrician to install one. You will need a transformer, which is mounted off the ground, to power your low-voltage system. From there, your individual light fixtures are connected by cable that can be run a few inches underground.

Before you purchase a lighting system and start digging up the yard, establish the goals for your exterior lighting. If you want to provide extra security by illuminating part of the yard, or if you want to accentuate a sidewalk or path, a row of fixtures that cast their light downward will do nicely. Upturned fixtures provide drama to your yard at night by illuminating some large feature of the landscape—a stone wall, for instance, an interesting planting, or a large tree.

Solar-powered landscape lights also are available. They recharge during the daytime and shine through the night. They're easier to install, since they require no wiring. However, the light they emit is rather soft and less useful for security and dramatic illumination. So make sure you get a good set that will

SHADES of GREEN

Use Flowers as a Finishing Touch

Once his vegetable garden is planted, gardening author Lance Walheim likes to add flowers to the borders of its beds—and even some flowers incorporated among the vegetable plants. This extra touch makes the garden a nicer place to visit for him as well as family and friends. Go a step further and place a table and bench nearby, he suggests, making your garden a nice place to hang out, read, or contemplate nature. Other gardeners use flowers to add bright dashes of color in front of evergreen shrubs and foundation plantings or attract birds to your feeders.

provide enough light to be actually useful. Solar-powered lights may be perfectly fine for illuminating a path or an entrance to the garden.

Crack open a couple of books. Having a couple of good reference books on your living room shelf will help enormously when you're creating a design for your yard, says landscape designer Flowers. One of his favorites is *The Essential Garden Design Workbook* by Rosemary Alexander. This tome walks home gardeners through the various stages of landscape design (assessing the site, drafting and improving a plan, using the right materials) with the goal of achieving a refined, cohesive look. The workbook provides hundreds of drawings and diagrams. You could also check out *Homescaping: Designing Your Landscape to Match Your Home* by Anne Halpin, and *Ann Lovejoy's Organic Garden Design School* by Ann Lovejoy. Another kind of reference that you will use time and time again: a thick pictorial plant book—one that's crammed cover to cover with color photographs and also provides information on the growth habits and preferences of each plant listed. Make sure it tells you how well each plant performs in your region. (For a few weeks, you won't have to keep buying detective novels to read at night.) Flowers recommends landscape plant books written by Michael A. Dirr, an expert on trees and shrubs and a professor at the University of Georgia. Look for his *Manual of Woody Landscape Plants* and *Dirr's Hardy Trees and Shrubs*. Another good all-around reference is *The American Horticultural Society A-Z Encyclopedia of Garden Plants*.

Don't forget the dirt. Many people dive into the artistry of home landscape design but forget about one of the fundamental keys to gardening success—getting the soil into optimum condition. This harkens back to the POTS principle (Priority One: The Soil) discussed in Chapter 1, which by now you have tattooed to your left forearm. You might put weeks or months into implementing your garden design only to find that your plantings aren't thriving because of poor soil, says horticulturist Adams. It's much more difficult to amend garden soil after planting is done and hard fixtures (borders, stakes, trellises, and such) are already in place. So if you skimmed or skipped over Chapter 2, flip back there and make sure that fixing your soil is an early, top priority before you implement a landscape plan. When he began implementing a design for

Consider the Shadows within Your Garden

Good—you figured out quickly that you need to put your garden in a spot that gets plenty of sun. But the sun considerations go further than that. As you plot out which plants will go where in your garden, make sure you take into account the height that your plants will be when they mature, says Joffee. If you are planning on sunflowers, trellises, or tall tomato cages, for instance, make sure they won't cast a perpetual shadow onto smaller, sun-loving plants. The easy way to do this? Just make sure tall plants are to the north of shorter plants.

his own backyard, Adams realized that his soil was heavily clay—so his first priority was to give the soil a major infusion of compost.

Protect your garden from wind. If a spot in your yard is frequently exposed to wind, that's probably not a great place for a garden, says Robert Hammond of Honeyman Creek Farms. A stiff wind can break tender plants. And wind during temperature extremes will interfere with growth and dry out the soil. If you must position your garden in a windy spot, use a windbreak to limit the damage. Your windbreak could be a hedge or a row of evergreen trees or tall shrubs, or it could be a hard structure such as a fence or latticework. Whichever type you use, make sure it doesn't block sun from your garden, and that it has open spaces for air to pass through. Don't use a solid wall as a windbreak—it will create strong air currents that can damage plants. If you choose a living windbreak, don't let such a planting compete with your garden for water.

Sketch out a yearly garden map. Just a couple minutes' worth of doodling on paper will help immensely in organizing your garden efforts. This garden-mapping idea works in conjunction with the master plan described above. It helps you track all of the little decisions you make each season, such as the placement of certain vegetables or flowers. Sketch out a map of your garden on an 8½-by-11-inch sheet of paper, indicating the positions of beds, borders, and any other permanent features. Photocopy this template several times and drop the sheets into a file folder. When spring approaches and it's time to plan your garden, write the date at the top of a blank map and mark what you want to plant in each part of the garden. (For the health of the soil, switch your plantings around from year to year.) In the margin of your map, jot notes about any purchases that your new plan requires, and work these items into your late-winter errand running. If you make changes as you do the actual planting, update the map. If you really want to get elaborate, note the variety of each planting, too. During the gardening season, keep a quick list of "Things to Remember for Next Year" on the map as well—your successes, failures, and reminders that will help you in planning next year's garden. "That's the best way to learn—to keep records," says Joffee.

FINDING THE RIGHT PLANT FOR THE RIGHT JOB

Nature is a very powerful force that never relents. So implementing a landscape that runs counter to the natural forces already at work will be a frustrating exercise. That's what landscape designer Tom Flowers calls "pressing a round peg into a square hole." Instead, "Respond to what the property naturally wants to be," says Flowers.

For instance, why try to create a shade area in a sun-drenched spot of the yard? And rather than building a patio over a watery part of your yard, turn that channel into a dry riverbed and put the patio off to the side. Keep pools and other water features away from trees, which will dump leaves and other debris into them and create maintenance headaches.

And don't try to control 100 percent of your landscape, Flowers says. You don't have to "do something" with every area of your yard—let nature decide how some parts will look. For instance, if you have a wooded slope on the backyard, why not just let it be . . . a wooded slope? This doesn't mean totally neglecting that patch of land—just give it occasional low-level maintenance such as clearing out underbrush, establishing a compost pile, and perhaps adding the occasional new tree. This is a relaxed, looser, low-maintenance approach. You might earmark this part of the yard for more extensive landscaping a few years in the future. In the meantime, this approach translates into more hammock time for you!

Leave some open spaces. Open space is important. Don't feel you have to fill up every inch of space on your property with gardens. Open space that has lawn, groundcovers, pavement, or water (like a reflecting pool) provides a neutral ground against which the shapes of your garden beds and borders, and the colors within them, are played. The contrast will make your gardens look better-defined and more important.

Here are more ways to make corner-cutting decisions when you're selecting and installing plants.

Match your plant choices to landscape conditions. Part of the early planning process is assessing the conditions in your yard. These factors include any hills or slopes, particularly wet or dry areas, and shade or sun exposure. These conditions will determine the "palette" of plants you want to choose from for your landscape. (For instance, horticulturist Edward Adams realized that a birch tree and a dawn redwood would thrive in his damp backyard.)

There are a number of ways you can find out about the growing conditions you have to deal with. You can consult the nearest Cooperative Extension office to get a fix on the ecology of your area. You can also ask gardening neighbors, or consult books and Web sites. But the best way to learn is to spend time outdoors in your yard, at different times of day, in different seasons, and just observe and pay attention. What path does the sun follow in spring? Summer? Fall? Where does water tend to collect after heavy rain? Where does snow or frost linger longest in cold weather? What kinds of weeds and native plants grow in untended corners of your property? All these observations offer valuable clues to your growing environment. And now you have one more reason to spend time in your hammock.

If you look closely at your land, you can find these clues. Then all you need to do is to look for plants that like the same sort of conditions. With a list of sure-to-thrive plants picked out, you're ready to pencil them into the drawing of your intended landscape.

Root for the local team. To make your gardening easier, love where you live and choose plants naturally suited to growing there. If you live in the desert, don't plan on a jungle look. If you live at the seashore, don't try an alpine meadow. If you're serious about keeping the maintenance of your garden and landscape to a minimum, you're going to have to overcome your own human nature, says Kathleen Cook, landscape designer for the Fort Worth Botanical Garden. People are naturally attracted to the exotic and unfamiliar, she notes. They may see a slick magazine photo (one taken thousands of miles away) and decide that they must have the plant depicted. To make matters worse, people tend to regard the native plants of their own region to be ho-hum and drab. These tendencies will lead you to select plants that will struggle in your yard and cause you ongoing headaches and hassles.

Instead of craving exotic plants that are not adapted to your local growing conditions, become a cheerleader for the beauty and richness of native plants. Make a habit of asking at your nursery for plants that are well adapted to local sun, soil, and rainfall conditions. Also get pointers from your local extension agent and botanical garden. Get in the habit of asking for varieties that require less water. Even if you live in a new development, think about what used to be there. If your subdivision is on the plains, think about trying a prairie garden. If you live in the woods, aim for woodland wildflowers and other shade plants instead of tea roses.

With a landscape stocked with plants that will naturally thrive in your region, you will be on the path to achieving that Holy Grail, the very-low-maintenance garden.

When plants fail, branch out. Persistence is an admirable trait in many pursuits—but not necessarily in gardening. Many gardeners repeat their mistakes over and over again, says Edward Adams—say, watching a plant fail, removing it from the garden, and then replacing it with precisely the same plant. Adams prefers a looser, more experimental approach: When one plant fails in the garden, try something else until you discover what works well with your landscape conditions. He thinks of this approach as letting the garden tell him what works best. Just don't frustrate yourself by repeating the failures.

That's not to say you should turn a blind eye every time a garden plant is struggling, Adams says. There are several easy, hassle-free ways to find out what may be ailing a downtrodden plant. Adams recommends taking a branch from the plant to your nursery, a local horticultural society, or an arboretum. These organizations routinely identify pests or diseases for gardeners. You may be able to identify your plant's malady yourself, too, by comparing a branch from your yard with photographs in a book about garden plant ailments. Your library may have exactly the reference you need.

Give your new tree a life raft. If you're going to plant new trees somewhere on your lawn, it's better to include them in planting beds, says Flowers. Don't plant trees that are "floating"—that is, by themselves in the midst of the yard. The roots and bark of such trees are too exposed to damage from lawn mowers and other yard work tools. Besides, you'll eventually be disappointed with the grass under a tree because the tree's root system will hog the nutrients and moisture in the ground and the grass will be sparse and anemic.

Under a mature tree, let the lawn go. People with shade trees that have been long established in the yard are often frustrated that they can't get grass to flourish underneath. The official *How to Cheat at Gardening and Yard Work* solution to this dilemma: Quit worrying about it and quit asking Mother Nature to deliver something she doesn't want to. There are two reasons that grass struggles under a shade tree. For one thing, the tree itself is taking up more water then you think, with a massive root system in the first foot or foot-and-a-half of soil. The low light makes growing grass difficult, too. There's nothing wrong with just letting the dirt under your tree go bare, says designer Cook. When the leaves fall, just leave them in place (yes, no raking!). If you prefer a tidier look in your yard, spread a bed of mulch under the tree. And if you're hankering for a swath of green that's reminiscent of lawn, Cook says, "Groundcovers are a lovely thing." She suggests ivy or monkey grass, both evergreen groundcovers that are famous for thriving in shade.

Cheat Sheet

Groundcovers—The Good and the Bad

Here are some great groundcovers to consider planting.

Baby's tears, grow in sun or shade

Bearberry, sun or shade

Bugleweed, sun or shade

Bunchberry, shade

Cotoneaster, sun

Creeping Jenny, sun or shade

Dichondra, sun or shade

Epimedium (barrenwort), shade

Wild ginger, shade

Green-and-gold, shade

Ice plant, sun

Lamium (deadnettle), shade

Leadwort, sun

Liriope, sun or shade

Moss pink, sun

Pachysandra, shade

Pulmonaria, shade

Salal, sun or shade

Snow-in-summer, sun

Sweet woodruff, shade

Thyme, sun

Tiarella (foamflower), shade

Vinca, sun or shade (Be careful: In some places this has invaded woodlands. Check with your local Cooperative Extension office to see if it is a problem in your area.)

Wintercreeper, sun or shade

Here are some groundcovers to keep *out* of your garden unless your soil is very poor—they're vigorous spreaders that can overwhelm other plants.

Aegopodium (bishop's weed)

Crown vetch

Houttuynia

Highway ice plant (carpobrotus)

English ivy

Ground ivy

Lamiastrum

Lily-of-the-valley

Groundcover: the no-hassle solution. One of the lowest-maintenance plantings you can add to your landscape is groundcover, says landscape designer Jon Feldman. Groundcovers—such as pachysandra, vinca, and various forms of ivy—typically grow 6 to 8 inches high. Because they're densely planted, weeds have little hope of survival in the midst of groundcover once it has grown and filled in any little gaps (one more yard work chore eliminated!).

Cheat Sheet

Good Companions in the Vegetable Garden

Here's a listing of some classic groups of plants that protect one another and enjoy one another's company.

Anise and coriander

Asparagus, carrots, tomatoes, and parsley

Basil, tomatoes, cabbage, beans

Beans, corn, carrots, cabbage, squash, marigolds, rosemary, and strawberries

Beets, cabbage, salad greens, and onions

Cabbage family (cabbage, broccoli, Brussels sprouts, cauliflower, collards, kale, Chinese cabbage), mint, dill, sage, rosemary, thyme, beans, marigolds, nasturtiums, onions, and potatoes

Carrots, tomatoes, cucumbers, radishes, peas, sage, and onions

Chamomile, cucumbers, and onions

Chervil and radishes

Chives, carrots, tomatoes, grapes, and roses

Coriander, anise, and potatoes

Corn, beans, peas, melons, cucumbers, squash, and sunflowers

Cucumbers, beans, cabbage, corn, lettuce, radishes, marigolds, tomatoes, broccoli, and onions

Dill, cabbage family members, corn, lettuce, and onions

Eggplant, tarragon, and thyme

Garlic, roses, cabbage family members, eggplant, and tomatoes

Grapes, beans, and peas

The best spot for groundcover is in front of a hedge, says Feldman. Shade-loving groundcover is a reasonable stand-in for lawn under trees, where grass may struggle. Use groundcover for erosion control on sloping ground, or in spots where using a lawn mower is treacherous. Use groundcover as a buffer zone, keeping lawn mowers, trimmers, and other potentially damaging tools away from tree trunks. It's also handy for creating a division between two distinct sections of your yard. Needless to say, every square yard of groundcover that you plant is a square yard of ground that doesn't need mowing.

Lettuce, beets, cabbage, radishes, and strawberries

Marigolds, potatoes, tomatoes, roses, cabbage family members, and peppers

Mints, beans, and cabbage family members

Nasturtiums, beans, cabbage family members, peppers, potatoes, and squash

Onions, beets, cabbage family members, lettuce, and strawberries

Peas, corn, carrots, cucumbers, eggplant, lettuce, peppers, spinach, tomatoes, and radishes

Peppers, carrots, onions, basil, marjoram, nasturtiums, and oregano

Potatoes, beans, corn, lettuce, onions, radishes, marigolds, nasturtiums, catnip, petunias, and coriander

Radishes, beans, cabbage family members, lettuce, tomatoes, peas, onions, and carrots

Roses, garlic, onions, parsley, chives, and geraniums

Sage, cabbage family members, carrots, strawberries, tomatoes, and marjoram

Squash, mint, nasturtiums, radishes, beans, corn, catnip, and sunflowers

Strawberries, beans, lettuce, and spinach

Sunflowers, beans, corn, and squash

Tomatoes, cabbage family members, asparagus, carrots, onions, dill, basil, parsley, and sage

Plant by the buddy system. Not all plants "play nice" together. For instance, two species may compete directly for water, sun, and nutrients. However, some pairings of plants are ideal. One plant may gobble up sun, while another may thrive in the shade its partner creates. One plant may naturally develop deep roots, while its companion may draw water and nutrients from the shallow soil. One plant may attract insects that turn out to be beneficial for the companion plant. The concept of "companion planting" takes into account these advantageous pairings and should be part of any garden's crop plan, says Daron "Farmer D" Joffee, manager of Georgia's Harvest Lake Farm. Our chart of compatible plants is on page 129, and others are easy to find online. (Conduct an Internet search using the term "companion planting.") Also check with your nursery or agricultural extension agent.

Break down a big planting job. Once the hardscape is finally in place, you're finally going to feel like you're gardening—because it's time to get some dirt under your fingernails and some plants into the ground. If you are planning a small landscaping project, you may be able to handle all of the planting at once. For something more ambitious—an entire backyard, for instance—break up the planting into smaller sub-projects, Adams says, and work methodically. In Adams's own backyard, he organized his planting by starting at the back fence and working towards the house. Then he planted along the fences on each side, and finally he planted beside the deck abutting the house. At last word, with the major planting done, he was back in the garden at large doing

ZERO-MAINTENANCE MARVELS

Save Yourself from the "Mulching Monster"

Many homeowners add new garden beds to their landscapes every season, and this proliferation of beds means they have to haul in more and more mulch every year. If you're a slave to "the mulching monster," as landscape designer Tom Flowers calls it, introduce more groundcover into your plant beds. Each time you do, you reduce the need for mulch. There is a caveat here—groundcovers need to be weeded until they fill in enough to really cover the ground. Till then, they take some work.

Plant your ornamental beds with a balance of high, middle, and low plantings—that is, trees and shrubs as the high level, perennials and ornamental grasses as the mid-level, and groundcovers as the low level. This kind of layered planting provides a cleaner look—and, of course, reduces the number of mega-size mulch bags that you have to haul around in the wheelbarrow. Back, monster, back!

Cheat Sheet

Bad Company

This is the flip side to the "Good Companions" list on page 126. Keep these plants away from each other.

Anise and carrots

Beets and pole beans

Cabbage family members and grapes

Caraway and carrots

Carrots and dill

Chives, beans, and peas

Coriander and fennel

Dill, carrots, and tomatoes

Garlic, beans, and peas

Grapes, cabbage family members, and radishes

Lettuce and broccoli

Onions and sage

Peppers, beans, and fennel

Potatoes, apples, and pears

Radishes and grapes

Rue, cabbage family members, basil, and sage

Sage, onions, and rue

Squash and potatoes

Sunflowers and potatoes

Tomatoes and fennel

---

some fine-tuning. Another way to break up planting chores is to start with the big structural stuff first—the trees and shrubs that form the skeleton of the garden plantings.

Plan for future growth. When you're fitting vegetation into the landscape plan you've devised, pay particular attention to the size your plants will reach once they mature. (Read the plant tags and labels to find this info before you buy.) One of the most common errors that homeowners make is over-planting, Feldman says. Two young shrubs or trees that might appear perfectly spaced when you plant them could grow together over the next several years, creating maintenance headaches. Having to move a big shrub or tree is a lot more hassle and expense than giving it enough space to begin with.

Plan for future growth: Take 2. The opposite problem is also possible:

leaving too much space between plants. For instance, if you position pachysandra groundcover plants too far apart, they take too long to fully cover the assigned area. That leaves the ground vulnerable to weeds.

Wrongly sized plants can create other headaches, notes Cook—for instance, a shrub that grows large enough to block the view through a window or high enough to touch an overhead power line.

When you receive planting instructions from the nursery, take a measuring tape outside to get a realistic read on how your plants will fit into the landscape when full-grown. A zillion planting mistakes have been made by homeowners who thought they could "eyeball" such sizes or estimate the fit without the concrete proof provided by onsite measurement. You also can double-check the nursery's planting instructions in a plant reference book.

Cut back on future trimming. What's your first idea when you want to create a little privacy for part of your yard? Install a hedge to screen the area? Hold up and consider what extra maintenance duties you're building into the landscape. A formal hedge requires trimming to keep it looking orderly—

Cheat Sheet

Perennial Combinations

These perennials look good together in the flower garden and are grouped according to their bloom season.

Achillea (or yarrow), Siberian iris, and Shasta daisy

Astilbe and heuchera (or coral bells)

Astilbe, ferns, and foamflower

Catmint, coreopsis, and summer phlox

Columbine and fringed bleeding heart

Hardy geranium and hosta

Heliopsis and butterfly weed

Hosta and ferns

Japanese anemone and sedum

Perovskia (Russian sage) and Autumn Joy sedum

Perovskia (Russian sage), black-eyed Susan, and asters

Salvia and Stella d'Oro daylily

Shasta daisy, daylilies, and veronica

Cheat Sheet

Invasive Plants to Keep Out of Your Garden

Some nasty plants to avoid include:

Bamboo

Japanese barberry

Oriental bittersweet

Scotch broom

Bluegum eucalyptus

Cogon grass, Japanese blood grass

Ribbon grass, canary reed grass

English ivy

Japanese honeysuckle

Purple loosestrife

Norway maple

Melaleuca

Russian olive

Porcelain berry

Princess tree

Chinese privet

Multiflora rose

Tamarisk

Tree of heaven

Water hyacinth

---

probably at least twice a year. On the other hand, you could plant instead a small tree and a couple of independent shrubs, or an informal screen planting or hedgerow, that would provide just as much screening—without requiring ongoing maintenance.

Give perennials preference. Reduce your gardening chores by favoring perennials over annuals, says Tom Flowers. Perennials, of course, reappear in your beds every year, while annuals must be replanted every year. Sure, annuals in general provide a wilder blast of color than the more sedate perennials. Nevertheless, guess which is the official *How to Cheat at Gardening and Yard Work* approach? To save more work, pick perennials that are long blooming and don't need constant deadheading. See the Cheat Sheet: "Low-Maintenance Plants" on page 102 for suggestions.

Don't plant invasives. Some plants are just thugs in the garden. If you plant these bad guys they'll grow fast, all right, but you'll have to spend plenty of time later on digging and pulling them out of places where you don't want them, or they'll take over your garden. Contact your local Cooperative Extension office for information on plants that are invasive in your area. Or do some research online—many states keep listings of invasive plants. And see the Cheat Sheet on page 131 for some known bad guys.

SCROUNGING MATERIALS FOR LOW COST—OR NO COST!

Horticulturist Edward Adams calls himself a "professional scrounger." He has learned to haunt the countryside and businesses where he is likely to acquire some of his favorite landscaping materials for either no cost at all or minimal cost. As a result, his yard is a charming display of found or low-cost landscaping—both plants and hardscape.

For example, he uses sediment rock for garden borders, scavenged from a construction site in a neighboring county. He uses lava rock acquired cheaply from a nearby stone supplier to line the sculptural dry riverbed that cuts across his backyard (a visually interesting feature that's functional, too, channeling water out of a damp area). The lava rock has high iron content and develops an attractive green patina over time outdoors. Also, a 6-foot height of 1-inch rebar stands in one of his garden beds, looking like industry-inspired sculpture (or an enormous tomato stake). But it's functional, too—he uses the rebar as a lever for moving those huge border stones around the yard.

Here are some other low-cost, low-effort ways to acquire and use materials in your landscape. It's up to you what you want to call it—scrounging, repurposing, or even recycling.

Rescue some plants. Adams's scrounging extends to plants as well. He has two areas of his backyard set aside as mini-nurseries. There, he temporarily plants small plants that he has acquired inexpensively—say, a scraggly plant tossed out by a commercial nursery, clippings offered by acquaintances, or plants that clients want removed from their yards. Adams chose special spots for his mini-nurseries, where fragile plants are protected from harsh sun and will get plenty of water. These are also fairly hidden beds, where less-than-perfect plants will go unnoticed. Adams lets them bulk up in the mini-nurseries, then he transplants them to an official home once they're strong and vibrant.

Organize a plant swap. Adams is a big believer in sharing plants with friends and neighbors. To stage a plant-swapping event, contact 20 gardeners you know and tell them when and where to take their extra plants. The idea is that each participant who contributes plants to the event will leave with plants of equivalent value. Appoint a committee to arbitrate the trade-offs between the gardeners to make sure that each participant is getting a fair exchange for the plants brought in.

Browse fund-raisers for bargains. Local plant sales can be a great source of unusual plants for a very reasonable cost, especially when the sale is a fund-raiser for nearby arboretums, herb societies, or horticultural societies, Adams says. You can expect to pay more for the larger plants being sold, but you often will find under-size plants for very low prices—what Adams calls "the Charlie Brown plants," the small, spindly plants he likes to nurse back to health.

Put retired items back to work. Use your imagination and put yard sale acquisitions or stored attic items to work as garden bed edgings or eye-catching centerpieces. Broken pottery or old plates that are retired from the dinner table can find a second life as a garden path, or a collection of upended wine bottles would make an amusing garden border. Ready to throw out a kitchen chair? Let climbing morning glories have their way with it for a season. Give Grandma's old headboard new life as a trellis or fence in your garden. Of course, you don't want to go overboard with the repurposed garden accessories lest your garden look more like a junkyard. But when you use them creatively, and not in abundance, they can be fun.

A less extreme form of recycling involves salvaged railroad ties. You can use them as a garden bed border or to create steps set into a slope. As with other treated timber, however, don't use creosote-treated railroad ties near plants that you're going to eat—impurities can seep into your food.

MAKE WATERING PART OF YOUR PLAN

As you're sketching out a plan for your garden and lawn, ask yourself how you intend to water them. Will you need to install underground sprinkler system pipes or a couple of new spigots? That kind of work will have to happen early in the implementation phase of your landscape design. Will a garden bed be situated on a slope? To prevent water runoff and erosion, run your plant rows and pathways across the slope of the hill. Are you planning to hand-water certain beds or containers—say, spraying from a hose or lugging a watering can around the yard? In that case, easy access to the water source is going to be crucial.

You have many approaches to choose from for watering your garden and lawn, including fixed sprinklers, drip systems, soaker hoses, and hose-end sprinklers. It doesn't really matter which type you choose, says landscape designer Tom Flowers. Just remember this: A good watering system is one that's controlled properly. What matters is that it delivers water consistently and equally over the areas that need it. But before you commit to a particular system for watering, here are some things you will want to know—the pros and cons of the most popular approaches, plus some tips for hydrating your landscape most efficiently.

Automatic Sprinklers: An Investment in Convenience

Having an automatic sprinkler system installed in your yard may sound like an extravagance, but consider the hassles that it saves you—season after season of dragging hoses and lawn sprinklers around the landscape, says landscape designer Jon Feldman. Also, when you go out of town, you will rest assured that your watering will be taken care of thoroughly and consistently (which isn't always the case when you hire that kid from down the block).

Feldman is such a big advocate of automatic sprinkler systems that if a homeowner doesn't have one, he won't guarantee the plants he puts into the landscape. A well-run automatic sprinkler system is the most efficient, water-conserving way to get the job done, Feldman says. Installation of an underground sprinkler system is not a job for the everyday homeowner, however. Use the HIRE principle. That is, if a job is Hard, Important, Rarely done, and Elaborate, then hire an experienced professional to do it for you. It's tempting to know that you can save more than half of the cost of a sprinkler system by installing it yourself. Don't kid yourself, however—the job requires some expertise with plumbing and a ton of backbreaking work, including digging foot-deep trenches and a lot of bending over.

An automatic sprinkler system should divide your landscape into different

SHADES OF GREEN

Wipe Out Water Waste

Water less often, more deeply. It doesn't matter much what kind of watering system you use for your yard and garden as long as it distributes the water well over the assigned area, says Tom Flowers, president of Sanctum Design Group in Atlanta and an instructor in low-maintenance landscaping at the Atlantic Botanical Garden. The most important thing to remember about watering, he says, is: Watering frequently is not the key— watering more deeply is. For example, rather than providing your yard one-quarter inch of water every day for 7 days in a row, water once a week—but more deeply. Deeper watering encourages healthier, deeper root systems for your lawn and garden.

Water early in the day. Always water your plantings early in the morning, says Flowers. That way, you will lose the least amount of water to evaporation. Avoid watering in the evening. If your plants sit wet overnight, you run the risk of inviting diseases and pests.

Prevent wasteful runoff. Learn how quickly your soil absorbs water. When you notice that water is pooling on the surface of the ground and is starting to run off, stop watering for half an hour or so to let the water soak in. Also, don't allow your sprinklers to drop water on hard surfaces such as the street, sidewalks, or driveway.

zones, each zone programmed to provide precisely the amount of water required for the plants situated there. (Lawn and shrubbery, for instance, will have different watering requirements.) This is a time when your landscape design and your watering system must work in tandem, because it makes sense to cluster plants with the same watering requirements into a zone together.

If you've had an automatic sprinkler system ever since you moved into your house, when's the last time someone checked it over for proper function? Several years, right? If that's the case, you could be wasting rivers of water and damaging your landscape with improper sprinkling. Here are some notes that could save you a lot of grief in the future, says landscape designer Kathleen Cook.

Take a stroll around your yard and inspect the entire sprinkler system, looking for leaks and broken sprinkler heads (some get hit by mowers).

Find out how much water lawns in your region require (if you don't know, check with your local Cooperative Extension office). Then check how much water your sprinkler system is putting out. To do this, spread several empty tuna cans around the yard in the different areas that get watered. Then run the sprinkler system for a half-hour and measure the water depth in each can. Also check the sprinkler system's control center to find out how often and how long it's set to water. If you found 1 inch of water in the tuna cans after a half-hour of watering and your system sprinkles the lawn for an hour three times per week, then you know it's delivering 6 inches of water every week. If lawns in your region require 1 inch of water per week, then you're pouring out six times the necessary amount of water! Time to reprogram that system controller.

Also, make sure that your automatic sprinkler's controller has a rain sensor and a freeze sensor. A rain sensor will cut back on watering when it detects rain, and a freeze sensor keeps your sprinkler system from freezing if temperatures drop, by shutting down the water flow when the temperature approaches 32°F. Some water companies offer rebates to homeowners who install new sprinkler systems if they include water-saving sensors. So check with your utility before you buy.

A Drip Does the Trick for
Beds and Containers

Installing a drip irrigation system does fall within the skill range of many homeowners. The setup instructions are "pretty much owner-friendly," says Cook. Drip systems use a network of rigid plastic pipes to deliver a low flow of water to specifically defined areas. As with any watering system, proper control of the system is the key to efficiency and waste prevention. So make sure the controller for your drip system has the same features you would look for in an inground sprinkler system, such as a timer and rain sensor. (Surprisingly, over-watering is one of the most common errors with drip systems.) Not only can you configure a drip system to service your vegetable or flower garden, but you can also set up a system to water the containers and boxes you use on the deck or patio. And as your needs change—say, you add a row to your vegetable garden—drip systems are easy to reconfigure accordingly.

Drip systems include emitters that slowly release the water onto the ground. Carefully follow the instructions for spacing and positioning the emitters so that the root systems of your plants are properly watered. The kind of soil you have will affect how closely you place your emitters, because clay in the soil will cause dripped water to drift laterally in the ground, expanding the area receiving water. In sandy soil, you will need emitters closer together (say, 1 foot apart), in ideally mixed soil (loam) the emitters can be more widely spaced (1½ feet apart), and in clay soil you would need them farthest apart (2 feet, for example).

If your drip system is fed water through an outside spigot, your hookup will likely include a backflow prevention device, a controller, a filter, and a pressure regulator. Installing a Y connector on your spigot will leave you an open spot for attaching a garden hose without a lot of hassle. Drip systems often are set to turn on for 1 hour of watering per week, but your own schedule will depend upon what your landscape's water needs are and how many emitters are hooked up to the system.

Drip systems do have drawbacks. It's easy for a drip system to miss the root systems of some of your plants and leave lots of dry areas in the garden. Also, drip systems become a maintenance hassle over the months and years when the water lines shift and are hard to adjust under layers of mulch. Landscape designer Kathleen Cook says drip systems work best in a shrub bed, where the lines aren't likely to be disturbed during the process of vegetable or flower gardening. That's also a decent way to use those "leaky pipe" soaker hoses, the kind that are riddled with pin-prick holes and provide close-to-the ground watering. You'll only get a couple years' life out of such a hose, Cook says— "Less if you put a shovel through it now and then, like I do."

Moving Sprinklers: What a Drag!

The other approach to lawn and garden watering, of course, is the time-honored, labor-intensive method—dragging a hose and sprinkler around the yard, turning it on for a while, and then repositioning it. Yes, this technique is kinder to your bank account in the short term—since you're not paying a few thousand dollars to have an inground sprinkler system installed. But that's what Feldman calls false economy. Watering by hand is imprecise and wastes water. Homeowners rarely manage to do it consistently, so over time their yards and gardens suffer as plantings get sick or die—a substantial cost in itself. On the other hand, hose-and-sprinkler watering may be the most practical method if you live in a rainy climate and you only need to add water to the landscape during rare dry spells.

PUTTING KIDS INTO THE PICTURE

To design a children's area in your yard, plot out the entire section on a smaller scale so your kids will feel naturally comfortable, recommends landscape designer Flowers. This means setting aside a smaller section of yard compared to the adult areas, installing smaller beds, a tighter path configuration, and selecting smaller plants. The exception to the small plants concept is the judicious use of sunflowers, those monster-size beauties that children are preprogrammed to adore.

Plants that Flowers likes to use in children's areas include lamb's ears, gumpo azaleas, sweetbox, and creeping gardenia. They're fragrant and kidsize, which means that children can study them more closely with a bird's-eye view than is possible with larger plants. Other good choices are marigolds (which are easy to grow), morning glories (perfect for covering a tepee or tunnel), strawberries, and celosia (which comes in screaming reds, pinks, oranges, and yellows).

Give the kids their very own downsize garden plots for the flowers and vegetables they most enjoy. Provide them with child-scale tools for working in the garden and fun structures (such as the bean tepee and sunflower hut described on the following pages). Amuse your kids with interactive features such as bird feeders and birdhouses, which will teach children to take care of the environment. Kids also love water features. Small fountains are a big hit, but avoid anything deep enough to be dangerous for a young child—a toddler can drown in just a few inches of water. Growing pole beans in a kids' garden area is a great idea because these climbing plants will quickly cover a simple framework, creating fantastic architectural features and hiding places for your children.

Here are three examples of structures for kids that Joffee suggests.

A bean tepee. Find three 6-foot-long garden stakes or bamboo poles (available at your garden store). In the appointed garden spot, use twine to tie the tops of the three poles together. Push the bottom of each pole into the garden soil. Two of the poles should be at least 2 feet apart, leaving room for the tepee's entryway. On the two other sides of the tepee, tie stretches of twine between the poles to serve as further supports for the bean plants. At the base of each pole, plant your pole beans (from seed or transplant). As the beans

For the door of your bean tepee, leave the bases of two poles 2 feet apart. On the other two sides, tie stretches of twine for your pole beans to climb onto.

grow, tie them loosely to the adjacent pole to guide their growth. In several weeks, your tepee "walls" will be well filled in.

A bean tunnel. This works much like the bean tepee. Use seven 6- to 8-foot poles to build a tunnel-like framework. For instance, position two vertical poles on either side of a path and tie their top ends together. Repeat 2 feet farther down the path and then again 2 feet farther. For stability, lay the last pole across the top of this row of supports and lash it into place. Tie lengths of twine between the vertical poles on each side of the pathway to create webbing that will support your pole beans. Plant the beans at the base of each vertical pole and tie them loosely to the poles as the plants grow tall enough.

Sunflower hut. In your kids' garden, use short stakes to mark off the dimensions of your hut—say, 5 feet for each of four walls. Along each wall of the hut, plant sunflowers, making sure to leave a "doorway" of 2 or 3 feet not planted in one wall. When the sunflowers reach about 8 inches in height, thin them to 2 feet apart. At this point, you can plant pole beans between your sunflowers. As the beans sprout, train them to climb the sunflowers, filling in the walls of your hut.

Note: Some gardeners like to add color to their kids' garden "architecture" by interspersing those famous and colorful climbers—morning glories—with the pole beans. To provide cushy sitting areas and to control weeds, cover the ground inside your structures with straw, other mulch, or planted clover. Make sure your children participate in each stage of the building process in their special garden, so they will learn about nature and gardening and will fully appreciate their special garden spaces.

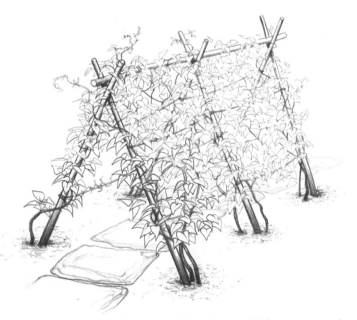

The side poles for this bean tunnel cross high over a garden path. They're connected by a horizontal top pole and twine on each side for the pole beans to climb on.

To create a children's sunflower hut, plant sunflowers in a narrow rectangular bed delineating the walls of the room. Leave an entrance open. Train pole beans and morning glories to climb the sunflower stalks and fill out the walls. Add straw or mulch for soft seating inside, or grow clover.

Tag a few plants. Speaking of environmental education, here's a sneaky way to slide a little book learning into a child's outdoor play. Buy some plastic or metal plant tags from your garden store or order them online, says landscape designer Tom Flowers. In the kids' area of your yard, label three plants with both the common name and botanical name on each tag. (More than three will scare the kids off.) Now and then check the tags and review the names with your kids. Every few months, consult with your children and select a few new plants to label. Your children will grow up at ease with the idea of plant names and the occasional Latin tongue-twister.

Assign kids their own digging areas. Kids love to emulate Mom and Dad, but you're not likely to turn a 5-year-old loose with a shovel in your prized garden. However, you *can* keep kids happy—and keep an eye on them while you work in the yard—if you set aside a couple of spots where the kids can dig to their hearts' content, says landscape designer Jon Feldman. Buy your children a few kid-size garden tools (or drag out the digging toys from your last beach trip) and point out the specific areas where they may dig and otherwise fool around in the dirt—say, a bare spot under a tree, or an inconspicuous area over by the woodpile. They'll love spending time outdoors with you, and you'll bring up your kids accustomed to working with soil and plants. Who knows—in a couple of years they might be ready for some productive work in the real garden.

Amuse your kids with gourds. Children are naturally drawn to the exotic look of gourds, so pick out a couple of funky-looking varieties to grow in your children's garden, Joffee suggests. Kids will love participating in the growing and preservation process. You'll find a wide variety of unusual shapes and colors available. Gourds vary in size from just a few inches in diameter to as much as 2 feet. They're ready to harvest when their stems turn dry and brown. Treat your gourds gently—scratches could expose them to rot. Wash your harvested gourds and set them aside to dry in a warm place. To protect your

SLEIGHT *of* HAND

Practice Mind over Maintenance

The "weekend warrior" approach to gardening and yard work is a path to misery. That is, saving up all of your maintenance tasks until a couple of afternoons and trying to get it all done well, without blisters or exhaustion. A much more sane approach, says Tom Flowers, president of Sanctum Design Group in Atlanta and an instructor in low-maintenance landscaping at the Atlanta Botanical Garden: Attack your outdoor maintenance daily as 5-minute mini-projects—5 minutes of pruning, 5 minutes of picking up trash, 5 minutes

of weeding, 5 minutes of picking up wind-blown leaves from the corners of the yard. The mini-project approach translates into less total time spent actually working, which is what *How to Cheat at Gardening and Yard Work* is all about. If you wait and try to handle all of your garden and yard maintenance in one blitz, all of those situations you were intending to control will have gotten worse—meaning more work and much more fatigue and frustration. It's better to stay ahead of the curve.

gourds from bacteria, apply rubbing alcohol or a bleach-and-water solution to their exteriors. Once they have dried completely, protect them (and enhance their colors) with a coat of clear, spray-on sealer.

Remember, connections count. When you design a children's area in your yard, make sure that it's directly connected to the broader, "official" lawn area of the yard, Flowers says. This ensures that kids can freely escape from their downsize nook and enjoy the larger lawn for wilder activities such as tag or an impromptu soccer game. Also, the ideal kid-friendly yard design allows for walkways (or, more appropriately, "runways") around the entire house for those inevitable chasing games that go 'round and 'round it.

ROCK PAINTING: INSTANT, ENDURING COLOR AND CHARM

The winter months can be long, boring, and brown while you wait for your garden vegetation to green up and for flowers to bloom. Lin Wellford, an artist in Green Forest, Arkansas, has a quick and simple solution for that: Introduce some color, interest, and whimsy to your garden anytime of the year by painting the stones that you use in your landscape—border stones, stepping-stones, or just large rocks hauled in for a sculptural effect. Her technique for painting stone is surprisingly easy and requires little in the way of special materials or artistic talent—just a lighthearted spirit and a willingness to experiment with an out-of-the-ordinary approach to garden design.

Wellford has authored a series of books providing instructions and patterns for her rock painting, including *Painted Garden Art Anyone Can Do.* Among her projects are:

- Scalloped flowerbed border stones painted to look like a parade of elephants. Each curving top forms an elephant's humped back.
- A fish-shaped flowerbed

- A tortoise created from several river stones
- Stepping-stones painted to look like huge flower blossoms
- A faux fishpond, complete with painted koi and lily pads, with a stone border (for once, raccoons will not tamper with the "fish" in your backyard pond)

To get started with garden stone painting, either pick up one of Wellford's books (available at bookstores, hobby stores, and online), or plunge in with projects of your own invention. If the process sounds scary or intimidating, starting with tried-and-true patterns will get you acclimated, and your fears will soon evaporate. One of Wellford's readers once wrote to her, "You know, this is more like coloring than art." She loves that comment because it points out how easy stone painting is.

Inexpensive brick edging can dress up a flowerbed in minutes. With just a few brush strokes, you can create a parade of pachyderms, using the scallop-top design for the elephant's back.

One of artist-author Wellford's favorite stone painting projects creates a parade of pachyderms along a common scallop-topped garden bed border. The primary outlines are done in black with a fine brush. The background is painted black. Shading around the ears and under the belly is created with a wash (black paint diluted with a little water). Paint the tusk and toenails white. Create your own pattern or, for detailed instructions, consult Wellford's book *Painted Garden Art Anyone Can Do*. Whether you purchase patterns or use your own designs, here are some things you will want to know about painting stone for display in your landscape.

Pick the right stone. Make sure that any stone you paint is sturdy (you don't want it to crumble) and also smooth (which helps you achieve the painting detail you will want).

Give them a bath. Remove all dirt and algae from any stone you want to paint. Wellford uses a scrub brush and a mildly abrasive bathroom cleaner for this.

Seal the deal. Before painting, coat your stone first with an acrylic primer that's labeled for exterior use.

Buy the right paint. When it's time to add color to your landscape stone, go to your hardware store or home improvement store and buy either latex exterior house paint or a product called patio paint. Using paint meant for outdoors ensures that your artwork will stand up to years of exposure to the elements. In many cases, you can now buy exterior paint in spray-on form, which makes stone painting go much faster. "You can do a garden full of these things really quick," Wellford says.

Stock up on dark green. For many stone painting projects that are intended for the garden, Wellford likes to start by covering the stone entirely in dark green (which also can be found in spray-on exterior acrylic). The bright-colored features are painted on over the dark green, and that base color helps the final work blend in well with surrounding vegetation.

Finish with a touch of gloss. Covering your finished stone painting with clear sealer will provide extra protection for your handiwork, Wellford says. It also will provide a glossy finish that's particularly effective for creating a watery effect (on a faux pond, for instance).

Save time with stamps. Using stamps in your painting will accelerate any project that requires repeated images such as leaves, flowers, or lizard scales. Stamps also will ensure that pattern details in your paintings are consistent. You can buy stamps in a zillion varieties at hobby stores for just a couple of dollars, or make your own. Save the thin plastic foam from the packaging of electronics products. Then use an art knife to cut it into the desired stamp shape. To use stamps in your outdoor artwork, spread a tablespoon of paint onto a piece of thick cardboard, press the face of the stamp into the paint, and apply it to your stone. Think strategically about what to paint first. For instance, Wellford likes to stamp out background leaves first, let them dry, and then add flowers.

Put petals on the path. If you have a spot of worn grass on a popular walkway around the corner of your house, dress up the path with a few round stepping-stones, each of them sporting an oversize painted blossom, Wellford suggests.

Take your sculpture for a walk. You can make an adorable backyard tortoise out of several painted river stones—a large flat one for the body, and others for the head, feet, and tail. Since the stones are never physically attached to one another, their positioning is a flexible matter. So to add a little whimsy and intrigue to your backyard, move your stone tortoise to a different position

SLEIGHT *of* HAND

Special Delivery for Small Garden Necessities

Mount an old mailbox on a post in your garden. Use it as a mini-supply depot, saving you scores of trips to the toolshed or the house during your gardening day.

Your garden mailbox is a great place to store twine, scissors, small shears, a pocketknife, a small garbage bag, and twist ties. Not to mention a packaged snack or two.

every few days. (Do this in the dark of night if you want to be sneaky.) Once your family members notice the occasional changes, they'll watch the tortoise's progress with rapt anticipation. You can typically buy smooth, rounded river rocks from a landscaping business.

Coat those pavers first. You can use painted pavers to great effect on a patio, a walkway, or in a garden centerpiece. However, if you're going to paint pavers, don't skimp on the first painting step—applying a coat of primer, Wellford says. That's because many new pavers carry a residue of silicon, which is used to help them slide out of their molds during the manufacturing process. The primer ensures that the residue won't interfere with your masterful paint job.

Consider the audience, front and back. There are no hard-and-fast rules for how you incorporate painted stone into your garden and yard design, Wellford says—it's your own style that counts. However, she has a rule of thumb that may help your decision-making: For front yards, which are usually fairly public, the more sedate treatments usually work best (a more formal "basket of flowers" made from a circled stone border or a fishpond painted on flat stones or pavers might be just the ticket). Likewise, the more whimsical and expressive treatments (caterpillars and butterflies galore) are likely to work better in the private areas of the backyard. Painted stones can be a real conversation starter for adults and loads of fun for children and budding artists.

Involve the entire family. For a personalized touch, turn the painting of stepping-stones into a family project—each family member decides the design and coloring of one stone. Use the stepping-stones in a kids' area of the backyard. Keep the kids interested in the garden by adding a new path or shortcut each summer and feel free to let them go wild with color and design. The goal is showing them that gardening isn't all hard work.

Consider the calendar. You are probably plenty busy with your garden and yard in spring and summer. Why not save stone painting for those dreary, monochromatic days of late fall and winter? It's easily done inside or in a basement or garage, and you'll feel like spring has sprung right there in your kitchen or craft room.

OFF-SEASON INTEREST

Most garden elements become more visible when it's *not* growing season. Fall, winter, and spring are just as much a time of beauty as when plants are in full bloom. When planning beds and designing planting areas for your yard, make special note of any views you want to obstruct and any areas you'd like to see more of when the leaves have dropped.

Bye-bye boat and hello hydrangea. If you store big items like canoes or campers in your yard, it's easy (well, sometimes easy) to hide them behind plants in full leaf. But now it's winter and the first thing you see out of the kitchen window is a canoe on sawhorses. When thinking about your garden design, take a walk around your yard and note what you'd like to disguise or screen year-round. There are a few easy ways to turn an eyesore into an attraction. If the object or view is relatively low to the ground, you could select a few large rocks and a few dwarf evergreens and create an island bed. If you need something a little taller, select a plant like forsythia, hydrangea, lilac, or viburnum. Even when their leaves fall, there's still enough plant structure to screen an unpleasant view. Disguising taller items may require more creativity, more work, and more money but you can find solutions in all price ranges, from trees and evergreens to lattice panels and fences.

Save the shearing for spring. Plant seedheads and old foliage heaped with snow or encrusted in ice are much more appealing than uniformly shorn stubble. As you plan your plantings with an eye to winter, be sure to include some perennials with attractive dried foliage or stems. Ornamental grasses, which will dry to lovely shades of buff and russet, will retain their plumelike flowers until spring. And added bonus is the graceful motion and gentle rustling of the grass blades in spring.

Seeing color in the white of winter. Shrubs can offer bursts of color against the bare browns or bright whites of the winter season. Shrubs like red-osier dogwood or Japanese kerria offer brightly colored bark. Trees and shrubs with winter-persistent fruits add sparkles of color and attract birds to the garden. Crabapples and winterberry are two of the best.

I hope you have gotten to the end of the design chapter with heightened confidence that you can plan out landscape improvements for your home in a way that will seriously reduce future work. After all, since landscape design is an outdoor concern, you have a powerful ally—Mother Nature. Once you understand what she has in mind for your garden and yard, and how to blend that with your own preferences, developing a low-maintenance, showcase exterior will be a walk in the park.

CHAPTER 6

Sub-Plots:
RAISED BEDS,
CONTAINERS,
ROOFTOPS, *and MORE*

|||||||||||||||||||||||||||||||||||||||||||||||||||||||||||||||||||||||||||||||||||||||||||||||||||||||||

I'll bet there's a certain rebellious corner of your personality that's attracted to abstract art, or to improvised music, or at the very least to coloring outside of the lines. After all, part of the how-to-cheat sensibility is the freedom to ignore the restricting rules set down for us, especially when the conventional approach is more labor intensive, more costly, and more—well—boring. The alternative forms of gardening, such as raised beds, containers, and rooftop gardening, do the same thing for us. They provide the opportunity to introduce the whimsical and unexpected to our landscapes—to place greenery or blossoms where the world expects to find drab grays and browns.

So here we have a collection of tips and tricks for making these forms of gardening work best for you. The great news is that these forms of growing are inherently easier to start up and easier to maintain than a conventional garden. They tend to be less costly. And you already knew that they were more fun, too!

A tip of my wide-brimmed gardening hat goes out to the advisors who contributed their thoughts to this chapter, including Michael Mastrota, landscape architect, and Stephanie DeStefano, grounds operations coordinator, both of American University in Washington, DC; Kathleen Cook, landscape designer for the Fort Worth Botanical Garden; Emily Shelton, horticulturist at the Chicago Botanic Garden; Tom Flowers, landscape designer and teacher at the Atlanta Botanical Garden in Atlanta; Annette Pelliccio, founder of the Happy Gardener organic gardening company in Virginia; Master Gardener Rebecca Kolls of *Good Morning America;* Lori Hayes, manager of the Horticultural Center in Philadelphia's Fairmount Park; Mel Bartholomew, author of *All New Square Foot Gardening;* Leslie Hoffman, executive director of Earth Pledge, a nonprofit environmental organization in New York City that advocates for sustainable practices; and Sharon Slack, head gardener for City Farmer in Vancouver.

CONTAINERS: GREAT GROWING IN SMALL SPACES

Container gardening is the famous solution for people who want to garden but have little space to do it because they live in apartments, condos, or townhouses. But containers also are a godsend for people who want the benefits of gardening without having to work too hard—for instance, people who would pick up a book titled *How to Cheat at Gardening and Yard Work.*

You might be saying to yourself: "What's the big deal about containers?

Find a pot with holes in the bottom, toss in some dirt, toss in some plants or seeds, water it, and you're done!" You're right—it's *almost* that simple. However, there are numerous easy ways to cut corners, to get maximum longevity out of your plants, and to use containers for maximum artistic impact. So if you want to know some fine points that will save you even more labor and anguish, read on.

Some bottom-line container rules. A creative gardener will convert all sorts of unconventional household objects into planting containers, but that doesn't mean you can throw all rules out the window, says landscape designer Kathleen Cook. Stick to these basics no matter how inventive your repurposed planting container might be:

■ The ideal container has drainage holes in the bottom. Otherwise, water can pool in the bottom and put your plants at risk for rot and disease.

■ Put a small patch of window screen over the drainage holes in the bottom of your container. A piece of paper towel works, too, and will biodegrade after a season. Either will act as a filter, preventing loss of your potting soil out the bottom of the pot and possible staining of your deck.

■ Many people add a layer of gravel to the bottom of their containers to enhance drainage. Unless you have some particular need to enhance drainage, don't bother. The gravel isn't mandatory and adds unwelcome weight to your containers.

No holes? Improvise. Lack of drainage holes can present a vexing problem to creative gardeners who occasionally love to use "found objects" as planters. Suppose you can't figure out how to drill holes in the bottom of that heavy porcelain tub? Here's a sneaky solution that may get you through, says Emily Shelton, horticulturist at the Chicago Botanic Garden: As noted above, in some cases a layer of small stones in the bottom of a container will help you out of a drainage problem. Fill the bottom of the tub with 2 inches of pea gravel or wood chips. Cover that with screening to act as a filter. Then pour in your potting mix and install your plants. When you water, the gravel or wood chips may provide enough drainage to keep the roots from sitting wet long-term. Note: This technique will only work in large containers.

Automate your watering. Sure, a container garden offers a number of conveniences. But containers still require maintenance every 2 or 3 days, says landscape designer Tom Flowers. If you're forgetful or easily distracted, your plants will deteriorate into a containerized wasteland. The surest way to prevent this: Irrigate your containers with a timer-controlled drip system. (For more on drip systems, see Chapter 5.)

Add time-release fertilizer. Most of your container plants' fertilizer needs can be taken care of right at potting time. Go to your garden supply store, buy some all-purpose organic fertilizer, and mix it into your potting soil according to the package directions. This will release nutrients into the soil over the next several months. For many plants, that's all the fertilizer they will need throughout the growing season. Check the fertilizing requirements that come with your plants, however. Some benefit from the occasional dose of fish/seaweed liquid fertilizer or compost tea for an extra boost.

Get the most from compost. Compost mixed into your container soil will work the same kind of magic that it does in your conventional garden bed, says Annette Pelliccio, founder of the Happy Gardener. The organic material allows your container to hold onto water better, meaning that drying out is less of a

|||||||||||||||||||||||||||||||||||||||||||||||||||||||||||||||||||||||||||||||||||||||||||||||||||||||||

Contain Those Penny-Pinching Ways

Don't skimp on the size of the containers that you buy for your plants, says Emily Shelton, horticulturist at the Chicago Botanic Garden. She once had a client who bought little quart-size containers for her seventh-floor balcony. The client proceeded to fill the small containers with enormous flowers. They immediately dried out in the sun and wind and the flowers died. Lesson learned: It's silly to spend money on plants but not on the containers that will keep them alive. "It's an investment," Shelton says.

|||||||||||||||||||||||||||||||||||||||||||||||||||||||||||||||||||||||||||||||||||||||||||||||||||||||||

problem. Also, when you add compost to your containers at the beginning of the season, you won't need to stir in fertilizer as well, Pelliccio says. (Some plants may still require occasional liquid fast-growth fertilizer, however.)

Read the fine print. Most garden supply stores now sell lightweight soil mixtures that are intended for containers or balcony gardens. Some of these mixes include fertilizer, however, so check. Unless the package specifies that the fertilizer inside is organic, skip it and mix in your own all-purpose fertilizer as described above, says Sharon Slack, head gardener for City Farmer.

Give your containers a lift. Stands that raise your containers several inches from the surface of the deck, patio, porch, or terrace are readily available at garden stores and home improvement stores. These are good to use wherever you place your containers. In the yard, the extra elevation keeps them away from pests. On the deck or other surfaces, the stand reduces the chances that water draining out of the container will cause stains. And either way, you don't have to bend over as far to reach your containers when they're elevated. Wheeled stands are available, too—a big help when you need to move heavy containers.

Plant with room to spare. When you have plants ready to take up residence in your container, fill the container halfway with your potting soil. Very large plants may need less soil underneath, so they can sit lower in the pot; small plants will need to sit higher, so put more soil underneath them. Arrange your plants on the dirt, leaving enough space between them to account for growth. If the rootballs are compacted, loosen them by applying gentle pressure with your fingers. Then add more potting soil around your plants until the container is all but an inch full. Now let your plants celebrate their new home with a nice drink of water.

Put a "diaper" in your container. Tired of checking the dryness of your patio's plant containers and watering them several times a week? Sure, you would expect outdoor containers to dry out quickly because they're exposed to the elements. However, you can easily improve their water retention and cut back on your watering duties. Buy water retention mats from your garden supply store, says Annette Pelliccio. A 12-inch-square mat will hold 4 cups of

Easy-Peasy Planting in Large Pots

Getting several new flower plants situated in a large patio container can be quite a juggling act. Here's the old way: You pour in the soil and then you have to decide how to arrange the plants. So you dig little holes, plant the rootballs, stand back and take a look, then re-dig and rearrange. Argh, it's frustrating!

Here's the cheating method: Sam Jeffries, one of the hosts of the radio show *The Garden Guys*, has a sneaky solution. First, fill your large container with potting soil up to the desired height (a few inches short of full,

accounting for the depth of your flowers' rootballs). Then take your flowers—still in the little plastic containers you bought them in—and position them on top of the potting soil. Switch them around to your heart's content. Then fill in more potting soil around the little pots until the soil is at the correct height.

With the potting soil heaped in place, lift each of the flowers out, remove their little plastic pots, then plop the plant right back in the same hole. There will be no more guesswork about what size holes to dig!

---

water, she says. The trick is to tuck a mat into your container when you're first doing the potting. (This will feel oddly like giving your plants a diaper.) First put 2 inches of soil into the container, then cut a mat to fit precisely over the dirt. On top of that, add the rest of your potting soil mix and the plants. When you water, the mat will puff up and absorb moisture, creating a reservoir that's slowly released to the soil and roots. (Roots will grow directly into the mat to reach the moisture it contains.) If you have a lot of containers in varied sizes, look for large rolls of water-retention matting that you can cut to the sizes you need. If you only need a few mats, buy pre-cut squares in packs. With water-holding mats in your containers, you will only need to water once a week, rather than the usual four or five times a week, Pelliccio says.

Quench plants' thirst with coconut. Subjected to sun, wind, and forgetful gardeners, container plants are particularly vulnerable to death by dehydration. Pelliccio has a cure for that—a secret ingredient she uses in her potting soil. It's coir fiber, the material left over from the processing of coconuts, which holds more than eight times its weight in water. This organic amendment, available from garden suppliers, is used much like peat moss. It takes a long time to break down, too—usually 3 to 5 years.

How do you use it in containers? Easy: Just mix together equal amounts of coir fiber and potting soil. An alternative: If you have been treating a garden bed with fertilizer all along, just mix some of that soil in equal amounts with coir fiber. Coir fiber will make your container soil lighter and looser—a superior medium for roots!

Gel it to keep your plants happy. You also can cut your watering duties in half if you have a high-tech, water-absorbing gel mixed into your container soil. This gel comes in powder or granular form and can hold 400 times its weight in water, acting as a nice reservoir for your container, says Pelliccio. Such gel comes in different forms and can be applied in different ways (so you're going to have to pay careful attention to the directions on the version that you buy). With one product, you simply mix a teaspoon of gel powder into the surface of the soil, or you can mix the powder into the soil at potting time. Another style of moisture-retaining gel comes in a rigid tube that fits

ZERO-MAINTENANCE MARVELS
Soil Simplicity

At a loss as to what kind of soil to use in your container garden? You'll do fine if you use conventional potting soil from your garden supplier, as long as it contains some organic material to hold onto moisture and lighten the soil, says Lori Hayes, manager of the Horticultural Center in Philadelphia's Fairmount Park. Without organic material, the soil will dry out too quickly. So you could add some compost or peat moss to your potting soil to keep your plants happy, plus an organic all-purpose fertilizer.

On the other hand, Hayes is a big believer in keeping your soil simple—which means buying a growing medium that's ready to use right out of the bag. One such mix includes peat moss, perlite, and limestone.

into your caulking gun. (You sink the nozzle a few inches into your container's soil and inject the gel directly into the soil.) Another type comes in the form of small crystals that swell up when wet, turning into little blobs of a clear gelatin-like substance. Follow the package directions precisely. If you put too much gel in your soil, the gel could swell so much that it pushes your plants out of their container.

Seal that terra-cotta planter. Terra-cotta plant containers have long been popular, and for good reason—not only are they relatively inexpensive, they're also beautiful and durable, and they have a classic look. Unglazed clay pots also allow air to pass through their walls—a benefit to the soil inside. Experienced gardeners have learned that there's a dark side to terra-cotta, however. It can be tough on your plants, because this porous material absorbs moisture that the plants dearly need. Since terra-cotta containers dry out faster than plastic ones, you have to work harder to keep your plants hydrated, especially if you live in a dry climate. There's a sneaky solution to this dilemma, says Pelliccio. At the beginning of the season, before you put soil and plants into your terra-cotta container, do this: Scoop a tablespoon of petroleum jelly onto a paper towel. Pick up the towel, and smear the petroleum jelly over the entire interior of the pot, adding more jelly as needed. This will create a moisture barrier inside your planter that will last throughout the growing season. At the beginning of the next growing season, replenish the barrier when you're changing plants.

Now, because I am psychic, I know what you're thinking: "Why not just buy those plastic plant containers that are made to look just like terra-cotta? The plastic look-alikes can be quite handsome, and surely they don't dry out as fast as genuine terra-cotta." Well right you are, smarty-pants. Except for this problem: Thin plastic containers only last a year or so. What typically happens is that you lift your heavy, soil-and-water-filled container by grasping that lip around the top—and the lip breaks. It's your choice, of course, but real terra-cotta is more durable.

On hot days, give plants a cool drink. Small pots dry out very quickly on hot days. If you'll be at work all day, you can water them well in the morning, then put some ice cubes on top of the soil when you leave. The ice will melt gradually and give the pots some extra moisture.

Pots need watering? Weigh the evidence. If you're not sure whether a pot needs watering, just pick it up, if it's not too big. For a hanging basket, put your hand underneath and lift up slightly. If the pot feels very light, it's probably dry. If it has some weight to it, it's probably okay.

To lighten your load, plant "peanuts." Large terra-cotta and stone containers get quite heavy once you add soil, plants, and water. So whenever you need to move your planters around, it's a backbreaking chore. There's a simple way to lighten that load, says Stephanie DeStefano at American University. When you're planting a really big or deep pot, first fill the bottom half of the container with those plastic foam "peanuts" that come in the mail with fragile

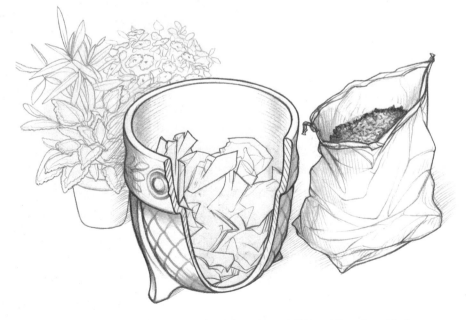

Cheat on filling up containers with potting soil by adding crumpled newspaper or foam "peanuts" to the bottom third of the pot.

shipments. Then fill the rest of the container with potting mix. This makes the container much lighter and also adds air to the soil, which roots will love. The technique also allows you to create container plantings that appear bigger without adding to cost or weight. Besides, you were looking for a way to recycle those plastic peanuts anyway. Another method for taking up extra space in a huge urn or pot is to put crumpled newspapers in the bottom of the pot—they recycle, too.

A couple of extra touches that will also help: At the very bottom of the container, lay a piece of filter fabric (landscape cloth or window screen will do). If your pot does not have drainage holes, pour in a few inches of gravel or river rock on top of that to improve drainage. Add your plastic foam peanuts and then cover them with another layer of filter cloth to create a barrier between the soil and the plastic filler.

Pick the right size pot. If you're not sure how big a pot your plant needs, a good rule of thumb is to choose a pot that's one-third as deep as the height the plant will be when it's fully grown (check the plant label when you buy to find the mature height).

Find a fun food theme. To add some fun as well as function to your containers or window boxes, select plants for them according to food themes, says Rebecca Kolls. Your pizza container might include green pepper, onion, and oregano. Your salsa window box might include garlic, tomato, chili pepper, and cilantro. And your salad planter would have a variety of mixed greens. For a tad more adventure, plant a box with edible flowers, she says—such as pansies, nasturtiums, and calendulas—embellished with some herbs.

Easy pickings: container salad. Put an entire fresh salad at your fingertips in your deck or balcony containers, says Pelliccio. A gourmet lettuce mix, easy to grow from seed in containers, will provide you with beautiful purple, red, green, and dark green foliage. To round out your salad, cherry tomatoes also are easy to grow in containers. In keeping with the theme, plant basil in the same container. Your containers will provide salad all summer long. (You'll have to supply the dressing yourself!)

Reap the fruits of minimal labor. Imagine taking your kids onto the patio at sunrise so you can all pick your own breakfast fruit. That's container gardening at its finest. Any berries will work well in containers, says Pelliccio, but strawberries and blueberries are the easiest to grow that way. Look for dwarf varieties so they don't outgrow their space. Pelliccio is particularly fond of Tophat blueberries. Tophat self-pollinates, so you don't need to buy more than one plant, and it grows to a compact 18 inches in height. Tophat also produces blueberries twice a year and has pretty red leaves in fall.

Create a layered look. Containers provide an opportunity to establish a creative layered effect with your plants, says Michael Mastrota, landscape architect at American University. This can be done using different sizes of round containers—say, 24 inches, 18 inches, and 12 inches in diameter. Stock the containers with plants that naturally grow at three different heights, creating the layers. You can plant one layer per container, or you can put all three layers in a single large container. Follow your artistic instincts! Don't be afraid to mix annuals, perennials, and grasses in the same pot—just remove the annuals for winter.

Here are some notes about tall, medium, and low layers.

Tall layer: Plant in the center or the back of the container. Good plant choices: hibiscus, sunflowers, fountain grass, canna lily, and Russian sage. Or try morning glories on a tripod or on a pot-size trellis.

Medium layer: Plant just about anywhere—around or in front of taller plants, or behind the lowest ones. Good plant choices include: *Rudbeckia hirta* (black-eyed Susan), Shasta daisy, salvia, sedum (taller ones, such as 'Autumn Joy'), coreopsis, geraniums, coleus, nicotiana, heliotrope, and dahlias.

Low layer: Plant near the edge of the container, where they will eventually drape over the side. Good plant choices are: catmint, strawflower (helichrysum), million bells (calibrachoa), verbena, vinca, wave petunias, and ivy.

In a similar vein, Pelliccio likes to combine fruit, vegetables, herbs, or flowers in the same planter. A particularly effective technique involves planting a tall, striking plant in the center of a round container and planting a lower plant around the outer edge—perhaps a plant that will cascade down the sides. Some examples:

- Broccoli is a striking plant at every stage of growth. Plant one in the center of your container, with petunias or impatiens around the edge.
- Instead of broccoli in the example above, use cauliflower or red-stemmed Swiss chard. (Hey, did anyone ever tell you that vegetables are good for you?)
- Rosemary grows high. So plant that in the center, with low-growing strawberries around the outside rim. Purple basil would make a good centerpiece, too.

Enhance your decorating with containers. Containers are an important element of the cheat-at-gardening lifestyle for another simple reason: They're mobile. This means that by rearranging your containers, you can give your patio an entirely new look every weekend if you want to. Incorporate containers into your interior decorating, too, rotating them as you wish from the deck to the living room and back again. And when part of a conventional garden bed is starting to fade late in the season, a couple of strategically placed containers will perk things up visually.

Extend your containers' season. Unless you have furnished your containers with particularly hardy plants, they're bound to suffer a "brownout" in fall after a season of faithful service. Rule No. 1 for late-season planters, says Lori Hayes, manager of the Horticultural Center in Philadelphia's Fairmount Park: "If it does not look good, I say lose it." So as part of your fall garden cleanup, cut down your failing container plants and yank them out.

You still have a few nice options for using these newly vacant containers, however.

- Install new plants that are known for late-season color—pansies and ornamental kale are good choices. Other cool-weather plants include chrysan-

4 Tips for Successful Container Improv

Converting "found" items into plant containers adds some whimsy and visual interest to the landscape—and appeals to the recycling enthusiast in you as well. However, not every yard-sale prize or Dumpster find makes an ideal plant container. Here are some notes on how to successfully convert salvaged objects into containers. A grateful garden-gloved salute for these goes out to Lori Hayes, manager of the Horticultural Center in Philadelphia's Fairmount Park.

1. Ask yourself how well your prospective container will drain water, so moisture will be less likely to collect in the bottom and stagnate. You can even convert an old work boot into a planter if you drill a few holes in the sole.

2. Your container must be made of a durable material that's held together securely. Likely candidates: sturdy baskets, buckets, dresser drawers, jugs, cooking pots, or wading pools. Remember how harshly the weather treats materials that were designed for indoor use.

3. If you're afraid that the soil will wash out of your container, use some kind of screening material (window screening or landscape cloth, for instance) to hold soil in while letting water drain out. This is the perfect tactic for converting a milk crate into a planter, for example.

4. Never think of your "found object" container as a permanent installation. Be willing to pour out the dirt, toss the object out, and start over after a few years. The novelty will inevitably wear thin for you and other observers. If the improvised container is showing signs of deterioration—such as rot or rust—get rid of it.

themums, African daisy (osteospermum), asters, sedum, ornamental grasses, and around the edge of the pot, sweet alyssum.

■ Miniature boxwoods, neatly clipped, make elegant plantings for winter containers in a formal garden.

■ Plant bulbs in fall to produce spring flowers—daffodils or narcissus, for instance. Petite bulbs are a nice, delicate touch, too—for example, miniature daffodils, grape hyacinths, or crocus. It's best to sink pots of spring bulbs into the ground or put them in a cold frame so they don't freeze and crack (these bulbs need winter cold in order to bloom in spring). Pull them out of the ground in early spring when it's time for the bulbs to grow and bloom.

■ Or just decorate your planters with evergreen boughs or berry-laden sprigs of holly.

Give castoffs new life in the garden. Container gardening provides an opportunity to employ fun and inventive thinking, says landscape designer Kathleen Cook. Objects that you were about to dispose of in a yard sale can find new life as a garden accessory on the patio, in a flowerbed, or among your growing vegetables. A freestanding towel rack becomes a trellis, for instance, a chair becomes a flower planter, and a file drawer becomes an herb garden. (In the same vein, keep an eye out for potential planters when you visit other people's yard sales. You'll score some plant containers for virtually nothing.) Such whimsy in your garden will draw a chuckle or two out of visitors and kids, and at the same time you'll be doing a good turn for the environment, since you're recycling materials. On the other hand, don't go overboard with this approach—you don't want your garden to look like a junkyard.

Thieves lurking? Play the heavy. In most cases, you want your plant containers to be lightweight so you can move them around easily. The exceptions are containers that you park in the front yard, where a vandal or thief might be tempted to snatch one up. You know your own neighborhood best, so if you're wary of such passersby, try this trick, says Hayes: Use large containers in the "public" areas of your yard. When you plant in them, weigh them down first by placing heavy rocks in the bottom. A passing ne'er-do-well will quickly decide that lifting such a container and running with it is impossible.

Get into the price-tracking habit. Don't assume that either your local nursery or your "big box" home improvement store will always have the best prices when you go to buy container plants, says Hayes. Prices fluctuate too much for

Container Plants Overly Thirsty?

If your container plants regularly dry out too quickly, it could be that your plants are rootbound, says Kathleen Cook, landscape designer for the Fort Worth Botanical Garden. This means that the root system has grown too large for the container and the plant needs to be repotted in a larger container. Some sure signs of a root-bound plant: roots extending out of the container's drainage holes, or the surface of the soil is firm and roots are visible there. Another way to check for a rootbound plant: Take the container into the yard, turn it on its side, and gently tap the plant out. A rootbound plant will show its roots all around the sides of the soil.

you to be sure. There's nothing wrong with buying from either type of store, she says, but your best defense financially is to keep a log of the prices you find, just as you would do between competing supermarkets.

Make your garden mobile. If you garden in large containers on your patio or deck, set the containers on small dollies. This way, you can easily move them if you're rearranging the outdoor furniture. You also can readily reposition the container plants to catch more sun during the day.

REST EASY WITH RAISED BEDS

Raised beds are a lovely hybrid of conventional gardening and container gardening. Basically, your garden soil is contained within a frame that lies on top of the ground. This allows you to build the garden soil several inches above ground level, an arrangement that gives you the following multiple advantages, says Pelliccio (who has eight 6-foot-by-4-foot raised beds in her yard).

■ When you have pathways around each raised bed, you have easy access to all of your garden plants.

Natural Clay Is a Bust

It can happen to even the most garden-savvy among us. Michael Mastrota, landscape architect at American University in Washington, DC, left his clay planting containers on his deck one winter. The moisture in them froze, then expanded, and all of the containers cracked. If you need containers that will stand up to arctic treatment, look for *heavy* plastic (thinner plastic pots aren't durable on a long-term basis) or fiberglass versions, Mastrota says. Yes, some people are turned off by the artificial look and feel, but containers are now being fashioned from man-made materials that are hard to distinguish from real clay or stone. Converting to plastic or fiberglass beats the heck out of hauling your containers inside every winter and outside again in spring.

Some terra-cotta planters are labeled as "frost proof," and sometimes they are, but they don't always hold up through a northern winter. There is always an element of risk involved with these pots—you can't assume they will get through a tough winter intact.

- There's less bending over when you work on a raised bed, meaning your back will be happy.

- The soil stays more workable and loose in a raised bed, meaning your garden *plants* will be happy.

- If you have clay soil or compacted soil in your yard, raised beds will help you achieve better drainage for plants, giving your garden plants a better growing environment.

- Raised beds automatically give your garden a neater, more orderly appearance.

- Raised beds help you efficiently rotate your crops, since it's easier to remember what was planted where within a nicely defined little rectangle. In a large garden, it's harder to remember where all of your plants were during the previous growing season. That increases the likelihood that you'll plant a crop in the same spot 2 years in a row—which can deplete the soil and risk disease.

Here's Pelliccio's simple method for building a raised garden bed.

1. Use 2-by-4's to build two identical frames, each of them 6 feet by 4 feet, held together at the corners by metal L-shaped brackets. Pioneering soul that you are, you may want to use different dimensions or a different size of lumber. However, don't use treated wood, which can leach toxins into the soil.

2. Dig a 3-inch-deep trench in your yard that's the same length and width as your wooden frames. Set one frame down into the trench, and stack the second frame on top of the first.

3. Now fill the frames with planting soil, mixed in these proportions: one-third compost, one-third regular garden soil or topsoil, and one-third coir fiber (a coconut processing by-product). All of these ingredients are available at garden stores.

(continued on page 170)

SHADES OF GREEN

Make a Handy Built-In Compost Bin

Making compost right in a raised garden bed is a two-way time saver. Just position bales of hay or straw to form a simple frame on your bed. During the growing season, this "bin" is conveniently located for easy disposal of weeds and other spent plant matter—no more time wasted shuttling compostables off to a remote location. In spring, this system speeds pre-planting soil improvement and mulch-ing. Simply disassemble the enclosure and spread the finished compost over your garden.

Using bales of hay or straw to build your bin makes this system doubly convenient—just break the used bales apart in spring and use them as mulch. Use fresh bales to form a new bin on another section of the bed and plant your vegetables in the enriched soil where the old bin stood.

Water Savers: Roll Out the Barrel

Rain barrels are a clever, Earth-friendly way to provide water to container plants, raised beds, and other garden plots. In general, they work like this: One of your home's downspouts is fitted into a hole in the top of a barrel (often with a capacity of 50 to 80 gallons). The barrel has a spigot on the side for filling watering cans or—in the cheat-at-gardening spirit—for feeding water to a soaker hose positioned in your planting bed.

Rain barrels are an excellent way to make use of water that otherwise would have been wasted in runoff. This protects our planet and lowers your utility bill at the same time. You can buy manufactured rain barrels, but you can also buy kits that enable you to do yet another good turn for the Earth. These kits encourage you to acquire a large plastic drum from a local business that wants to dispose of it (a restaurant, for example). Just make sure the drum held a nontoxic substance in its previous life, and that you clean it out thoroughly before you use it as a rain barrel. Then all you have to do is install the spigot and the fitting at the top that accepts the downspout. This recycles the drum, of course, and it also saves you the shipping costs of ordering by catalog or online. And don't forget that rainwater is the stuff your plants crave—it's usually more pure than your tap water (depending on what your roof is made of, and how polluted your air is). Your Cooperative Extension office should know where you can pick up a free or low-cost drum to convert into a rain barrel, says Annette Pelliccio, founder of the Happy Gardener organic gardening company. Don't try to adapt a plastic trash can to this use. It won't withstand the weight of the water for long.

A few rain barrel issues to think about:

- Look for a childproof top to prevent a curious youngster from injuring himself—and to keep pets and other critters at bay as well.

- Use fine-mesh screening that will keep debris and breeding mosquitoes out of your barrel.

- To add water storage capacity, use more than one barrel and connect them with PVC pipe so that one spills over into the other.

- Set up your rain barrel on solid, level terrain. A full, tipping-over rain barrel is not fun to deal with.

🌲 Make note of where the overflow runs from your rain barrel. Just as you would do with a downspout, direct any barrel overflow well away from your home's foundation.

🌲 When you turn off your home's outdoor spigot to keep it from freezing in winter, that's a good time to disconnect your rain barrel, empty it, and turn it upside down for the cold season. Otherwise, water freezing inside could crack it.

To capture runoff water, a downspout is typically redirected into the top of a rain barrel. Set your rain barrel on firm, stable ground. Lay out a drip hose for your planting containers or garden beds and attach it to the barrel's spigot.

While a wood frame is most often used to establish a raised bed, other possible materials include "timbers" made of recycled plastic, cinder blocks, stone, or bricks. Here are even more pointers that will make your raised garden beds carefree and easy.

Keep your beds narrow. You may like a king-size bed indoors, but extra width is actually a handicap in a garden bed. Make your raised bed no more than 3 or 4 feet wide so that you can easily reach the center of the bed from the sides. (Remember: No stepping on the planting soil—that compacts it.)

Don't overbuild. How high you want your raised garden beds is largely a matter of personal preference. However, to keep your soil workable, don't elevate your beds any more than 4 feet above ground level, says Pelliccio. A foot or two is probably plenty.

Plan with a compass. Orient the longer sides of your raised beds so they run east-west. This way, your bed will get the best sun exposure because the plants will be facing south. Ideally, pick a spot that gets at least 6 hours of sun a day. Position your taller plants on the north side of the raised bed so they don't cast shadows on shorter plants.

Wet your bed weekly. Water your raised beds in the morning, once a week, says Pelliccio. The best way to water such beds is to run a drip hose right down the center of each one. Bear in mind, though, that how often to water depends a lot on climate and weather conditions. Watering weekly is a good idea if it doesn't rain, and if your soil is loamy. But conditions vary, depending on your climate. Where the air is dry and sun is very strong (like the Southwest or Colorado) or the soil is sandy (in seashore gardens, for instance), once a week watering is not enough in dry weather. Gardeners in these climates may have to water every day or two when no rain falls, especially in July and August. If your soil is sandy, it's important to add compost every year—it will get used up quickly.

Confine renegade plants. We all know stories of land-grabbing crops that take over an entire garden. Watermelon and cantaloupe love to spread out that way. Oregano and mint are famously ground-greedy as well. Raised beds are an excellent way to keep such renegades on their best behavior—they're simply confined within the bed frame, and the garden plants growing in other beds get to thrive without worry of invasion. So if you've been reluctant to turn melons and mint loose in your backyard, you may now put those worries to bed.

Skip the sides on raised beds. Radical? Maybe, but it's a true cheater's method. When you mound soil, organic matter, compost, and mulch about 8 to 10 inches high to make a raised bed, simply slope the very perimeter of the bed. Gravity keeps the soil in place, and you'll rarely have to tidy the edge. Simply press on the edge area to firm it in place, or dig a V-shaped trench around the bed. The soil will settle over a few weeks, stabilizing the bed; adding a thin layer of mulch will protect the bed from erosion during a hard rain.

Less watering for low beds. If you're building raised beds in hot or dry climates, plan for a frame just a few inches high. Building a higher bed in a hot climate means the soil will dry out quickly and you'll need to water more often. With the shorter-height frame, you'll still get the benefits of amended soil and good drainage but there's not as much soil exposed to the heat.

Deep beds have advantages in northern climes. Build deep beds in colder regions for a lower growing season. In cold climates, the soil in raised beds warms up more quickly in the spring and drains better than in-ground beds, so you can plant earlier. An earlier start on the season means an increase in the number of crops your beds can produce.

Limitless choices for bed materials. Frugal-minded gardeners can find a variety of materials to use for raised beds. Of course, there's inexpensive pine and rot-resistant cedar available for purchase but don't overlook found materials. A yard sale may yield a broken-down dresser with perfectly sized drawer fronts and sides that can be reused; drawers can act as the raised bed itself once the bottom is removed. You can also find lightweight plastic or engineered lumber, composite decking planks, or closely spaced pickets that can be transformed into a raised bed frame.

SQUARE FOOT GARDENING: ENGINEERING A REVOLUTION

When How to Cheat books starts handing out its lifetime achievement awards, the first one probably will go to Mel Bartholomew. He's the guy who turned his engineering background loose on the messy, inefficient overplanting that he observed in the typical home or community garden. He turned vegetable gardening on its cabbage head with his best-selling book *Square Foot Gardening*. It demonstrated that through careful planting in controlled little plots, you can grow the same amount of produce in just one-fifth of the space. And his system requires commensurately less time, toil, and expense. I'll give you a quick overview of how Square Foot Gardening works, but for detail and the fine points, pick up the latest version of his book *(All New Square Foot Gardening)* and visit www.squarefootgardening.com.

Basically, Square Foot Gardening is container gardening—without the containers. Your Square Foot Garden is contained within a garden box made of untreated lumber (2-by-6's or 4-by-6's work well). The size can be quite variable, but a good starter dimension for a garden box is 4 feet by 4 feet. Fasten together the boards, set on edge, with deck screws. If you're setting the box on top of your lawn, cover the ground inside the box with cardboard or weed barrier fabric to kill off grass and weeds. Fill the box with several inches of garden soil (you may need a foot of soil if you want to grow root crops), prepared as you usually would with plenty of organic material (see Chapter 2). Or

SLEIGHT *of* HAND

Keep Those Roots in the Dark

Whenever you're preparing to put plants into the ground, turn your back to the sun and keep the plant's bare roots in shadow, recommends Mel Bartholomew, author of *All New Square Foot Gardening*. Direct sun will quickly dry out a plant's exposed roots and kill it, he says.

MYTH-BUSTERS
Misconceptions That Drive Away Gardeners

The gardening world is just jam-packed with misconceptions that inspire home gardeners to waste wheelbarrow loads of time, energy, and money—or that drive them away from gardening altogether. Here are some such misconceptions, offered by Mel Bartholomew, author of *All New Square Foot Gardening.*

🌳 *You need to buy hefty, expensive tools that will last for decades.* No, Square Foot Gardening only requires three simple tools: a trowel for minor digging, scissors for trimming plants, and a pencil for creating planting holes. And speaking of expense, a $1 trowel from your discount store will serve you nicely. Take a pass on the pricey, stainless steel import.

🌳 *Gardening requires a long row of each vegetable, with rows spaced 3 feet apart.* This old-fashioned approach to laying out a garden encourages over-planting, a waste of effort and materials. Square Foot Gardening requires one-fifth the space of conventional gardens.

🌳 *Children are stuck with the weeding.* Sure, when Bartholomew was a child, it seemed like adults got all of the fun duties while the kids were assigned the weeding. Square Foot changes all of that—kids can handle any of the tasks. They'll enjoy themselves more, they'll learn more, and they'll be more likely to pitch in.

🌳 *Elderly people can't garden—they have to throw in the trowel.* Wrong, says Bartholomew. No matter your age or physical condition, there's a form of gardening that matches your physical abilities. Tabletop gardening, for instance, works great for people in wheelchairs or people who can stand but have trouble bending over.

• •

instead fill your box with a mix recommended by Mel Bartholomew, of equal parts peat moss or coir, coarse vermiculite, and compost blended from a variety of ingredients.

Now fashion a crosshatch grid that divides your garden box into square-foot plots. In the 4-by-4-foot example, you'll end up with 16 squares. Make the grid out of any slatlike material (thin strips of wood or used Venetian blinds will work nicely) and fasten them together with twine, baling wire, or screws where they intersect. Your choice: Make the grid wide enough to rest on the top edge of your garden box, or make it just narrow enough to lie on top of the ground within the box.

How you plant within each square foot plot depends largely on the space requirements of the plants you want to grow—a detail you learn from the seed packet or from the planting instructions that come with a transplant. All plants fit into the square foot box with either 1, 4, 9, or 16 plants-per-square-foot spacing. If a plant requires 12 inches of clearance, place only a single plant smack in the middle of one square. If you're using seeds, poke a hole in the dirt with your finger, tap some seeds out of the packet into your palm, pick up a few with your fingers, and drop no more than two or three seeds into the hole. (This prevents the gross overplanting—and subsequent required thinning—that happens when a gardener shakes an entire seed packet over a garden row.) The less spacing a plant requires, the more of them you can comfortably fit within 1 square foot—but be careful not to crowd them. When harvest is done within one square, pull out the old plant, add a little more of your soil or compost mix, and plant something different for a late-season harvest.

By now, the advantages of the Square Foot method are piling up in your cheat-at-gardening mind. Your squares will grow more produce than a conventional garden that covers five times the area. This means you need much less of just about every kind of gardening material and much less in the way of ongoing maintenance. These compact and orderly gardens are easy to fit into your yard. Watering by hose or watering can is quick and simple. You have no need for heavy gardening equipment. And the grid system makes the what-to-plant-where organizing issues easy and intuitive.

In later growing seasons, you may want to expand your Square Foot Garden by adding more planting boxes. Make sure to leave ample pathways between the boxes so you always have easy access to every gardening square.

Here are several more sneaky gardening tricks offered by Mel Bartholomew.

Grow all of your vine crops vertically. Vine crops are notorious space hogs, rambling around your garden gobbling up ground that less aggressive garden plants would like to get nourishment from. Square Foot Gardening will help to control such wanderers, but you also can benefit from your viney aggressors by encouraging them to grow vertically rather than laterally. Here's how: Build strong vertical frames for your vines. Don't use wood for the frame (it will rot)

Welcome Transplants with a Warm Bath

Plants are in a delicate state when they're small and are being transplanted from a little container into an actual garden bed. Here's how Mel Bartholomew, author of *Square Foot Gardening,* likes to introduce transplants to their new homes. First, pick up the plant and set its container in a pan or bucket of water that's been warmed in the sun. Leave the container in the water until bubbles stop forming (about 2 minutes), which means its soil is saturated. Turn the container over and gently shake the rootball out of it.

Take your garden scissors and trim off the bottom tips of the roots. You'll be clipping no more than $1/8$ inch off the bottom of the rootball. Each trimmed root will divide and send out two roots, and your new plant will grow much more vigorously this way.

Use your trowel to dig a planting hole that's just slightly wider and deeper than the plant's rootball. Sprinkle some of the warm water inside the hole and place the rootball

into it (the rootball should go slightly below the surface of the ground). With your hand or a pencil, pull some more dirt over the rootball. With your hand, dig a small trough around the plant and pour a cup of the warm water from the pan or bucket into the trough and let it soak in.

Now provide shade for your new plant for 2 days, especially if the weather is hot and sunny. The shade will give the plant time to acclimate to its new environment. Otherwise, your plant could wilt and go into shock. One way to provide shade: Stick a wooden shingle into the ground next to the plant on the south side to put it in shadow. Alternatively, put a wire cage over the plant and use clothespins to affix cloth or plastic to it. (Overseas, Bartholomew used banana leaves to shade his plants.)

If you follow this procedure, Bartholomew says, your transplants will grow vigorously, they will be healthy, and they will take off quickly.

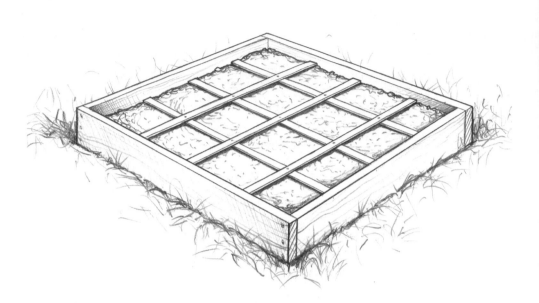

A simple way to start your Square Foot Garden: a 4-foot-square box made of untreated lumber. A grid divides the interior into square foot plots.

or plastic (it will eventually turn brittle in the sun). Bartholomew likes to use metal electrical conduit pipe. Affix to the frame a covering of nylon netting (available at garden stores). Plants such as tomatoes, pole beans, cucumbers, squash, melons, and pumpkins will climb up the netting and dangle their fruit in the air where you can easily pick it. With this arrangement, your plants get more sun and the fruit will not lie against the ground and rot. For heavier fruit, you will need to fashion support slings out of fabric, more netting, or old panty hose.

Keep your seeds happy. Since you're no longer planting every seed that comes in a seed packet, you're going to wonder what to do with the leftover seeds. Fortunately, if stored properly they will be good for years, says Bartholomew. To remember the conditions that will preserve seeds long-term, think of the conditions that cause them to sprout—and then provide the opposite. To sprout, seeds like warmth and moisture. So to preserve seeds, keep them cool and dry. The best place to do this is in the refrigerator (no, the freezer is too cold).

Position your garden close to the back door. Here's yet another advantage of Square Foot Gardening. It's easy to put a 4-foot by 4-foot gardening box or bed near the back door of your house (not so easy if you're planting conventional garden rows). Because your garden plot is near a popular exit, you'll pass the garden more often. This higher visibility will inspire you to spend more time in your garden. You will harvest more often from your garden—therefore you will eat more healthful food, you will eat less junk food, you will lose weight, and you will be healthier. This will be a good lesson for the entire family. Also, when you can see your garden out the back kitchen window, you will get more pleasure from it, and you will be in a better position to protect your garden when critters invade it.

Give kids their own garden boxes. Children are capable of handling just about any Square Foot Gardening task. If you give them their own garden box where they can plant whatever they want to grow, your kids will learn, have fun, and pick up a lifelong gardening habit. If you have more than one child, let them have separate gardening boxes—watch them compete!

UP ON THE ROOF

A chapter about alternative gardening practices wouldn't be complete without a discussion about rooftop gardening.

Rooftop gardening is most often associated with urban areas where few residents have access to a ground level yard. For a city apartment dweller, a rooftop garden can provide a chance to interact with nature, to show some creativity, to provide visual relief in a barren landscape, and perhaps to raise some fresh herbs and veggies for the kitchen at the same time.

Besides bringing beauty and a bit of produce to your urban environment, rooftop gardens do other good things for the planet, says Emily Shelton, horticulturist at the Chicago Botanic Garden. They reduce water runoff. The soil and foliage absorb sound, reducing noise pollution. A rooftop garden will help insulate the building, lowering heating and cooling costs. And such gardens provide a small extension of habitat for the birds and insects that live in nearby green areas. And if you grow flowers, you'll have something colorful to look at, too.

People living in the suburbs or rural areas will have less call for rooftop gardening—unless you've been hankering to add some greenery to a high terrace or the flat roof of your carport. (In which case you could use a reality check: You're contemplating a lot of work that few people will see, while you probably have easy access to a perfectly garden-worthy yard all around the house.)

The official cheat-at-gardening way to go about rooftop gardening is to use a few containers and flower boxes. But serious rooftop gardening, in contrast, is no casual undertaking, and it is fraught with complications. In case you're tempted, here are some things you should know about it.

To create a serious garden on the roof, you need a structural engineer to determine how much weight the roof can bear. You need a way to waterproof it. You need to build beds in which to plant. You need to use lightweight growing medium (like a peat-based soilless mix). You need a way to haul everything up onto the roof. You need a handy water source. And you need to get permission from the landlord or co-op board unless you want to be sued. It's serious stuff and not to be entered into lightly.

If you still think you do want to get into serious rooftop gardening, do yourself a favor and start small the first year.

Now, don't pout. I know you have an independent streak, and you want to garden where you want to garden. So no matter whether you're a city mouse or a country mouse, here are some rooftop gardening pointers that will save you time and aggravation.

Extensive rooftop gardening. The layer of growing medium is only 2 to 6 inches deep. This means you use more shallow-rooted, low-growing plants, such as salad greens and herbs. An extensive garden weighs 15 to 40 pounds per square foot. Use only drought-tolerant plants with this approach. After planting, watering with a temporary system (hose or watering can) will suffice. Long-term, normal rainfall might provide all the water you need.

Intensive rooftop gardening. The growing medium is more than 6 inches deep. This gives you a greater variety of plants to choose from, but weight becomes a bigger concern: 50 pounds and up per square foot. (Essentially, you're re-creating the ground, only it's up in the sky.) Also, the deeper your planting soil is, the more water you will need. Hand watering probably won't be practical. Install a drip irrigation system, possibly one fed by a cistern or rain barrel. Watering by an overhead sprinkler isn't a good idea, because the water can get blown about in the wind and will evaporate quickly. And don't use water-swilling tropical plants—they aren't practical on a rooftop. This is the more extreme end of rooftop gardening, seen more in commercial operations. Installations could even include trees and patios.

Rooftop gardening is not solely gardening, says Leslie Hoffman, executive director of Earth Pledge, an organization that advocates for sustainable practices. Rooftop gardening is actually a blend of gardening and roofing, and some of the critical considerations are beyond the ability of the average homeowner or apartment dweller. Look at it this way: You could send a 5-year-old out to work in a conventional garden, and the potential for damage would be minimal. However, even reasonably intelligent adults can create a disaster by being reckless with rooftop gardening. To forestall calamity and heartache, Hoffman says, get two professionals involved in your project: a structural engineer or architect, plus a roofing consultant. You may not need them involved in your project from beginning to end; hire them just to get you started out right. Also, ask your local government whether a permit is required for the project you have in mind.

Rooftop gardening is generally done using one of two systems.

- **Modular.** Low planting boxes tied together to create the garden space. Each box is self-contained.
- **Integrated.** The garden runs from roof edge to roof edge and looks pretty much like a garden on the ground. It's installed in layers, typically (starting

from the bottom): an insulating layer, a waterproof membrane, a root barrier, a drainage layer for excess water, a filter layer to prevent soil loss, and the planting mix.

The weight of your rooftop garden and the structural integrity of your roof are the No. 1 considerations. You've heard of roofs collapsing under the weight of a heavy snow, right? Well, adding thousands of pounds of moist soil to your roof's load isn't much different—and just imagine what could happen when you add snowfall to that weight. Keep the materials used in your rooftop garden as lightweight as possible, including a light planting soil and lightweight plastic containers. As handsome as they might be, resist the temptation to use pavers for a walkway or a patio. They may be pretty, but they're pretty heavy, too!

Another crucial consideration: Make sure you don't damage the roof's waterproofing. When you're wielding tools and heavy objects, there are scores of opportunities to crack or to puncture the membrane that keeps water outside of your building. So take it easy up there.

Here are some more tricks for minimizing the work that goes into your rooftop garden.

Get approval first. Make sure you have formal permission to install your rooftop garden, says Sharon Slack, head gardener for City Farmer in Vancouver. This won't be a problem if you own the building, but you would have a mess on your hands if the manager of an apartment building or condominium demanded that you dismantle an elaborate garden.

Include irrigation in your planning. Work out in advance how you're going to water your rooftop garden. Such gardens are more exposed to intense sun and wind, which means they dry out faster than ground level gardens. Also, a lightweight growing mix with less organic content is usually used in rooftop gardens. This stuff drains more quickly and dries out faster than regular garden soil. For a sizable rooftop garden, hauling watering cans up the stairwell is not practical. Better to have a plumber install a spigot near your garden. Best of all: Irrigate your garden with an automated drip system. (In a suburban situation where the rooftop garden is only a story or two off the ground, you could rig its irrigation system as one branch of your ground-level drip system, says landscape architect Michael Mastrota.) The hot and dry conditions on a rooftop also mean that a late-summer planting isn't likely to thrive.

Save effort, go ornamental. Part of the early planning of a rooftop is answering this question: What's the purpose of this garden? Is it purely ornamental, or are you going to put some fresh produce on the table? As mentioned previously, the conditions in a rooftop garden are more extreme than in a ground level garden. Growing vegetables and fruits requires deeper soil and more watering, all of which translates into more work for you. So the official *How to Cheat at Gardening and Yard Work* approach is: Damn the tomatoes! Full speed ahead with the low-effort, ornamental approach.

Pick the right plants. Your choice of plants to grow could make all the difference between success and failure in your rooftop garden. Basically, you are accommodating a windy, sunny, dry environment that's not very different from a mountaintop, says Emily Shelton, horticulturist at the Chicago Botanic Garden. Some good plant choices: sedum, allium, and hens and chicks (sempervivum).

SLEIGHT *of* HAND

Put Excess Herbs on Ice—Or on the Hot Seat

If you have grown more herbs than you can easily consume, chop them up on a cutting board and pour them into an ice cube tray. Then fill the tray with water and freeze. When the cubes are solid, dump them into a zip-closing bag, label the bag, and return it to the freezer until you need the herb cubes for cooking. Just drop cubes as needed into soup or stew.

Or, if you prefer, that heating mat you use for starting seeds indoors can do double-duty and dry out herbs for you. Just put a cardboard box on the heating pad and spread your herb leaves over the bottom of it.

For a more intensive rooftop garden (deeper soil and more water), try phlox, evening primrose, and ice plant (delosperma). Drought-tolerant Mediterranean herbs (such as thyme, oregano, and rosemary) are excellent rooftop gardening plants, too, since they play a dual role—they're both ornamental and they provide a bit of produce.

Track down your soil supplier. Natural soil isn't suited to rooftop gardening, says Shelton. The ideal growing medium is lightweight aggregate that contains less than 10 percent organic matter. Typically, it's mostly a water-holding material such as shale, slate, pumice, and vermiculite. It might include sand, too. This mixture isn't a common item at your neighborhood gardening store. A consultant who works with rooftop gardens would be able to point you toward sources, or you could conduct an Internet search to find suppliers.

Feed your plants at the outset. Fertilizing a rooftop garden is a simple matter, says Shelton. Just start your plants out right by mixing an organic, slow-release fertilizer into their growing medium on planting day. That's all you'll need to do, unless you have a plant or two that specifically requires the occasional dose of liquid fertilizer.

Don't skimp on waterproofing. Make sure the waterproofing membrane underlying your rooftop garden is high quality and truly waterproof, says Shelton. You really don't want to get your garden into place only to discover that the membrane leaks and you have to dismantle your work.

Install wind protection. If your rooftop garden gets lots of wind, put up a solid railing, lattice panels, or some other structure to shield your garden. This is a particularly important consideration when your plants are in the vulnerable seedling stage, says Sharon Slack of City Farmer. A trellis supporting beans or tomatoes will also serve as a windbreak, she says.

Keep gardeners and visitors safe. Railings are a critical safety measure for a rooftop garden. Use them to keep visitors and distracted garden workers away from the roof's edge.

Plan for some shade. If you have plants on your rooftop that can't stand intense sun, pair them with taller, hardier plants that will provide some shade, says Slack. For instance, position sun-loving beans in front of lettuce.

Watch your back. If you're carrying heavy loads up to your rooftop garden—say, bags of soil mix or full watering cans—know your limits. Making multiple trips to carry smaller loads is better than risking your back or risking a fall by trying to carry too much.

Stash a small tool kit nearby. Once your rooftop garden is planted, you should only need a few small tools on hand, such as pruners, a trowel, a hand weeder, kneeling pads, gloves, and a hat. Keep these in a small bucket that you can easily grab on your way to tend the garden. Also keep a watering can handy for the occasional plant-dying-of-thirst emergency.

It's nice to see your creativity and independence rewarded, isn't it? By that I mean that so many of the alternative forms of gardening—containers, raised beds, Square Foot Gardening, and such—are not only departures from the conventional row upon row in the backyard: They're actually easier to implement and require less ongoing maintenance. So don't hold back any longer. Put some beauty, some green, and some produce into the world where nobody expected to find it. Take some chances and make people smile!

CHAPTER 7

The Rot Stuff:
The WORLD'S EASIEST COMPOSTING

||||||||||||||||||||||||||||||||||||||||||||||||||||||||||||||||||||||||||||||||||||||||||||||||||||||||||||||

Composting in your backyard is a lot like sailing on open water. For the most part, nature does all the work, and you sit back and take advantage. Oh, for both pursuits you need some equipment—and that equipment can be extremely simple or a hundred times more complex than you have patience for. And for both pursuits you need to understand a little underlying science. Not deep science, mind you, just some basics that anyone can grasp.

It's a shame that a lot of people don't compost. Some form of composting is even feasible and easy for people with small apartments and little or no yard. You gain the satisfaction of keeping household waste out of landfills and also of being part of a natural process—and of course you are rewarded with a nutrient-packed soil booster that your garden and houseplants relish.

"I think people are afraid of composting," says Clea Danaan, author of *Sacred Land: Intuitive Gardening for Personal, Political, and Environmental Change*. But composting actually is easier than managing your household garbage, she points out—while you have to remember which day is garbage day, nature goes to work every day on your compost pile whether you remember or not. "Composting is a process—and you gain so much just in being a part of the process," adds Jodie Colón, a compost educator for the New York Botanical Garden and the Bronx Green-Up program.

Let's take a quick look at what composting is and how it works. Compost is the dark, dirtlike stuff that results from the decomposition of plant-based material. When added to your garden soil, compost slowly releases crucial nutrients that your flowers and vegetables depend upon for growth and health. This organic material also improves the soil by making it drain more readily, making root penetration easier and providing space down there for water and air. Equally important, organic matter supports and nourishes soil life, such as beneficial microbes, bacteria, and earthworms.

The breakdown of this plant-based stuff is work done by living creatures—visible ones such as worms, millipedes, and other critters, as well as microscopic organisms including bacteria and fungi. They all have important roles to play in a healthy underground ecosystem that is the basis of a thriving garden. And *you* get the best end of this bargain. All you have to do is manage your compost pile to meet the conditions that your little worker bugs need—basically providing them with food, moisture, and air. When you do, your happy little workers thrive and multiply, which means you then have even *more* organisms working for you.

Yes, there is science involved in composting—but don't let that intimidate you, says Colón. It may be science, but it's not rocket science. The basics are easy, and there is no finicky "right" way to do it. Remember, the very same composting process happens all the time out in the woods—without any participation from human beings whatsoever. The most common problem in home composting is that the gardener gets flustered and gives up too quickly. So be patient and let nature take its course.

Composting can be divided into two broad categories: outdoor composting and, believe it or not, indoor composting. For the newcomer, taking up either requires getting past some mental barriers. So this chapter is devoted to laying aside myths and misconceptions about composting. And, as you would expect from How to Cheat books, we'll explore the easiest, least expensive, most hassle-free ways to go about it.

In the end, getting used to the idea of indoor composting may be your biggest challenge. That's because it involves, well, keeping a box of live worms in your house. If that idea makes your tummy turn flip-flops, do yourself this favor: Read that passage from top to bottom and think about it for a while. You'll soon recognize worm composting to be a simple, rewarding process. I'll bet that your resistance breaks down. And need I mention that you'll never want for fishing bait again?

YOUR BACKYARD PILE: GIVING NATURE A LITTLE NUDGE

As a cheat-at-gardening enthusiast, you're determined to pare unnecessary labor out of the composting process, right? So keep this crucial fact in mind: Compost happens just fine without your help whatsoever, says Colón. So why bother fretting over the right structure of compost bin, how often to turn your pile, and pouring on "accelerant" formulations to speed the process? Forget all of that. Wait for nature to take its course. Colón calls herself an "efficient" composter, "Which I spell l-a-z-y," she says.

Marvin Duren, owner of Marvin's Organic Gardens in Lebanon, Ohio, also is no fan of barrels, bins, and other structures intended to help composting. He believes that such devices require too much work. His approach to composting: Just find a spot in the yard and start piling your compostable materials there. It might seem counterintuitive, but Duren recommends including in your compost pile a layer of bulky limbs and brush. This will allow air circulation through your pile to help the rotting process along.

Duren favors composting with a minimum amount of equipment and a minimum amount of work on your part. "The organisms are the ones doing the work," he points out.

Make it convenient. Where's the best place in the yard to establish your compost pile? Your No. 1 priority should be to find a spot that's extremely convenient, says Colón. Likely candidates: a screened-off corner near the garage or next to the garden, or a closed bin next to garbage cans, or outside the kitchen door. The harder your compost pile is to get to, the more often you will find excuses not to carry new material to it. Eventually, you will abandon the project. Otherwise, consider the needs of the organisms that do the actual work of composting—they need moisture but not sopping wetness, so a low spot in the yard that puddles up frequently won't do.

Gardening author Danaan agrees that convenience is the top priority. For her, composting is an informal, throw-everything-into-a-pile process. (She once inherited a compost bin made from wooden pallets, but found that the structure made the finished compost hard to get to.) Her structureless compost pile is right next to her garden, so it's very easy to shovel the spoils right onto the garden soil. "It's not pretty, but I don't mind it," Danaan says. "Frankly, I'm a lazy gardener." Bottom line: It works!

Try compost the lazy way. Here's a really easy way to make compost. Fill a wire bin with leaves, grass clippings, weeds you've pulled that haven't yet gone to seed, and other plant debris, dust with bone meal, and moisten with a hose until the stuff is as wet as a wrung-out sponge (in other words, moist but not dripping wet). Wet down the pile when it gets dry, but otherwise leave it alone. In a year or so, you'll have compost!

A pile is the easiest way of all. Compost happens. It's as simple as that. If you do nothing but throw your leaves, grass clippings, and kitchen scraps together in a pile, eventually all of the parts will decompose and turn into dark, crumbly compost. Forget about making neat layers of materials, mixing, and stirring. Just make a pile of ingredients you have on hand. Keep adding materials as you get them until your pile reaches about 3 feet tall. Then start a new pile.

Okay, weigh the advantages of a bin. Maybe you're a traditionalist, and you feel strongly that you're just not composting unless you have built or bought a formal compost bin of some sort. Even though such structures are not required at all, in some cases they might provide an advantage or two, says compost educator Colón, who includes the subject "To Bin or Not to Bin" among her lecture topics. So in the interest of full disclosure, here are advantages that a formal compost bin *will* provide.

- Going without a compost bin can take up more space in your yard. A loose compost heap will tend to spread, while a bin will contain it. (Consider the difference between a loose pile of laundry on the floor and all of the clothing stuffed into a laundry basket.)
- When you go without a compost bin, the breakdown process generally takes longer (not that we're in a race).
- A compost bin that contains or disguises the rotting debris might help you with "neighbor issues." Colón has two compost bins in a corner of the parking lot of her apartment building. The bins look like garbage cans, and none of her neighbors appears to know what they are.

Buy a premade composter. You're looking for shortcuts. When it comes to outdoor composting, here's one of the best, says Annette Pelliccio of

Cheat Sheet

Qualities of a Good Compost Bin

Before you buy a compost bin (or before building your own), make sure it has the following features.

- Passages for air to get in and out, since composting requires aeration
- A wide opening at the top, to make it easy to add ingredients
- An easy way to empty it when the compost is finished
- A lid to keep out vermin and other wildlife

the organic gardening company the Happy Gardener in Virginia: Forget about building your own compost bins—buy one ready-made. Yes, there are various structures that you can make with chicken wire and a pile of 2-by-4's. Such bins often produce stinky compost and can attract rodents, she says. Instead, save yourself the hammering, nailing, and lumber hauling—invest in a pre-made, freestanding compost bin from your garden supply store. Often made from recycled plastic, such bins are solid, weatherproof, rodent proof, stink proof, and blend into your landscape easily (won't your neighbors be happy!). Pelliccio's compost bin has a hinged lid for convenience. Another handy feature: a small door near the bottom that allows you to scoop out the oldest compost when you're ready to toss some onto a garden bed. ("Easier is better," she says.)

Stuff it in fall. If you have decided to acquire a formal compost bin, fall is a great time to set it up, since you typically have lots of leaves available. Just pack your new bin with leaves and sprinkle on a few gallons of water, making sure the moisture gets well distributed among the leaves. Toss in some soil or completed compost and you're ready to start adding kitchen trimmings (cover them with leaves when you dump them in).

Give rotting leaves a head start. For faster compost, shred the leaves you use in a shredder or by running over them (spread out on the lawn a few inches thick) with a lawn mower a few times. To keep decomposition going, make sure the pile of leaves stays moist all winter, or until it freezes if you live in the North.

Shoot for a critical mass. "Pile" is part of the term "compost pile" for a

SHADES OF GREEN ————————————————

Ask About a Free Bin

Call your local government and ask whether it makes free compost bins available to residents. Many municipalities do this to lower the amount of waste that is sent to their landfills.

reason. That growing mass of plant stuff that you have accumulated serves a function—holding in moisture and preserving the heat inside that helps the composting process along. A compost pile that's 3 feet wide and 3 feet high is big enough to contain its own moisture and heat, says Colón.

Mix your "browns" and "greens." When you read about composting for a while, you'll inevitably come across the terms "browns" and "greens." Don't panic—this is easy to understand and actually even useful. "Brown" stuff is plant material that has dried up and no longer has any life in it, says Colón. (Examples are old leaves, twigs, wood chips, pine needles, shredded paper, shredded cardboard, coffee grounds, and straw.) "Green" material is fresh, moist, and still appears to have some life in it. (Examples are newly pruned branches, grass clippings, and vegetable and fruit scraps.) Some compost theorists say you should build a compost pile with alternating layers of browns and greens. You see, the decomposition happens at the point where the dry and moist materials meet. Well, don't spend another moment fretting about this issue, says Colón. It's much easier to simply mix the two kinds of plant material in your compost pile as you go along rather than worrying about layers. Remind yourself: If it once was alive, it will break down all on its own.

You can use this brown-vs.-green knowledge to make adjustments in your compost pile. For instance, if you have been piling up lots of dead brown leaves in your pile, you will notice that they tend to break down slowly. To compensate, hold back on the leaves for a while and add a greater component of green stuff, or thoroughly wet down the leaves just before you add them. On the other hand, if you find that your compost pile is heavy on wet and squishy food scraps that are starting to stink, compensate by adding more of the dry leaves for a while to absorb the excess moisture and balance things out.

Don't fret about turning. If there's one thing you already know about maintaining a compost pile, it's that every few days you need to haul out some tools and turn the darned thing, right? Well, rest easy, says Pelliccio. Yes, turning your compost pile will move the decomposition process along more quickly. But guess what? Composting doesn't have to be a race! Without turning, the rotting will still happen. Be patient and let nature take its course.

Give Your Compost a Pick-Me-Up

Strike up a conversation with the manager of your local coffee shop. She might be happy to let you cart away a bucket or two of used coffee grounds— a great addition to any compost pile. Garden author Clea Danaan picks up grounds from her local Starbucks for composting.

Ignore the undone chunks. When you shovel your rich, black compost onto your garden bed, you may notice the occasional bits and pieces of vegetation that haven't completely rotted yet. For finicky gardeners, the solution goes like this: Nail some chicken wire to a wooden frame, set the frame at an angle (perhaps against a cinder block), and shovel the compost from your pile onto the screen, pushing it through. Toss the sifted-out chunks on top of the screen back onto the compost pile, and scoop the finer stuff onto your garden bed.

As you might suspect, the official *How to Cheat at Gardening and Yard Work* approach is a wee bit simpler. Namely: Quit fretting about the chunks in your compost. Shovel that stuff onto the garden bed anyway—it won't harm anything, and the larger bits will rot eventually on their own, says Pelliccio.

Hold back the invasive plants. Invasive plants are one brand of vegetation that doesn't make its way into author Danaan's compost pile. Seeds from the likes of bindweed, Oriental bittersweet, or Japanese honeysuckle could too easily find their way back to her garden, so that's the rare bit of plant material that goes straight into the trash at her house. Contact your county Cooperative Extension office for info on plants that are invasive in your area.

Take eggshells straight to the garden. The eggshells from Pelliccio's kitchen often go straight to an outdoor garden bed. The eggshells add calcium to the soil, a mineral that's often not included in commercial fertilizers. Bulbs in particular love eggshells, she says. Here's Pelliccio's procedure: When she is cooking, she places any eggshells onto a paper towel. She folds the paper towel over the shells and crushes them with her fist. Then she takes the paper towel out to a garden bed and shakes the crushed shells straight onto the ground. A side note: With kids in the house who love to decorate Easter eggs, in spring her garden becomes a bright, beautiful mosaic of pastel eggshells.

Keep a leaf bag handy. Even without turning, your compost pile will rot more efficiently if you alternate the daily food scraps from your kitchen with a layer of leaves. Here's a trick from Dr. Kenneth Mulder at Green Mountain College in Vermont: Keep a few bags of the fall leaves you rake up and store them near your compost bin. When you haul out a bucket of kitchen trimmings to add to your pile, scatter on a layer of old leaves at the same time. The combination of old brown leaves and fresh "green" material from the kitchen helps the rotting process.

Toss in some plain ol' dirt. Add a few shovelfuls of common soil to your

Keeping a bag of leaves handy makes it easy to add a layer of leaves to your compost pile whenever you empty your kitchen scraps.

compost pile, says organic gardener Marvin Duren in Ohio. This will add "the background biology" to your pile—a host of natural organisms you need to gnaw away at that organic matter.

Rein in the animal waste. If you have access to livestock manure from a local dairy or horse farm, for example, you can use that along with green matter in your compost (never, ever use pet waste!). Livestock manure, especially if it comes from a small farm where animals are raised without antibiotics and hormones, can be a great source of organic matter and nitrogen. But don't use too much of a good thing. Many people try to use too much animal waste in their compost piles, says Duren. Excessive manure raises the salt levels in your compost too high, he says. "The solution is dilution," he says. Follow a one-third rule: No more than one-third of a compost pile ought to be animal waste, even if you have easy access to a horse stable. The other two-thirds should be vegetation—the "green" and "brown" ingredients described earlier.

Forget deadlines. Ignore any advice that puts time pressure on your compost pile, says Colón. You might read in an article that if you do certain things you will have garden-ready compost within 11 days or within 3 months. What's the hurry? Just enjoy the slow and steady, tortoiselike rhythm of stacking up plant-based waste materials. "Just piling them up, compost will happen," says Colón.

In a hurry anyway? Add nitrogen. If you're just not the patient sort, you

THE *MOST* LIKELY PROBLEM
Keep Out Scavengers

If neighborhood pets, rodents, or raccoons are regularly raiding your outdoor compost, review what kitchen waste you're allowing into the pile. Don't use any animal by-products—meat scraps, fat, bones, or oily foods—as they attract scavengers and don't decompose well anyway. When you do put kitchen trimmings (fruit or vegetable) into compost, bury them under several inches of composting material, such as dry leaves, straw, or grass clippings, to make them less accessible to intruders.

can speed composting in your pile by adding nitrogen. Soybean meal, corn gluten, cottonseed meal, and dried blood are good sources, says Duren. These materials are available at many garden centers. Or just add more fresh green plant material. Or get out your pitchfork and turn that pile once a week, forking materials from the outside of the pile to the inside. Consider it an upper body workout that gives you a pass from the gym.

To compost, recycle that trash can. A lot of the compost bins available for sale are so fancy you'd think they were designed and price-tagged by NASA. Keep your money in your wallet and do this: Take a beaten-up plastic trash can and drill about 75 half-inch holes all over its sides. Position the can near your back door, with an old tarp or a stretch of old carpet under it in case of leaks. There it will be easy to toss in vegetable trimmings from your kitchen. Add the occasional armload of cut grass and the occasional armload of leaves. Secure the lid with a bungee cord to keep the raccoons and other critters at bay. If you want to move the composting process along, once a week stick a shovel inside and stir the rotting gunk around. If you have the kind of trash can with wheels, lucky you—just cart it over to your garden now and then and shovel out the rich black compost.

Or downsize to a bucket. To compost outdoors on a small scale, mix your compostable materials in a 5-gallon bucket—both the "brown" stuff (leaves, sawdust, plus a little soil) and the "green" stuff (such as vegetable trimmings). For convenience, leave a trowel in the bucket. A lid on the bucket will discourage pests. Whenever you add compostable material, use the trowel to chop and stir the contents. If the compost gets too sloppy, wet, and stinky, add more of the "brown" ingredients to compensate. You probably will have garden-ready compost within a few months.

Feed your garden a smoothie. Here's another way to turn your kitchen scraps into garden gold. Once each day, put your kitchen scraps—potato peels, carrot tops, coffee grounds, eggshells, used tea leaves—in a blender or food processor with enough water to cover, and puree them. Dig a hole or trench in the garden alongside plants or in a currently empty area, pour in the puree, and cover with dirt.

Ditch those unwanted plant materials. A trench bordering one side of your garden—or even running through it between beds—makes a handy composting device. This makes it easy to toss waste from your garden straight into composting, and also to shovel the finished compost straight onto the beds. It also eliminates the need to add a bulky structure to your backyard in order to compost. Dig your trench as deep as 3 feet and spend the summer filling it with spoiled vegetables, garden trimmings, yard waste, and kitchen scraps. Each time you add food waste, cover it with a layer of soil to keep bugs and vermin at bay. Now and then, cover it with a layer of grass trimmings, shredded leaves, or straw—you'll be able to walk on the trench without getting your shoes messy. Next spring, shovel the rich black compost onto your garden and start the cycle over again.

Keep some shears handy. You probably have handy any number of yard and garden tools that will quickly cut down the size of plant stuff that you toss onto the compost pile. Give long stalks or branches a few snips with pruning shears, for instance, before you add them to the stack. This creates extra surfaces for the composting organisms in your pile to work on, says Colón.

Test it for doneness. Wondering whether your compost is "done?" Here's a simple test, says Colón. Finished compost has an earthy smell and looks like rich, dark dirt. If you have some material like that at the bottom of your compost pile, scoop about a half-cup of it into a sealable jar or a zip-closing plastic bag. Leave it for 3 days, open the container, and give the compost a sniff. If you detect an ammonia-like stench, the compost isn't done yet.

SHADES OF GREEN

Cover-Crop Your Pile

Here's an easy way to give your compost pile an extra boost of nitrogen: Sow an annual cover crop such as crimson or berseem clover on top of it in fall or early spring and water it in. Dig the crop into the compost when it flowers in early summer.

The Incredible Vanishing Compost

Jodie Colón, compost educator for the New York Botanical Garden, often has students who complain that they try and try and never actually achieve that rich black compost that will enhance their garden soil. More often than not, this is the real problem, says Colón: These gardeners do have compost, but they're looking for it in the wrong place!

"It's at the bottom of the pile," she says. Think of mixed nuts in a can. Shake them up, and the smaller peanuts fall to the bottom. The same happens with the tiny particles of finished compost. So she instructs her students to go home and look at the very bottom of their piles. "I have had some home gardeners amazed when they got back home," Colón says.

Just shovel it on. Taking compost from your pile and applying it to your garden is not a complex process. Remember, you essentially have created healthy new soil—not fertilizer—and it doesn't need to be turned into your garden bed, says gardening author Danaan. Just lay it over the top. If you have a mature garden bed, just an inch or two of compost across the top in spring will do nicely. If you have a new garden bed, try shoveling as much as 1 or 2 feet of compost across the surface of the soil in spring.

Hold back those sick garden plants. If you have garden plants that are struggling with disease, keep those plants out of your compost pile. Otherwise, you may just perpetuate the problem by transferring the disease right back to your garden in your compost. Instead, bag up diseased garden trimmings and set them out with the trash.

Add some dirt. Keep a bucket of dirt from your garden near your compost pile. When you add fresh vegetable scraps from the kitchen, toss on a handful of dirt as well to give the scraps an instant infusion of those composting microbes. This measure—and covering the food scraps with yard trimmings—will also keep annoying flies at bay.

Use a recycled cover. If you have an open compost pile, covering it over is

Use a Bag Instead of a Bin

If an unstructured compost pile is too loosey-goosey for your taste and buying a commercial compost bin isn't in your budget, try trash bag composting in your backyard. Load up a large trash bag with your "brown" compostables (leaves, straw, and such) alternating with layers of "greens" (grass clippings, spent flowers, kitchen vegetable trimmings). Toss in a few shovelfuls of dirt. Some bloodmeal and lime will help as well. Moisten all of these contents with the garden hose (about a quart of water should do the trick). Tie off the top of the trash bag and poke several holes in its sides for air circulation. Once a week, as you're working in the yard, grab the bag by its neck and give it a good shake. After several months, when you notice that the volume inside your composting bag has seriously collapsed, open it up to check whether your compost is done.

---

not essential, but it will help to preserve moisture in the pile and discourage pests to some degree. Be creative and find some material that you can repurpose as a cover for your compost pile—an old tarp, a shower curtain, or a discarded piece of carpeting, for instance. Remember to pull it off on rainy days so the moisture can get in.

INDOORS: COMPOSTING WITH A TWIST—AND TURNS AND WRIGGLES, TOO

You say you would love to protect the planet by composting, but you have no yard space to do it in? Composting your kitchen scraps indoors is a convenient, low-maintenance way to recycle plant material into rich soil for your garden or houseplants. As mentioned at the beginning of this chapter, the trickiest part of indoor composting may be getting used to the fact that it entails keeping a bin full of worms in your home. But don't dismiss indoor worm composting as the province of fringe extremists. Everyday sober-minded folks such as yourself are gleefully taking up the practice.

So let's take a look at the basics of indoor worm-assisted composting—with an emphasis, of course, on how to do it with the least amount of effort, hassle, and yuckiness.

A couple of semantic notes: You will also find worm composting referred to variously as vermicomposting and vermiculture. And you will hear the final product of worm composting referred to as "castings." This is a term used by people who are too genteel to say "worm poop."

This time, definitely get a bin. For outdoor composting, a specially built bin is not a requirement. For indoor worm composting, you do need a container to keep your wriggly little friends from exploring the reaches of your kitchen or laundry room. While some people modify conventional plastic storage bins and use them to contain their worm beds, you might be happier buying a bin specifically designed for this purpose. Working with a conventional storage bin will be harder, says Pelliccio, while it's easy to work with a commercially made worm bin that has all of the desirable features built into it. (And you're more likely to start indoor composting if it's easy, right?) Whichever route you take, you will want to be sure that your worm bin includes these features.

- **A lid that snaps down securely.** This will discourage escapees from inside your bin and intruding pests from outside it.
- **Ventilation holes.** Air circulation through your bin will let the worms breathe and will also reduce odors. By the way, indoor earthworms are able to deodorize a new serving of kitchen scraps within 10 minutes, says Duren. They do that for competitive reasons—not wanting the odors to attract insects that would eat their food.
- **Opaque construction.** Worms like darkness, so don't use transparent or translucent plastic.

- **The right size.** Worm composting is done in bins of many different sizes, but for the average household, a bin measuring 2 feet wide by 2 feet long should do nicely. Count on the contents of your bin taking up at least several inches in depth. Make sure your bin fits comfortably in the intended space (under the kitchen sink, on the floor of a hall closet, or on a sturdy basement shelf, for instance). Also, ask yourself whether the size of your bin is a good match for the volume of food scraps that you will be loading into it.

You can find worm bins at some garden supply stores or on the Internet (search using the terms "worm composting," "vermicomposting," or "vermiculture").

Get the right worms. The ideal worms for indoor composting are known as red wigglers—also called tiger worms, dung worms, red worms, and other names. They're recognizable for their red and brown stripes (thus the "tiger worm" name). You can buy them by the pound (1,000 worms per pound). If your kitchen produces about a half-pound of trimmings for the worm bin each day, 1 pound of worms will be able to keep up with you. Under ideal conditions, they will double in number within 3 or 4 months. They like the same temperatures that humans do, between 60° and 80°F. Some garden centers sell worms. They're also available from worm growers, bait shops, and the Internet. Whatever source you buy your worms from, make sure you're getting the species *Eisenia fetida,* says Colón. There are other kinds of red worms, but *Eisenia fetida* is ideally suited to indoor composting. Not only do these worms like the same temperatures that you do indoors, but they thrive in crowded, shallow containers, they love moist food scraps, and they eat a lot.

Tuck them in with newspaper. Keep your indoor worm bin one-third full of bedding. There's no reason to buy special bedding for your worm bin. Instead, turn to that steadily growing stack of newspapers that you usually hand over to recyclers. Tear up the newspapers by hand into long, thin, fluffy strips and drop those into your worm bin, says Colón. You'll have the best-read wigglers in town. Resist the temptation to empty your office shredder into the worm bin, however. Unlike newsprint, the paper and inks in such refuse are too likely to include chemicals you don't want in your compost. (Although you *could* use an office shredder to make quick work of ripping up conventional newsprint if you wish.) Also, avoid slick paper, such as glossy advertising circulars.

Some people add shredded leaves to their worm bins. The disadvantage: Leaves brought in from the outside might include bugs that will multiply in your worm bin.

Keep the bedding damp. Your worms' bedding should be moist, but not wet. Keep a spray bottle of water handy for spritzing the bedding as needed. If the bedding appears to be too sodden, add some fresh, dry, shredded newspaper to it. Fluff up the bedding once a week to make sure that air is circulating well.

Keep a regular schedule. One

MYTH-BUSTERS
Hundreds of Hungry Surprise Guests

Jodie Colón, compost educator for the New York Botanical Garden, was preparing to teach a class on indoor composting—that is, tossing kitchen trimmings into a bin of worms, which break the food down into rich dirt. So she proposed starting a bin of her own in her apartment. Her husband, Audie, said there was no way he would share his living space with a boxful of worms. So Jodie cheated—she secretly started up a worm bin anyway and hid the little operation in the coat closet.

When class time rolled around, Colón's husband volunteered to help. He was videotaping the session when a student asked Colón whether worm bins start to stink after a while. No, she replied—this one's been in the coat closet for a month. Her surprised husband piped up, "*Whose* coat closet?"

He's now accustomed to the idea of living with a worm bin in his midst. And the worms are out of the closet now. They're parked in the kitchen right next to the recycling bin, appropriately enough.

• • • • • • • • • • • • • • • • • •

key to successful worm composting is to feed your worms in a consistent way, says Dr. Kenneth Mulder of Green Mountain College. If the amount of food you give to your worms is variable, your population of worms will fluctuate accordingly. If your kitchen produces more scraps than your worms can keep up with, take some of your waste outside for composting there. You don't want the excess food rotting in your indoor worm bin—that would start to stink.

Give them some grit. Sprinkle a cup or two of potting soil, garden soil, or sand into your worm bin. The grit will help your worms with their digestion.

Stick to vegetarian fare. Worms prefer fruit and vegetable scraps, bread, cereal, other grains, crushed eggshells, coffee grounds (toss in the filter, too), and tea bags. Don't feed them fatty or oily foods, meat, dairy products, or pet waste.

Keeping your wigglers on a vegetarian diet helps avoid odors and bacterial problems. Red worms tend to reject spicy foods, such as garlic and onions. Banana skins, apple peels, and wilted lettuce are earthworm favorites, and they also love eggshells that have been rinsed well and crushed. Cut vegetable and fruit scraps into small pieces before putting them in the bin, or whirl them in a blender or food processor to make a slurry. Include paper coffee filters (unbleached ones are ideal!) and tea bags (remove the staple, please!) when feeding worms coffee grounds or tea. In summer, add a few handfuls of fresh grass clippings to the worm bedding materials. And anytime you want to energize your worms, a light sprinkling of cornmeal will do the trick.

Learn from watching. If you take your time and observe your composting worms now and then, you'll learn how to keep them happy, says Colón. For instance, if you find all of your worms clustered in one place, the conditions in that particular spot are what your worms prefer. Colón discovered that for some reason her worms hate spinach (perhaps they're toddler worms?).

Keep the fruit flies at bay. Here's the No. 1 reason that people give up on composting indoors with worm bins: Their bins develop an annoying and persistent following of fruit flies, says Colón. But this is a surmountable problem, she says.

First, you'll have to bite your lip and absorb this little tidbit from the Things I'd Rather Not Know Department: Fruit flies lay eggs on the skin of commercial fruit at some point along the growing-and-distribution process.

That's how they hitchhike into your home in the first place. When you drop fruit peels into your worm bin, the eggs have time to hatch and those pesky little bugs take wing.

Some people go to extremes to eradicate those eggs before they drop fruit trimmings into their worm bins, says Colón. They wash the peels off, freeze, or boil them. That's way too much bother, she says. Here's her secret: When adding fruit scraps to your worm bin, push them down to the bottom and bury them under several inches of moist newspaper bedding. If fruit fly eggs hatch down there, the larvae will simply die—they can't survive in that environment.

Take the dirt—but leave the worms. Once your worms have been doing their work for a while, you'll inevitably encounter the quandary of how to collect the compost from the bin without mistakenly grabbing up a few worms with it. Some bin systems solve this problem by dividing the bin into separate compartments. You feed your worms in one compartment for a while, then you remove the divider between compartments and start putting the food in the other compartment. The worms migrate to the new "dining hall" and leave the compost behind in the first compartment.

Other worm bins are designed with a small door at the bottom. When worms rise in the bin to get to food, you can pop the door open and scoop the compost out without extracting any live critters. (The newsprint will have gotten all mixed in with the compost.)

If that all sounds a tad complex, here's Pelliccio's simple approach: Your worms prefer darkness. When you open up your compost bin and light strikes the interior, the worms will immediately crawl to the bottom of the bin, out of the way. Then, like Pelliccio, just use a plastic measuring cup to scoop out the compost.

Or try the start-over-from-scratch approach: Lay out a tarp in the backyard and dump the entire contents of your worm bin onto it. Get your kids to help you pick out the worms and return them to the bin (with freshly shredded, moistened newspaper bedding). Save any little worm cocoons, too—little light

(continued on page 206)

Stop the Messes! Caddy Liner Origami

When you collect kitchen waste in a caddy for later composting, you'll inevitably accumulate drips and messy flecks of food in the bottom of the container. Annette Pelliccio, founder of the organic gardening company the Happy Gardener in Virginia, avoids this hassle by making a simple liner for her kitchen waste caddy out of folded newspaper. Her kids race to see who can complete a liner first. When the caddy gets full, she just dumps the scraps—liner and all—onto her compost pile. Here's how to make the liner.

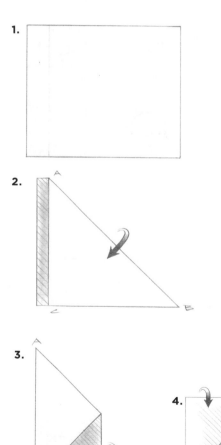

1. Open up three or four separate sheets of newspaper and stack them.

2. Fold the top right corner of the stack down to the bottom left, to form a large triangle. Trim off the left-hand edge that doesn't fall within the triangle.

3. Fold the bottom right corner (B) of the triangle to meet the bottom left corner (C) and crease the paper at the fold.

4. Fold the top left corner (A) down to meet the bottom left corner (C) and crease this fold, too. Your creation should be square now.

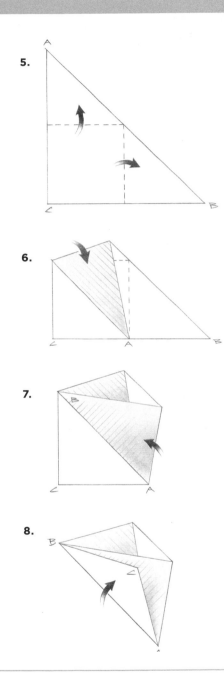

5. Undo those last two folds to return to the large triangle. Those creases will serve as guidelines.

6. Fold the top left corner (A) down to meet the bottom of the vertical crease.

7. Fold the right-hand corner (B) of the triangle to the left, meeting the left-hand edge of the horizontal crease.

8. At the lower left corner (C) of your creation, separate the sheets of newsprint and fold them over the sides of your bin liner.

9. Open up the bin liner and fit it into the bottom of your kitchen compost caddy.

This creates a cup-shaped liner that fits perfectly into Pelliccio's kitchen compost caddy, which is 12 inches tall, 8 inches wide, and 6 inches deep. If your caddy is a different size, experiment with the folds to adjust the liner's shape.

Beginners, Take the "Plant Pledge"

If you are just starting out with composting, Jodie Colón, compost educator for the New York Botanical Garden, recommends that you take the "Plant Pledge." So right now, raise your right hand and read this aloud.

"I PROMISE TO COMPOST ONLY THINGS THAT COME FROM PLANTS—UNTIL I KNOW WHAT I'M DOING."

Congratulations! Now that you are officially sworn in and authenticated, you might well wonder what the point of the "Plant Pledge" actually is. Colón devised it to focus the attention of composting novices on a couple of important points. First, if you stick to composting the likes of garden plants, leaves, grass clippings, fruits, and vegetables, you run a low risk of encountering frustrating problems in your efforts—and therefore you'll be more likely to stick with it. Also, the pledge reminds you that there's a big, wide world of composting beyond the basics once you see for yourself how compost improves results. You can look forward to learning, experimenting, and teaching others what you know.

brown ovoids the size of a match head. Then drag the tarp with remaining compost to your garden bed.

Use the compost indoors or out. What do you do with the compost that you harvest from your worm bin? There are three main uses for this rich dirt. The one that involves the least work on your part is rejuvenating your houseplants with it, says Pelliccio—indoor compost for indoor plants. Otherwise, dump your worm compost onto a garden bed or just spread it on your lawn.

Share the wealth. Sourdough bread culture takes on an eternal life as it gets passed from one kitchen to another. In the same vein, you can spread the joy of composting worms. If you have dazzled a friend with your worm composting operation, it's a simple matter to share the wealth. A beginner can start home composting with as few as 20 worms, says Dr. Mulder. In just a few months, those worms will increase in population enough to keep up with the food scraps provided by their new owner's kitchen.

Keep a caddy near the kitchen sink. When you set aside kitchen waste for future composting—whether inside or outside—you need a mess-free way to store this stuff temporarily. For many people, the solution is a plastic storage bin with a snap-on lid tucked under the sink. Unless the lid is easy to pop off and on, you might prefer a product called a "compost caddy," a handled bin with a hinged top that you can flip open and closed with one hand—since you're likely to have a cutting board or chopping knife in the other. If you buy a compost caddy, says Pelliccio, look for one that includes a carbon filter in the lid to keep odors down, and that can be safely cleaned in the dishwasher. This type is available online from recycling suppliers.

Hit the road with confidence. Being a caring and responsible worm owner, you want to know what's going to happen to your little darlings when you go on vacation. Time to hire a worm sitter? Relax, says Colón. If you just check their food and moisture levels before you leave, your worms will fare just fine by themselves for a few weeks. If your worms run out of food scraps while you are sitting on the beach, they'll get by while eating their bedding or even their own castings (sorry, but it's true). In fact, trying to be overly attentive to your worms could put them in the greatest danger, says Colón. If you try to leave them 2 weeks' worth of food, the bin could become too soggy for your worms to live in. Also, don't leave your worm bin where it will be subject to temperature fluctuations. (Worm pie, anyone?) The best thing of all: You don't have to bring home vacation souvenirs for your little worm friends—unless you have an apple core or two.

CHAPTER 8

FLOWERS MADE EASY— *Even for* LATE BLOOMERS

|||||||||||||||||||||||||||||||||||||||||||||||||||||||||||||||||||||||||||||||||||||||||

Fresh garden vegetables may delight the taste buds, but nothing in the landscape will delight the eyes like a flower garden. As a cheat-at-gardening enthusiast, naturally, you will want the simplest, most efficient techniques for coaxing blossoms out of the ground. As is often the case with gardening, the easiest way to success with flowers is finding plants that fit your growing conditions. There also are bushels of sneaky ways to design a flowerbed, to plant your little beauties, and to care for them throughout the growing season—plus ways to get more and buy less. Boy, are your neighbors in for an eye-popping surprise! With forethought and smart plant choices, you can create gorgeous plantings and beds that don't demand lots of maintenance.

SELECTING SURE-TO-SUCCEED FLOWERS

Selecting the flowers that will grace your garden is a little like selecting a spouse. Choose well, and you can look forward to a gratifying life together. Choose poorly, and there will be plenty of misery to go around—for you and for your spouse . . . er, flower. If you're serious about removing the work and aggravation from flower gardening, it all begins with selection. So, if you cheat right up-front (choosing appropriate plants), you'll be growing carefree down the road. Here are some pointers.

Whittle down the field of candidates. As a cheater at gardening, you're looking for ways to simplify flower growing. Since there are thousands upon thousands of flower varieties available, this calls for a quick and easy process for deciding which varieties to plant. So here's how to whittle down the decision-making process to a manageable size: Before you start paging through catalogs, browsing the Internet, and cruising the aisles at the nursery, assess the spot where you intend to plant your flowers, says Barbara Arnold, horticultural designer for the Franklin Park Conservatory in Columbus, Ohio. This will give you a firm set of criteria that will enable you to reduce the flower candidate pool immediately. After all, what's the point in ogling and daydreaming about some exotic blossom you see in a magazine if it's destined to fail in a garden like yours? So make a cheater's checklist of four simple things.

1. The type of soil in your flowerbeds (sandy, clay, or the ideal loam)
2. The amount of sun and shade the beds get during the day
3. How dry or wet the planting beds tend to be
4. Whether the plant is appropriate for your garden's hardiness zone

When a flower variety is offered for sale at a commercial nursery or garden center, you'll typically find the cheater's information right on the plant label or nursery signage about the growing conditions the plant prefers. When you encounter a variety that's not a good match for your conditions, don't give it another thought—no matter how enticing the prospect is. Life is too short to spend it nursing a struggling plant or trying to recreate an entire ecosystem that will be to its liking.

Insist on a plant tag. If a plant at your nursery is missing its tag, don't buy it, says Ellen Covner, landscaper and owner of Custom Gardens in Wynnewood, Pennsylvania. Sure, a staffer might tell you what variety the plant is, but unless you are sure that the staffer is really knowledgeable, you can't count on that information—the staffer could be guessing in order to make a sale.

Check out growth patterns first. There's more you need to know about a flower variety before you buy it, says Arnold. Take a measuring tape to your flowerbed so you will have a clear idea of how much space you have to fill. Then see what size your chosen flower will be in maturity. Spacing out your flowers correctly will spare you some major embarrassment in the middle of the growing season—say, when monster plants start overwhelming their neighbors, overlapping each other, and spilling over the border of the bed onto the sidewalk. (It can happen—for instance, some perennial geraniums can spread to 6 feet across if you let them.)

Another item to check on a flower's plant label, says Arnold, is how aggressively it grows and spreads. If a flower is described as having a "vigorous" growth habit, watch out. It's the kind of plant that will spread rapidly in your flowerbed. It will be choking its neighbors within a month, and it will be hard to rein in if it gets out of control. An example is the flowering groundcover bishop's weed.

Go native. Susan Gottlieb is renowned for her home garden in Beverly Hills, California, but she's a laid-back, laissez-faire gardener who attributes her success to one core strategy: Gardening is much easier when you rely on plants that are native to your region. Native plants are naturally resistant to the local pests, they love the soil as it is instead of supplemented, and they're accustomed to the amount of water provided by nature (a particular advantage in a dry climate such as Gottlieb's). Right now, you're nodding appreciatively, because you see that stocking your garden with native plants is in keeping with the SAIL approach to working with Mother Nature (that is, Stand Aside, Interfere Little) that was introduced in Chapter 1. "I come at gardening as a conservationist," says Gottlieb, who owns the G2 Gallery featuring nature photography, in Venice, California.

When she first moved into her home, the yard was heavily planted with ivy, which required a substantial amount of water. She pulled up the ivy. Now more than 150 different native plants bloom in her garden, including California lilac (Ceanothus), an evergreen known for its color, fragrance, and drought tolerance. The advantages to Gottlieb's native plant strategy pile up quickly.

- She never needs to fertilize. Though she might add compost to her garden soil occasionally, her native plants do better without fertilizer.
- Gottlieb's garden requires minimal water. She has a friend who loves exotic ornamentals from all over the world, but that "pour" soul is out in the garden at 6 a.m. every day to get her watering duties done. The water-intensive garden is inarguably beautiful, Gottlieb says, but who needs all that work?
- She never uses insecticides, and pest infestation is rare.
- Gottlieb is happy to attract and provide a habitat for local wildlife, including birds and butterflies.
- Her native plants have strong and deep root systems that stabilize the soil of her steep yard.

Ease into the native lifestyle. Susan Gottlieb offers the following further pointers for people who are just getting started with native plants in the garden.

- Start small. Trying to replace your entire garden with native plants all at once is too intimidating a project. It will feel too much like work. So start with a small cluster of native plants here and a small cluster there. As you get accustomed to the new (and reduced) rhythm of gardening, you can expand from one season to the next. But take it easy. A common home-owner mistake is over-planting, Gottlieb says. The more plants you have in your garden, the more maintenance your garden requires.

■ Even natives need water when you first plant them, until they establish themselves. If you have a drip system, turn it on for the first few weeks after you plant. Or just get out the hose when the soil feels dry an inch or so below the surface. After that, you probably won't have to water your natives except in prolonged drought conditions. After their first year, you'll only have to water when conditions are extreme.

In keeping with her laissez-faire gardening approach, Gottlieb lets her plants tell *her* when they're thirsty. If a plant is looking stressed, she just gives it a drink of water and sees how it responds.

■ If you're pressed for time and want to quickly select plants that are native to your region, ask a local horticultural society, arboretum, or Cooperative Extension office for recommendations. If you're interested in learning more, "I would definitely read books," Gottlieb says. Check for native plant books at your library, your nursery, and your local bookstore.

■ Another place to learn more about native plants is the Web site of the North American Native Plant Society at www.nanps.org. This Canadian group lists local organizations all across North America.

■ If you ever need a landscaper's services for help in your garden or yard, ask first about his or her familiarity with native plants. You may find a professional or a garden center that specializes in natives, but you may also find that many in the landscape industry are barely acquainted with the topic and won't provide the kind of help you need.

Target your buying to reduce labor. When a gardener keeps buying plants without restraint, the labor required to maintain those plants increases exponentially. Instead, focus on buying flowers that can bring bursts of color to a small area, and use low-maintenance shrubs and trees—rather than more flowers—to provide background and height. Some gardeners believe buying perennials is the answer to saving work, on the theory that they require little upkeep. That may be true for some well-chosen varieties (see Cheat Sheet: "Low-Maintenance Flowers," on page 219), but not for the great majority. Tearing up lawn to make space for your expanding garden will be the least of your problems. With every purchase, remind yourself: Each of these plants is going to need watering, fertilizing, deadheading, and pest control. Do I have time for that? As author Phyllis McGinley famously observed "The trouble with gardening is that it does not remain an avocation. It becomes an obsession."

Look for lifestyle compatibility. The success of any flower depends a lot on how well suited that plant is to the person tending it. And finding the plants that are best suited to you is tricky business, says publicist and garden blogger Katharine Hall, based in Ukiah, California. In fact, it's almost as complex as finding friends or soul mates. So as you search for new candidates for your flowerbeds, keep in the back of your mind a permanent checklist of your own situation, attitudes, and abilities. For instance, if you have a jam-packed work schedule and you're always on the go, you need easy-care, can't-fail plants—for instance, nasturtiums and Mexican primrose, Hall says. Other good choices include bleeding heart, hosta, Russian sage, artemisia, and yucca. Ornamental grasses are good bets, too.

Steer clear of troubled plants. If you're choosing among the flowering annuals at a nursery, it's easy to be dazzled by those gorgeous blossoms. However, you're better off choosing a plant with buds that are showing just a little color—they'll adapt more easily when you plant them in your garden. Also, focus your attention on the rest of the plant as well—you want deep green foliage with no signs of pests or disease (spots or leaves turning yellow). Check the root system, too. (Press on the sides of the container to loosen the rootball inside, then gently slide it out.) Ideally, you will find a half-and-half mixture of roots and soil. If the roots are compacted, twisting inside the container, or growing out of the container's drainage holes, move on to another plant.

For smooth spreading, go for bulbs. Your perennials may keep producing flowers year after year, but they're not quite maintenance-free. The problem is that they're spawning more plants down there in the dirt, and after 2 or 3 years they get so crowded they don't grow well anymore. This is why you have to dig up or divide your perennials every few years and separate them. There are a couple of shortcuts that every cheat-at-gardening enthusiast will want to know. First, flowers that grow from bulbs are much easier to separate than other perennials. So even if you didn't like them before, I'm sure that lilies and tulips are taking on a whole new beauty in your eyes right now. Second, when you're separating bulbs you generally have a choice: You can replant the separated bulbs right away, or you can store them for later planting. Storing them means hanging them in a mesh bag in a cool, dark place—where, likely as not, you will discover them several years later when you're packing to move. You might as well replant them on the spot, as long as you're already on your knees, with your digging tools out and dirt already under your fingernails.

Give bulbs a quick checkup. Be picky when you buy bulbs. Choose bulbs that have a healthy look to them. Avoid dry, shriveled-looking bulbs. They should be firm, not squishy. If they have cracks, deep scratches, or other obvious damage, pass them by. A healthy bulb will feel dense. If you run across one that's surprisingly lightweight for its size, that bulb is probably dried out.

Learn from mistakes—quickly. If you try out a new plant in your garden and it fails, resist the temptation to try again and again, says native plant gardener Susan Gottlieb. Sure, patience is a virtue, but persistence can also prolong misery. Even with native plants, sometimes your chosen species will not be a good match for the conditions in your garden, or perhaps pests such as aphids take too much of a liking to that particular variety. Just shrug it off and try a new plant in that spot. Remember to SAIL with nature (Stand Aside, Interfere Little).

Narrow your choices and plant in masses. Many gardeners make the mistake of planting every flower they fall in love with at the nursery and every variety that dazzles their eyes from the pages of a seed catalog. The saner, easier, and more artistic approach, says landscaper Ellen Covner: Choose several key plants and several colors that you will stick to and position these in repeating groups of five or more plants each. (Groups of three work well in a small garden.) Always use an odd number of each plant in these groupings that are called drifts. Then passersby will mistake you for a disciplined, sophisticated, artistically talented flower gardener!

Don't buy trouble. Now and then you will inspect a flower's tag at the nursery and read, "This plant is prone to . . ." and a list of several diseases, pests, and other maladies. That's your signal to move on and find another plant, says Covner. Any plant with a résumé like that is more trouble than it's worth.

Let neighbors do the watering. Occasionally Susan Gottlieb adopts a garden plant that requires more water than natural rainfall provides. But she has a low-labor solution for that situation: You see, her neighbors water their gardens heavily. So Gottlieb positions any water-needy plants along the side of her property, where they will benefit from the watering next door. Yup, sounds like cheating to me.

CLEVER DESIGN STRATEGIES FOR YOUR FLOWERBEDS

Flowers and foliage are your "paint," and your flowerbeds are your "canvas." Here are some shortcuts to achieving an outdoor masterpiece.

Stagger those blooming seasons. It's a shame to have a showcase of dazzling flower color in spring, only to have your beds wither into a brown tangle by mid-summer. (Unless you like decorating early for Halloween.) The solution is to select and position your plants according to their blooming season, information that's usually included on the labels of plants you buy at the nursery. For instance, you might plant a bed with a combination of plants that bloom in late winter (crocuses, for instance), early spring (pansies), mid- to late spring (irises and peonies), early summer (foxgloves and astilbe), midsummer (bee balm, phlox, and daylilies), and late summer to early autumn (asters, chrysanthemums, and sedum). Use your artistic instincts—cluster several plants of each variety together to provide maximum impact, and separate the

Cheat Sheet

Long-Blooming Perennials

These perennials bloom for many weeks—some of them will go from spring to fall.

Achillea (yarrow)

Anthemis (golden marguerite)

Mongolian aster (Kalimeris)

Fringed bleeding heart (Dicentra)

Coreopsis

Shasta daisy

Daylilies: Stella d'Oro, Happy Returns, and related varieties

Echinacea (purple coneflower)

Geranium (hardy ones, not the annual flowerpot kind)

Nepeta (catmint)

Perovskia (Russian sage)

Physostegia (obedient plant)

Platycodon (balloon flower)

Rudbeckia (black-eyed Susan)

Salvia: May Night and Blue Hills varieties

Scabiosa (pincushion flower)

Tradescantia (spiderwort)

Veronica

---

varieties that will be blooming at the same time so the bed will have a nice balance of color at all times.

Throughout the growing season, treat your flowerbed like a forever-unfinished masterpiece. When noticeable gaps appear in the bed (say, when a cluster of early-blooming perennials dies back in summer), make up the difference with some fresh annuals. Even the most accomplished gardeners manage their flowerbeds on a trial-and-error basis—a perpetual learning experience!

Or go for long bloomers. Another strategy is to seek out flowers that bloom for a long time. Lots of annuals bloom all summer. But some perennials also flower for longer than the 3 to 4 weeks that's typical. See the Cheat Sheet above for a list of long-blooming perennials.

Plan for waves of color. Plant your flower garden in "waves" of color, suggests landscaper Ellen Covner. Creating a continuous swath of the same color is a more sophisticated look than planting in alternating colors, she says. Such expanses of color also are more likely to attract the attention of bees and butterflies. Individual plants of varying colors are harder for these friendly flying bugs to see.

Plant a buffer between competing colors. When brightly colored flowers display two clashing colors side-by-side (say, blue and orange), they rob each other of visual impact. To let each cluster of flowers bloom in full glory, create a visual buffer between such color beacons by planting flowers in a subdued color. White usually works quite well as a buffer between two more vibrant colors.

Plan for a little overlap. The easiest weed control ever? Space plants so that your flowers overlap their leaves by just 1 inch by the time they are mature, says Barbara Arnold, the horticultural designer. Your plants will do a better job of blocking out weed growth this way. Otherwise, in the spots where you *don't* put a plant, Mother Nature surely will. As an added benefit, the shade created by the overlap will keep your soil cooler and moister. A mere inch overlap will do no harm to the plants, Arnold says, and this kind of spacing gives your flowerbed a more polished look.

Minimize maintenance. Some flowers are just easier to take care of than others and need less fussing. You won't have to deadhead impatiens or wax begonias. See the Cheat Sheet on "Low-Maintenance Flowers," on the opposite page, for more easy-care candidates for your garden.

Focus on foliage to save work. Plants with distinctive foliage provide a pleasing contrast to your flowers, suggests landscaper Covner. Such foliage plants save you further labor, of course, since they don't need deadheading. Some of the artemisias are a good bet—they've got greenish gray or whitish gray foliage and don't need a lot of water. Other good choices include alternanthera, helichrysum, lamium, New Zealand flax, and setcreasea (purple heart). In shady beds, try ferns, hostas, wild ginger, coleus, heuchera, polka-dot plant, caladium, lamium, pulmonaria, and Hakone grass.

Also, strategic use of evergreen shrubs in your flowerbeds will provide some year-round color and interest, as opposed to that "brownscape" that's typical of fall and winter.

Cheat Sheet

Low-Maintenance Flowers

These plants are durable, easy to care for, and need little—or in some cases no—deadheading (trimming faded blooms).

ANNUALS

Sweet alyssum

Wax begonia

Catharanthus (Madagascar periwinkle)

Celosia

Coleus (its leaves are its best feature)

Cosmos

Dusty miller

Globe amaranth

Impatiens

Morning glories

Nasturtiums

Polka-dot plant

Portulaca

Salvia

Sunflowers

PERENNIALS

Achillea (yarrow)

Amsonia

Japanese anemone

Aster

Astilbe

Baptisia (false indigo)

Bleeding heart (Dicentra)

Columbine

Threadleaf coreopsis

Echinacea (purple coneflower)

Ferns

Gaura

Ornamental grasses

Heuchera (coral bells)

Hosta

Nepeta (catmint)

Perovskia (Russian sage)

Sedum (stonecrop)

Tradescantia

Veronica

Get easy color from shrubs. An easy way to get color without dealing with lots of perennials and annuals is to create a bed or border of flowering shrubs—they need less overall maintenance than herbaceous flowers. Focus on long-bloomers like hydrangeas, butterfly bush, and Japanese spiraea, or plan a seasonal succession of spring, summer, and autumn bloomers. See the Cheat Sheet on page 220 for ideas.

Add some annuals. Yes, you have to plant them every year. But many annuals bloom all summer long, and they don't all need a lot of fussing and

Cheat Sheet

||||||||||||||||||||||||||||||||||||||||||||||||||||||||||||||||||||||||||||||||||||||||||||||||||||||||||||||||||||||||||||||||

Seasonal Flowering Shrubs

If you want to make a border of flowering shrubs, here are some choices that bloom in different seasons.

Abelia, spring to fall

Azalea, spring

Bougainvillea, summer to fall

Butterfly bush, summer to fall

Camellia, fall, winter, or spring

Caryopteris (blue-mist shrub), late summer

Ceanothus (California lilac), spring to summer

Clethra (sweet pepperbush or summer-sweet), late summer

Daphne, late winter or spring

Deutzia, summer

Flannelbush (Fremontodendron), summer

Forsythia, early spring

Gardenia, summer to fall

Witch hazel, late winter or early spring

Hibiscus, summer

Hydrangea, summer

Kerria, spring

Kolkwitzia (beautybush), summer

Mock orange, spring to summer

Oleander, spring to fall

Rhododendron, spring

Roses, 'Flower Carpet' and 'Knockout', all summer

Spiraea, Japanese, spring and summer

Viburnum, spring or summer

Vitex (chaste tree), late summer to fall

---

deadheading. See the Cheat Sheet on "Low-Maintenance Flowers" on page 219 for some easy-care choices.

Use shorter plants to hold up taller ones. Support floppy plants with shorter, sturdier plants instead of stakes and string. You'll get a beautiful, casual, cottage garden look as the leaves and flowers mingle.

Let instinct play a role in planning. Many gardeners overcrowd their flower plants simply because it's hard to imagine each plant at full size—you feel like you're wasting acres of space when you space your new flower plants according to the mature size described in the planting directions. But if you plant too closely, you'll just have to dig and move plants in a year or two when they become overcrowded. The sanest approach to planning is to accept the fact that flower gardening is more art than science and to use plant marker information—and your instinct—to guide you from the get-go. Particular planting conditions (type of soil, moisture level, sun exposure, and such) may make some varieties grow like gangbusters while other varieties will struggle, but just take a leap of faith and do the best you can with spacing. Then sit back, watch, and learn.

To win with color, clip photos. Do you have trouble envisioning the potential flower colors and combinations in your head? Try this trick: Take a pair of scissors to a few of those stacked-up seed catalogs. Lay those beautiful flower photographs out on the kitchen table. Mix and match to your heart's content.

Consider the view from inside. Choose a spot for your garden that's visible from inside your house, landscaper Covner says. That way, you get double the pleasure out of your flowers, admiring them from inside the house as well as outside.

Plan for a fragrant garden. The visual display of a flower garden is not the only payoff for your efforts—the fragrance is a considerable benefit as well. If you want to enhance these olfactory rewards, position the most fragrant flowers, whether they be trees, shrubs, or bed plants, near your house. There the scents will more easily waft inside, so people both inside and outside will benefit. Furthermore, reflected heat from the house and surrounding structures will enhance the fragrance provided by flowers. Also, when flowers are planted near a wall, fence, or other windbreak, the scent is less likely to dissipate into the air. Flowers for a fragrance garden include sweet alyssum, roses, lavender, heliotrope, hyacinth, mignonette, stocks, lilac, phlox, dianthus, and jasmine.

Hide it with height. Tall flowers are great for hiding unsightly features in the landscape, such as a utility meter. With this approach, you have no need to install such features as a lattice fence or faux rocks. You can also use flowers of varying heights to create artistic accents in your flowerbeds, says Covner. One of her favorite tall plants is the spiky foxglove. Other tall plants to use for screening include hollyhocks, sunflowers, and Herbstonne rudbeckias. Or try morning glories or honeysuckle on a trellis or lattice panel. Ornamental grasses are also terrific for camouflage, and the only care they need is cutting back once a year and watering during prolonged dry spells.

Let less visible beds fill your vases. If you're an avid flower gardener, it's likely that you have more than one flowerbed. If that's the case, you have the luxury of assigning different roles to the separate beds. Pick one flowerbed, the most prominent one in your front yard, to be the showcase bed that all of the passersby will ogle. That one highly visible bed is where you will devote most of your time and creativity—featuring lovingly balanced large plants and small ones, the most striking color combinations, and the most endearing little border flowers.

The hidden flowerbeds—say, those along a side wall of your house or bordering the backyard—can play an entirely different role in your flower gardening. These flowers are destined for the vases inside your house and the bouquets you give to friends. Because these beds are less visible, it matters little whether you leave the occasional gap where you have clipped out a few blossoms, and the balance of sizes and colors need not be so precise either. This means less effort on your part. Also, since your bouquet beds are less formal, they're a great place for experimenting—for instance, trying out that scruffy little plant you picked up at the arboretum plant sale or the orphans you salvaged from a friend's overcrowded garden. You can stick such foundlings in any ol' corner of your bouquet garden and let them do what they will.

Pick the right bulb bed. Most bulbs thrive on full sun, so when you're planning your flowerbeds, pick a spot where your bulbs will get a minimum of 6 hours of sunshine. Soil that drains well is another bonus—bulbs tend to rot if they sit in excess water too long. Plant bulbs 6 to 8 weeks before the ground freezes in your region. Sure, you're eager—but don't plant bulbs earlier than that. In a warm fall, they might start growing prematurely, only to get damaged by the deep freeze later.

Show restraint on ornaments. Another item from the Department of Taste and Discipline: Covner pleads with you to limit your use of garden gnomes, balls, toads, pinwheels, and other ornaments. One or two will take you a long way. Think of your restraint as a shortcut to a polished look. Simple is good. (Now, perhaps we should discuss your flock of pink plastic flamingoes . . .)

Give your beds an edge. Some kind of edging material will not only define the borders of your flowerbeds, it will also keep mulch from drifting astray and will keep the lawn mower away from your garden plants. Covner's favorite edging: the common heavy, black, pliable plastic kind. Visually, it "disappears" in the landscape, she says. The colorful kind of edging made of rigid plastic that sticks up from the lawn is too distracting, in her opinion.

Step on stones, not flowers. If you have a large flowerbed, a few strategically placed stepping-stones provide a great advantage, Covner says. They allow you to enter the bed and maintain your plants without stepping on foliage and without compacting the soil. You can buy flagstone or prefabricated stepping-stones at a home improvement outlet, or pick up an artsy and pricier version at a garden store.

Keep records without a map or pencil. If you want to remember what you have planted, do this, Barbara Arnold says: Take all flower plant tags into the house, slide them into an envelope, and label the envelope something like "Front Yard Bed." Stash the envelope in a handy drawer in the living room. Then, if you need to identify your flowers for friends, you can quickly sneak inside and look in the envelope. Arnold likes a clean and neat look in a flowerbed, and doesn't think gardeners should leave those little arrow-shaped plastic tabs stuck into the soil as labels for their plants. "Plastic doesn't grow, plastic doesn't rot," she says, so don't leave little scraps of it lying about your beds.

"DIRTY" TRICKS: WHEN FLOWER ROOTS MEET SOIL

Now you have mastered the selection of low-maintenance flowers for your garden, and artistically—well, you're a horticultural Claude Monet now. So let's roll up our sleeves and get some dirt under our fingernails as we actually plant some flowers.

Decide if you need more or less before you dig. It's flower planting day. You're standing over your vacant flowerbed, at your feet are a score of transplants fresh from the nursery, you have a trowel in hand and a wide-brimmed hat on your head—ready to dig some planting holes? No, not just yet, says Barbara Arnold, horticultural designer for the Franklin Park Conservatory in Columbus, Ohio. She suggests positioning and spacing all plants (even separating the multi-packs) in the bed and deciding if you have too many or too few plants *before* you dig a single hole. Now is the time to buy more plants if you don't have enough to fill the bed, or to find other homes for your extra plants if you bought too many. It's best to decide right then and there to head back to the garden center if you need to find the same plants while they're still available. And if you have too many plants, don't make the decision to crowd a bed that will need uncrowding 2 years from now; just find another appropriate spot or pass along the bounty to another gardener.

A shallow trench will give you an edge. When Sam Jeffries creates a new flowerbed, he has a couldn't-be-simpler way to delineate between lawn and planting area. Jeffries, a horticulturist and cohost of the radio show *The Garden Guys*, uses a heavy-duty garden spade (a shovel-like digging tool with a wide, straight cutting edge) to dig a shallow trench around the bed. This cuts grass away from the planting area, creates the desired visual separation, and also allows him to altogether skip wrestling with plastic edging. Most likely, he won't have to re-dig the trench until the next growing season.

Mark the border with limestone. When plotting out the border of a new flowerbed, many people like to lay a garden hose along the intended edge, Jeffries notes. A simpler approach: Mark off the edge of your new bed by sprinkling a line of pulverized limestone (inexpensive, at about $2 per bag). You can leave the limestone in place when you have finished preparing the bed—it's good for the soil.

Cheat Sheet

||||||||||||||||||||||||||||||||||||||||||||||||||||||||||||||||||||||||||||||||||||||||||||||||||||||||||||||||||||

Annuals—The Easy Route

Annual flowers are famously easy to plant from seed. Here are some pointers to keep in mind.

- Just about all of the planting details you need will be printed right on the seed packet, including when to plant, how deeply to plant, and the spacing required between plants.

- Remember that the traditional method of tapping seeds straight out of the packet will lead to overplanting. You will end up with crowded plants, which will cost you more work when you have to thin them out. You'll feel guilty about destroying young plants, you'll struggle to find homes for them, and you'll end up with overcrowded beds anyway. The low-labor approach: Tap seeds out of the packet into your cupped palm. Then pick out no more than two or three seeds with your thumb and forefinger and plant them together. If more

than one sprouts, thinning will be a simple matter.

- Remember the POTS principle (Priority One: The Soil) and treat your flower beds to plenty of organic material (see Chapter 2 for more info).

- Plant your seeds to the prescribed depth, smooth loose soil over them with your hand, and then tamp the earth a little to improve the seed-to-soil contact.

- Water with a gentle sprinkle.

- Some annuals, defying their 1-year-and-done reputation, will do you the favor of reseeding and sprouting again the next year. (Examples are sweet alyssum, cosmos, poppies, some morning glories, and zinnias.) Just thin out or move those that pop up in the wrong spot—and don't mistake them for weeds.

Build a bridge for your wheelbarrow. Do you find yourself carting multiple wheelbarrow loads of mulch into your new flowerbed—and messing up your newly dug border trench (described earlier)? Jeffries has an easy answer for that, too. Take a few handfuls of mulch and use them to build a little bridge across the border trench. Push the wheelbarrow across the bridge as many times as you need to. When you have all of your mulch in place, scoop out the mulch bridge with your hands and toss it onto the flowerbed as well. Your border trench will survive unblemished.

Erase your footprints. When you're done spreading mulch over a flowerbed, turn a leaf rake upside down and use it to erase the footprints you have left behind. This is purely a cosmetic touch, says Jeffries, but it gives your new bed a professional look.

Plan with mowing in mind. The layout of a flowerbed can make your lawn mowing more difficult if you're not careful. Here are tricks from Sam Jeffries for keeping mowing hassles to a minimum.

Don't run the border of a new, curved flowerbed straight into the driveway. This creates a situation where you have to stop and turn your lawn mower around. Instead, end the border of the bed in an S-curve that trails off parallel to the driveway. Then you will naturally mow with the contour of the S rather than stopping. Also, do not leave a wedge-shaped patch of lawn between the edge of the bed and the driveway—that's awkward to mow.

Prevent disease with good spacing. Good air circulation keeps disease from developing in fungus-prone plants, like hybrid tea roses and phlox. Give them plenty of room for cleaner leaves and blooms and plant mildew-resistant varieties.

MYTH-BUSTERS
Simple Division for Perennials

Barbara Arnold, horticultural designer for the Franklin Park Conservatory in Columbus, Ohio, says many perennials need dividing every 3 to 5 years, but some don't need it at all (perennial geraniums, for instance). Here's how to tell whether your perennials need to be divided: Have they lost a lot of their former level of flower production, or is there an empty, dead spot in the middle of the plant? If so, it's time to divide. Also, check the interior of the plant. When a perennial needs dividing, its interior leaves will grow close together, looking tight. This happens in particular with daylilies.

For lots of bulbs, use a drill. If you have just a few bulbs to plant, a garden spade or a trowel is probably the only help you need. However, if you have scores of bulbs to plant, that's backbreaking on-your-knees work, which means it's time to cheat. Buy a tool called a bulb auger from your nursery or over the Internet. This super-quick hole digging device attaches to an electric drill and will bore planting holes up to foot or so deep and a couple of inches wide. Using the cordless variety of drill will move the project along even faster, since you won't have to bother with extension cords. Make sure that the planting hole you have dug bottoms out with nice, loose soil that drains well. If the bottom of the hole is hard-packed clay, it will hold water, and a bulb down there will be in danger of rotting.

For planting depth, measure your bulb. How do you know how deeply to plant a bulb? Here's a rule of thumb: Measure the width of the bulb and multiply by 3. So a bulb that's 2 inches across should be planted 6 inches deep.

Tuck in your bulbs lovingly. When you plant a new bulb, provide a little fertilizer at the very bottom of the planting hole and cover that over with a layer of regular soil so the bulb doesn't have direct contact with the fertilizer. Drop the bulb into the hole with the pointy side up and the flatter root side down. Then fill the hole the rest of the way with soil and add water.

CARING FOR YOUR FLOWERS

By now, most of your work is done. You have well-chosen plants ensconced in good soil, all laid out to provide optimum visual impact. There's a little more you can do to pamper your flowers during the growing season, however, so adopt the following habits to give your little lovelies their best shot at full glory.

Adjust for the humidity level. You know that the hottest days of summer will be a touchy time for your flowers. But the protective measures you take will vary a lot according to how humid your climate is in summer. If you live in an arid region with plenty of heat but not much humidity, your emphasis should be on preserving moisture. So making sure your soil has plenty of water-hugging organic material is a good move. Become a master of mulch to prevent evaporation from the soil. And use windbreaks—such as fences, shrubs, and the walls of buildings—to prevent arid breezes from snatching away your flowers' water.

On the other hand, if you get particularly humid summers, your flowers are at greater risk for mildew and diseases. So prune the surrounding trees, shrubs, and other vegetation to allow in plenty of drying air circulation and sunlight.

Just remember—every 2 days. Make it easy on yourself and water newly planted annuals every 2 days for the first month. Annuals need to be watered regularly until they're established, which takes about 3 weeks, says horticultural designer Barbara Arnold. Your watering should total 1 to 1½ inches of water per week on average. If your soil is heavy clay, your plants may need a bit less water; in sandy soil they'll need more. If your flowers are in containers, water them every 2 days until the weather gets hot, and from then on water them every day, Arnold says. Smaller pots may need watering twice a day in hot, dry weather.

Save your deadheading labor. Deadheading flowers is a practice with a grim name and beautiful consequences. When you deadhead, you eliminate blossoms that are starting to fade—and the plant responds by regrouping and producing even more flowers. Deadheading can be time-consuming, painstaking work. But try these cheating strategies.

For plants that produce lots of flowers at once, you can shortcut the process by shearing back the entire plant at one go. For small plants use household scissors. For bigger, woodier plants, hedge shears are ideal. Plants to deadhead by shearing include sweet alyssum, lobelia, baby's breath, dianthus, lavender, and Russian sage (perovskia).

Another way to beat deadheading chores? Skip them altogether and fill your garden with flowers that don't need deadheading, either because they drop their spent flowers without help from you, or because their seed heads are attractive to you or your local bird population. See Zero-Maintenance Marvels: "They're Blooming Easy" on the opposite page for suggestions.

ZERO-MAINTENANCE MARVELS

They're Blooming Easy

To cut back on your flower-tending duties, select plants that don't need deadheading (trimming off faded blooms). Here are some to try: amsonia, astilbe, wax begonia, boltonia, ceratostigma, threadleaf coreopsis, daylily, gas plant (dictamnus), gaura, impatiens, love-in-a-mist, mignonette, purple coneflower, black-eyed Susan, rose campion, tansy, turtlehead, and tradescantia (spiderwort).

Make your bulbs happy. When your bulbs' flowers are spent, cut off just the stems at ground level. Let the leaves die back on their own, however. That green foliage is happily making new food and storing it in the bulb for next year's growth. And speaking of food, give your bulbs some organic fertilizer right when their blossoms begin to fade. Work this bulb food (it's high in potassium and phosphorus, and is available at your nursery) into the surface soil near the roots and then water.

Make dividing as easy as slicing bread. Conventional gardening wisdom advised you to dig up the entire plant when it was time to divide a large perennial. No more of that with the cheating mind-set—just sink the spade into the plant crown and slice off an outside portion of it (or two or three portions). Be sure to get a healthy chunk of roots attached and replant the slice in a new spot. One note of caution: If the perennial is really overdue for division and there's an empty, dead area in the center of the plant clump, it's best to dig up and fully divide the plant to remove the worn-out section.

Cut down on mulch purchases. Want to buy and haul fewer 40-pound bags of mulch? Don't go overboard with the mulch, says horticulturist and radio host Sam Jeffries. Here's the problem: When you add mulch to a bed year after year, it will mount up more and more, creating strangling volcano-shaped mounds around the base of your plants. Instead, put no more than 1 inch of mulch around the base of the plants and use 3 inches of mulch in the outlying areas between plants.

Protect perennials in winter. Sure, you're planting flowers that are hardy for your region, and you keep your eye on first frost dates to protect your flowers from the ravages of cold. But what if you typically get long-term snow cover where you live? Do you just throw up your hands in despair? Actually, you can throw up your hands and cheer! For perennials hunkering down in your soil, the crucial factor for survival is the underground temperature, not the aboveground air temperature. And a blanket of snow actually provides a layer of insulation from the brutally cold air. So think of snow cover as a gift from Mother Nature and let her play to your advantage.

If nature isn't so kind as to blanket you with snow throughout the winter, you can still protect your perennials during sub-zero (Fahrenheit) weather. Pro-

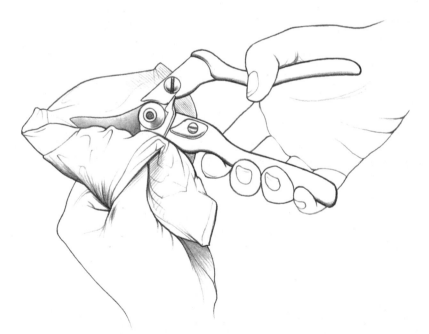

No cheating allowed when it comes to garden sanitation. Prevent the spread of diseases in your garden by regularly wiping your pruning shears with a disposable hand wipe.

vide your own insulating layer—namely, mulch, wood chips, straw, evergreen branches, or leaves raked up in fall. Wait until the ground begins to freeze before spreading your winter mulch. The idea is to keep the ground frozen to protect the root systems of your perennials from exposure to frigid, drying air when the earth is disturbed by alternating freezing and thawing that can happen in winter cold snaps and warm spells.

Wipe down your cutting tools. When you're deadheading flowers and otherwise trimming in your flower garden, carry a pack of disposable hand wipes with you, says San Francisco-based organic gardening columnist and "dirt diva" Annie Spiegelman (she writes under the slogan "Critics will be composted"). As you move from one section of your garden to another, give the blades of your shears a quick wipe so you won't spread diseases around your garden.

Give cut flowers a sweet drink. Don't just plop your cut flowers into a vase of plain ol' tap water—they'll last longer with a little sugar, some citric acid, and a touch of bleach to

MYTH-BUSTERS
Potting Soil Mix-Ups

Containers and window boxes are popular with flower gardeners, of course, but a lot of people misuse the potting mix that's commonly sold for such applications, says Sam Jeffries, a host of *The Garden Guys,* a popular radio program that airs in the northeastern United States. Keep these pointers in mind as you plan your containers for the season.

- Potting soil is one of those you-get-what-you-pay-for products. There's a huge difference in quality between the cheap stuff and premium potting soil.

- Many flower gardeners reuse potting mix from one season to the next. Stop that! Throw out the old mix and substitute a fresh supply. Otherwise, you run the risk of perpetuating diseases from one year to the next.

- Before potting, sterilize your container with a solution of 1 part liquid chlorine bleach to 9 parts water. Then rinse and dry.

- Soilless potting mix does not work like real soil. It contains no nutrients for your plants. Stick with regular potting soil.

- Use organic fertilizer, liquid fish or seaweed solutions, or compost tea to keep plants looking their best.

Let the Garden Shows Design Your Beds

A garden show is a great place to look for beautiful color combinations and new ways to use familiar plants. Study how garden features, pathways, and arches are used in the show garden designs. Use a notebook, and write down or draw what impresses you, in order to re-create the idea back home. This is where a camera can really come in handy, too.

For example, say you saw a flower show garden featuring a river of blue grape hyacinths edged with yellow daffodils that snaked through a very impressively designed garden. Obviously, not many gardeners have the room or the time to plant a river of daffodils and grape hyacinths. But jotting down a note in your garden notebook about such a classy plant combination may be enough to remind you to add a cluster of grape hyacinths to an existing stand of daffodils next fall.

You can also use garden show scenes as inspiration for your own designs. You may see a beautiful display of irregularly shaped flagstones meandering through a cutting garden. If you like the look of the textural stones next to the tall stems of cut-flower plants, you can "take it home" in your notebook by drawing a rough sketch of the way the flagstones fit together and were placed among the flowers. At home, perhaps you can use broken chunks of concrete or concrete pavers to lay a path in the same casual fashion in your own backyard.

The lesson to be learned here is to record what appeals to you, using any combination of written notes, photos, and drawings from your flower show visits. You can then use these great ideas to create something different, original, and often more practical than the thing you originally admired at the show.

Garden and flower shows are held all over the country. Among the biggest are the Philadelphia Flower Show, the New England Flower Show in Boston, and, in Seattle, the Northwest Flower and Garden Show. On a small scale, you can find garden shows and fairs held almost every spring weekend though-out the country at local public gardens, garden centers, and historic sites. To find out about local shows in your area, call the local garden club or your county extension agent. Both groups are usually affiliated with local shows.

discourage the growth of bacteria. So try this longevity formula: Fill your vase halfway with warm water and the rest of the way with a clear, non-diet soft drink such as Sprite. Then add 1½ teaspoons of chlorine bleach.

Or just change the water. An even easier way to extend the life of cut flowers in the vase is to change the water and snip ½ inch or so off the bottoms of the stems every day.

Trim stems underwater. If your cut flowers have hollow stems, air in the stem can prevent them from drawing water out of the vase, and the blossoms will wither quickly. So when you cut such flowers in the garden and bring them into the house, immerse the ends in a pan of water and snip the bottoms off again underwater with kitchen shears. Then place the flowers into their vase immediately. Another trick for helping your flowers draw water better: Cut the stems at a 45 degree angle.

Keep leaves out of the vase. Strip away any leaves from the stems of your cut flowers before you place them in a vase. Foliage will prompt the development of bacteria, which will age your flowers prematurely. Also, remove any dying blooms immediately. They release a gas that will degrade neighboring blossoms as well.

Keep your cut flowers hydrated. Fill a squirt bottle with water, set it on "mist," and spritz your arranged flowers daily to keep the blossoms hydrated—and therefore longer-lived. Another measure that will keep your flowers hydrated: Keep them in a cool room and away from heat sources, including sunlight.

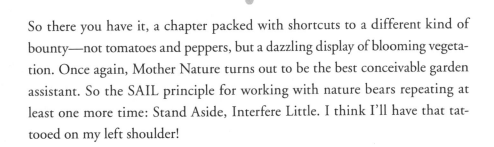

So there you have it, a chapter packed with shortcuts to a different kind of bounty—not tomatoes and peppers, but a dazzling display of blooming vegetation. Once again, Mother Nature turns out to be the best conceivable garden assistant. So the SAIL principle for working with nature bears repeating at least one more time: Stand Aside, Interfere Little. I think I'll have that tattooed on my left shoulder!

CHAPTER 9

Grass:
BRINGING PEACE *to*
the TURF WAR

‖‖‖

Felder Rushing learned to hate mowing lawns at a young age. It was sweaty, dusty work, and not only did he mow grass for his parents, he also had to mow for his grandmother and great-grandmother. So wouldn't you know he became a horticulturist, a specialist in turfgrass management, and host of radio's "The Gestalt Gardener." Now when Rushing has to mow his own lawn in Jackson, Mississippi, he reaches for little hand clippers. That's because his "lawn"—the only grass he grows—is in a container.

Oh, Rushing still has lawnlike shapes in his elaborately landscaped yard. One is a big round deck that's painted teal green, and the other is a round patch of mulched soil. Both fulfill the visual requirement for open areas in the yard. "And last time I checked, teal and brown are colors, too," he says. However, your finely tuned cheat-at-gardening sensibilities have deduced by now that no mowing, watering, or fertilizing is ever required for these "lawns." As a bonus, Rushing can sleep at night knowing that his turf is so much more environmentally friendly than a yard that requires heaps of chemicals, fertilizing, watering, and mowing to stay in shape.

I mention Rushing's yard because it illustrates how severely many of the rest of us are bound up by convention. Powerful forces indeed compel us to coddle these enormous green carpets of grass that cover our yards. Ads, TV shows, and magazine photos pelt us daily with the message that expanses of lush green are a required part of the homestead. Our neighbors do it, so we have to as well. And of course there's the all-purpose, overriding sentiment "I've always done it this way." This quixotic drive leads us to all sorts of time-wasting procedures that drain our wallets and our energy.

Am I going to tell you to bulldoze your lawn and replace it with walls, decks, fountains, and fishponds? No, that's more work than you want on your to-do list right now. Instead, I consulted a host of lawn care experts in search of some kind of balance—tips for having the kind of lawns we can feel proud

SLEIGHT *of* HAND

Save Work with a Smaller Lawn

To cut down on your lawn mowing, replace part of the lawn with groundcovers. Groundcovers can be a big help on slopes and hillsides, too, where it can be tricky or downright dangerous to mow. See the Cheat Sheet on page 125 in Chapter 5 for some suggestions on plants that make good groundcovers.

Lawns have been traditional in the United States, and we tend to just assume that we need them. But you can think outside the box. Here's the bottom line: The smaller the lawn, the less work you'll have to do to keep it up. So if you want to do less work, think about where you really need to have lawn grass. If you want grass under a picnic table or swing set, you don't need a big lawn. Use groundcovers or pavement where you don't really need grass. Then congratulate yourself from your hammock when you observe how great your yard looks with a lot less work on your part.

of without, of course, having to work very hard for them. So how can we simplify the lawn care process down to the core necessities, and what are the big misconceptions about nurturing turfgrass? Let's take a look.

WEEDS: MIND OVER WHAT DOESN'T MATTER

The ideal residential lawn, we were brought up to believe, is a smooth and deep-green continuous carpet of silky grass blades—every one of those grass plants hailing from the very same species, by the way. If you're like television's obsessive-compulsive detective Adrian Monk, the unholy amount of work required to meet such standards of perfection might seem worth the effort, time, and expense. But if you happen to be the sort of person who would, well, read a book like *How to Cheat at Gardening and Yard Work,* then you'll be glad to hear from Trey Rogers, author of the book *Lawn Geek* and professor of turfgrass management at Michigan State University: "What it takes to *keep* it green is more important than what *is* green," he says.

Preference about what mixture of plants should make up a lawn is a highly personal matter. There is no law that says your lawn must be purely of one variety, and there are no lawn police who will arrest you for practicing otherwise. (Wasn't that the plot of the movie *Blade Runner*?) So the official cheat-at-yard-work stance on lawn composition is: If it's green and it's not harming anything, then keep it.

Weeds are an inescapable fact of life. Rogers estimates that in a square foot of his own lawn he easily has 10,000 crabgrass seeds. (He keeps the turfgrass thick enough that crabgrass has trouble germinating.) So save your heart some wear and tear and quit fretting about lawn purity. And by the way, when did clover become a bad thing? It doesn't look bad, it fixes nitrogen in the soil, and it gives your kids a chance to look for a lucky four-leaf stem. If you've got it in your lawn, leave it.

Besides, grass seed that you buy at the garden center is typically a mixture of varieties anyway. You'll find a blend of quick-sprouting annual grass to provide some instantaneous green, along with the "real" perennial grass, which will mature later and stay in your lawn long-term.

Rushing calls this relaxed attitude about what's growing in your lawn the "mow what grows" approach. Rushing says "mow what grows" is more in keeping with our heritage anyway. "Meadow lawns" were once perfectly acceptable—until the companies selling fertilizer, seed, herbicides, and mowers started persuading us that meticulously manicured swaths of single-species turf were the only socially acceptable goal. "There were ads during World War II that actually claimed that if you didn't show civic pride by caring for your lawn, you were unpatriotic. Really." says Rushing.

Some of the plants we think of as weeds today served as perfectly good groundcovers in generations past, Rushing says (for instance, dichondra on the West Coast and ground ivy in the Southeast). Besides, the very definition of the word *weed* has long been debated among backyard (and front yard) philosophers, Rushing says. The conventional view is that a weed is a plant in the wrong place. Ralph Waldo Emerson observed, "A weed is a plant whose virtues have not yet been discovered." But Rushing's definition will change your lawn care outlook altogether: "A weed is any plant having to deal with an unhappy human." So if a plant in your yard doesn't bother you, "It ain't a weed—even if a neighbor or expert says it is," the horticulturist says.

LAWN CARE, TRIMMED DOWN TO THE BASICS

When you cheat at yard work, your goal is to achieve the kind of environment you can be proud of—for a minimal amount of effort. In respect to lawn care, that calls for an extremely simple, bare-bones system that will reliably result in healthy grass—turf that will make your home and landscape look great. Such a system not only must be effective, but it also must be devoid of the myths

The Lowest-Maintenance Lawn of All

For a really easy-care lawn, plant a lawn of native grasses suited to your region. These grasses are tough and undemanding, and they're naturally suited to growing conditions in your area. They might need to be left just a little bit higher than a more traditional lawn, but they're a lot less work.

Note that some lawn grasses grow in cool seasons—spring and fall—and others in warm seasons—summer. Cool-season grasses can go dormant in summer, while warm-season grasses go dormant in winter. If you live in a warm climate where you've got a lawn all year, you'll need to plant both cool- and warm-season grasses. If you live in a cool climate, a warm-season grass that grows in summer may be all you need.

Here are some native grasses to look for.

Bent grass (Agrostis): Well-drained soil; suited to meadows and woodlands; sun to partial shade; cool season

Common bluestem (Andropogon): Dry to moist soil; tolerates poor soil; warm season

Little bluestem (Schizachyrium): Dry to moist soil; adaptable; warm season

Buffalo grass (Buchloe): Dry soil; adaptable to a range of soil types, tolerates poor soil, prefers clay; tolerates drought and cold; warm season

Red fescue (Festuca): Adaptable to a range of soils; tolerates shade; cool season

Sheep fescue (Festuca): Suited to moist but well-drained soil; cool season

Blue grama (Bouteloua): Best in drier soils; tolerates drought; warm season

Sideoats grama (Bouteloua): Best in drier soils; tolerates drought; warm season

Junegrass (Koeleria): Poor soils of low fertility; tolerates drought; cool season

Sedges (Carex): Adaptable, but prefer evenly moist conditions; most species tolerate or prefer shade; not considered seasonal

Tickle grass, winter bent grass (Agrostis): Dry or moist soil; suited to open forest conditions; partial to light shade; cool season

MYTH-BUSTERS
Set Your Mower for a High Cut

It sounds like a great idea at first blush—reducing your lawn-cutting time by mowing your grass as short as possible. The longer your grass takes to grow back, the less often you have to mow, right? Actually, you're inviting a world of trouble with that approach. First of all, you're weakening the grass plants with extreme mowing—making them vulnerable to pests and disease. For optimum health of the grass, never cut off more than one-third of its height. Otherwise, you will inhibit its full blade and root development. Furthermore, longer grass can more easily crowd out the weeds that are vying for the same sun, nutrients, and moisture. The ideal height for grass depends on what variety of turf you have, but in general, 2 to 3 inches is a good height for most lawn grasses. When grasses are growing actively, aim for no more than 2 inches. In shade, drought, or other stressful conditions, go higher. If your lawn is planted with native grasses, such as buffalo grass, mow even higher—3 to 4 inches. Never mow your lawn shorter than 2 inches.

and misconceptions that cause homeowners to spend countless hours and dollars in an ill-fated quest for the perfect lawn.

Here's that system, as described by Trey Rogers, author and professor of turfgrass management. First, think of lawn management as a three-legged stool. There are three core activities—none of them difficult or particularly time-consuming—and they all work together to produce the kind of lawn you can be happy with. The three activities are mowing, fertilizing, and watering. Now, before you grab your sun hat and run outside, understand that there are a few details you need to know about each of these tasks. After all, if one of the three legs of your stool falls short—or is oversize, for that matter—the stool will be out of balance. In a lawn, that will mean pests, disease, and weeds will have a field day. (Okay, those nasties are probably present to some degree anyway, but you don't have to make life easy and comfortable for them.) So here are the simple basics you need to know about mowing, fertilizing, and watering your grass—your best shot at achieving a satisfying, low-effort lawn.

Mowing. Each time you mow, adjust your lawn mower to a height that allows you to remove no more than one-third of the grass blade (this usually means setting the mower blade at 4 to 5 inches high). This way, your grass will remain thick enough to block light from reaching emerging weeds. Furthermore, a grass plant makes its food in the parts aboveground, so a severe cut is depriving it of nourishment. Mow often, every 5 or 6 days, whether or not your lawn appears to need it. (Some lenient souls say allow 10 days at most.) The longer you let your lawn go uncut, the easier it is for weeds to creep in.

You probably recall the famous quote from comedian and film director Woody Allen: "Eighty percent of success is showing up." Well, success with your lawn is much the same and just as simple. Consistent mowing is 80 percent of the job, says Rushing.

Fertilizing. Carefully apply an organic nitrogen fertilizer to your lawn twice a year while the grass is growing. This will depend somewhat on what kind of grass you have. Cool-season grasses—that is, grasses that thrive in colder climates, such as Kentucky bluegrass, ryegrass, and fescue—like their fertilizer in spring and late fall. On the other hand, warm-season grasses—those that thrive in warm climates, such as zoysia grass and Bermuda grass—like their fertilizer in late spring and summer. Carefully follow the package directions for your fertilizer. Resist the temptation to add more fertilizer than prescribed. Overfertilizing will prompt excessive growth, which means you will be chopping off an unhealthful amount of the grass plant when you mow.

Watering. The basic rule of green thumb is that your lawn will need about 1 inch of water per week (and you have to calculate rainfall as part of that total). You may have to adjust that a tad to account for such factors as a dry or wet climate, how water-needy your type of grass is, and how well your soil holds onto the water it gets. So be prepared to observe, improvise, and adapt. Water early in the morning, so you will lose less moisture to evaporation and wind. If you water at midday, much will be lost to evaporation. If you water in the evening, the moisture could sit too long on the grass and encourage disease.

FOR YOUR LAWN, THE KINDEST CUTS

Good mowing isn't about being finicky or fanatical about your lawn. It's about establishing some simple, easy habits that pay off handsomely in the long run. Make these tips and tricks a part of your regular yard work repertoire.

Streamline your mowing. When you design your landscape or make changes affecting the layout of your lawn, remember to make the lawn mowing easy. After all, when you streamline a task that's repeated many times over, the time and effort saved build up to a considerable benefit. Here are some pointers from landscape contractor Doug Boyd of Greenville, North Carolina.

- Don't build into the lawn a lot of little island beds—or plant individual trees and shrubs scattered around the lawn—that you will have to mow around every time.

- Make sure you can mow between obstacles in your lawn, such as trees, birdbaths, bird feeders, or benches. Alternatively, simplify your mowing pattern by combining such features into a single planting bed. A bed along the outer edge of your yard, one that you don't have to mow around, is ideal.

- Avoid designing acute angles into the border of your lawn that will force you to stop, back up, and make sharp turns with your lawn mower. Rounded, soft edges are easier to mow than precise rectangles and squares with straight sides and sharp corners.

- Confine trees and shrubs to the outside perimeter of your yard, framing the lawn and providing a simple mowing pattern.

- Prune away a tree's lower branches if they interfere with efficient mowing. The pruning will also let more light reach the grass, which is good.

- When you mow, keep the discharge chute of your mower directed toward the lawn so you won't have a driveway, sidewalk, or street full of clippings to clean up later.

Measure your blade's height. It may not be readily apparent how high or low your lawn mower's blade is set, but this is important to know so you can cut your grass properly. Here's an easy way to figure out your blade's height for sure, says Peter Sawchuk, home editor at *Consumer Reports* magazine. Get a ruler and park your mower on a hard, level surface. Make sure the mower is safely shut off. Tilt the mower up and turn the blade to a spot where it's visible through the grass discharge chute. Set the mower back down, get down on your hands and knees, whip out your ruler, and measure the distance from the blade to the ground. If you use a riding mower with two sets of blades, remember to position both sets at the same height.

Many people cut their grass too low, damaging their turf in an ill-conceived quest for a putting-green-style lawn. (Remember, never mow away more than a third of the grass height.) Taller grass means deeper roots, says Sawchuk, and deeper roots mean your grass will be more resistant to heat and better at gathering moisture. (He ought to know—his company maintains 6 acres of test grass in Florida.) Ideal mowing height varies with the kind of grass you have, but 2 to 3 inches is a good bet; you can go to 4 inches if your lawn contains native grasses. When the summer starts getting hot, your grass will better weather the heat with a little more body, so allow it to grow an extra ½ inch.

SHADES OF GREEN

Let the Clippings Fall Where They May

Think about how much time and money—not to mention environmental damage—you rack up by fertilizing your lawn. Here's an easy way to lighten that duty: Trim your lawn with the kind of mower that's designed to chop up the grass into fine bits and leave it on the ground, where it will decompose and return nutrients to the soil. When you use such a "mulching mower," you can reduce by one-third the amount of fertilizer that would otherwise be recommended for your grass (grass clippings, as they decompose, add almost 2 pounds of nitrogen per 1,000 square feet of lawn). And with this approach, there's no grass-clipping bag to empty every 10 minutes!

Gas up your mower over concrete. We're creatures of habit, but sometimes accomplishing the same task in precisely the same way over and over again works against us. Think about the way you gas up your lawn mower, for instance. When you pour gasoline, there's inevitably a little spillage, notes Barbara Arnold, horticultural designer at the Franklin Park Conservatory in Columbus, Ohio. That spilled gasoline will kill your grass. So to avoid doing your lawn serious damage where you habitually gas up the mower, at the very least choose a different place in the yard every time. Even better, move your mower to a concrete sidewalk or a concrete driveway before you pour. (Gasoline will damage an asphalt driveway, so that's not a good location for filling the tank.) Best of all, use a no-spill gas can to avoid any spillage or runoff.

Peek at the dipstick. Before you start up your lawn mower, check the machine's oil level. Yes, do it every time. Nothing will wear down your mower's engine and kill it more quickly than running low on oil. Letting your lawn mower die from neglect is an expensive hassle.

Before you start, scope out the yard. Before you start mowing, take a 45-second tour of the yard. You're looking for anything you can do to prevent having to stop the mower once you have started. This means picking up bits of litter that you don't want to shred into confetti, tossing stones and sticks out of the way, and dragging any footballs or plastic dinosaurs over to the toy bin. Every time you prevent an unscheduled stop of the mower, you win TWO

SHADES OF GREEN

Clear the Air with a New Mower

Is your lawn mower 5 years old or older? Sure, you might be able to get a little more mileage out of it without spending a dime, but know this: When you *do* buy a new lawn mower, you're doing the planet a big favor, says Peter Sawchuk, home editor of *Consumer Reports* magazine. The new models spew significantly fewer emissions (in the form of exhaust that includes a hefty component of carbon monoxide) into the atmosphere.

points on your mental scoreboard. (That stands for Thinking Wins Out.) Also, check out any of the movable obstacles that you're going to have to cope with. Map out a mowing pattern that allows you to mow part of the backyard, take a break to slide the lawn chairs, the grill, and the hammock onto the trimmed turf, and then finish mowing the grass that you have freed from obstructions.

Don your armor. I know, wearing protective clothing sounds like a Pollyannaish thing to do. But prevention of injuries—even small ones—is definitely worth the effort when you consider the pain, inconvenience, and embarrassment of hurting yourself while mowing. So pull on a brimmed hat and long sleeves, and smear on the sunscreen (you don't need a lecture about skin cancer, do you?). Wear sunglasses to shade your eyes and to keep flying grit out of them, too. Wear sturdy, closed-toe shoes with a tread that won't slip on grass. And, having been stung by a number of excited bees while mowing, I recommend long pants as well.

Squirt your mower's underside. Store an aerosol can of cooking oil spray in your garden shed. Before you mow the lawn, tilt the mower over and give the cutting blade and interior housing a quick spritz. The grass blades will fall to the ground where they belong, rather than clinging to your mower.

Get a clean cut. A dull lawn mower blade will shred your grass rather than cutting it cleanly. This leaves ragged ends on your grass blades, which will turn an unhealthy brown. So keeping your mower blade sharp is one simple way to make your lawn happy, and this practice needn't be a big hassle.

For starters, keep a sharp backup blade on hand. The next time you buy a mower, purchase a second blade to store in the shed. If your current mower will last several more seasons, drop by the dealer where you bought it and get a new blade that fits your model. Check your mower owner's manual—changing the blade is generally an easy operation involving an adjustable wrench or pliers. (For safety, disconnect the spark plug wire first.) Then take the dull blade for sharpening at a mower service center. If you're lucky, they'll quickly hand you a presharpened replacement blade, just as companies do with refilled propane tanks. (As long as you have the mower tipped onto its side, take the opportunity to scrape off some of the caked-on grass clippings with a garden tool or putty knife.)

If you're handy with tools, you can sharpen your own mower blades using either a file or a sharpening wheel that attaches to a power drill or Dremel hand tool. With this approach, you don't even have to remove the blade from your mower. If you keep your sharpening tools stored near the mower throughout the summer, you won't even mind spiffing up your mower's blade every month or two—which would make a big difference in the health of your lawn, Sawchuk says.

Streamline your mowing chores. Make a quick survey of your yard and identify all of the features that force you to slow down and turn sharp, tricky angles or circles. This survey will give you a checklist of weekend mini-projects that will remove the frustrating twists and turns from your mowing. Got a birdbath in the middle of your yard? Lift it up, plop it into the middle of a flowerbed, and reseed the bare patch to restore the grass. Got a grouping of trees or bushes that you have to mow around? Cluster them together with a landscaping border (plastic edging or pavers) and fill in the interior of this space with a maintenance-free groundcover.

Let the grass dry first. Don't bother mowing your lawn when it's damp from dew or a recent rain. That whirling blade cuts more cleanly when it buzzes through dry grass, and that's healthier for the plant. What's more, wet grass trimmings tend to clump up, leaving wads of messy green inside your mower and ugly mounds of the stuff all over your yard.

Overlap as you mow. As you crisscross the lawn with your mower, you might tell yourself that you're saving a few minutes' work if each swath you cut just nudges the edge of the previous swath. No sense in mowing little sections of the lawn twice, right? Actually, you'll be much happier with the mowing job—and save yourself some repair work later—if you overlap the previously cut row by 3 to 5 inches. This gives your mower a second chance to trim those pesky little blades that originally laid flat under your mower's wheels and never got cut. It also provides a more even distribution of the grass clippings over the lawn. Trying to hurry through the job will just leave your lawn looking ragged and sloppy. If you don't go back and re-mow right away, you won't be able to stand the look a few days later as those rebellious blades stand up like a Mohawk haircut.

Capture those spring nutrients. When you mow your lawn for the first time in the season, those clippings contain more nutrients than at any other time of the year. They come with the lowest concentration of weed seeds, too. To take advantage of those attributes, make sure your clippings make it onto your compost pile, or leave the clippings on the lawn where they'll return those nutrients directly to the soil.

Give your mower a shower. When you're using a mulching mower, it's important to keep the interior of the blade housing clean, Sawchuk says. If a thick deposit of grass blades builds up inside, that crusty gunk will interfere with the cutting action. So do this: When you're done mowing for the day, shut off the mower, turn it onto its side, and wash it out with the garden hose. Every time. Some mowers now have a hose attachment site where you can hook up the water, turn on the hose, turn on the mower, and clean it all out in a flash.

Let Mother Nature sweep up after you. When you mow your grass, there's inevitably a smattering of trimmings left behind on your driveway and sidewalk. If you like making extra work for yourself, go ahead and spiff things up with a leaf blower or push broom. But if you like cutting corners, here's a can't-miss approach: When you mow, make a point of cutting next to the driveway and sidewalk first. On a hot day, there's a good chance that the offending trimmings will dry out somewhat, and therefore they'll be lighter by the time you have finished mowing the rest of the lawn. Then, with your mower still on, make a final pass up and down the driveway and sidewalk. The helicoptering blade will disperse the trimmings well enough that no one will notice. Or even better: Just leave the trimmings baking in the sun. Soon they'll be light enough that a passing breeze will do the sweeping for you. If leaving a few grass trimmings lying around offends your sensibilities, get over it—we're cheating, remember.

Trimming Back That Herbicide Habit

Being an eco-friendly kind of gardener, you don't want to add to pollution by using unnecessary chemicals on your lawn. So here are some observations from Trey Rogers, professor of turfgrass management at Michigan State University, about weeds and the herbicides that are designed to control them.

- The very best way to avoid the temptation to use weed-controlling herbicides is this: Mow, fertilize, and water your lawn properly (you'll find details throughout this chapter). The resulting lush lawn will be too thick to allow much space for weeds.

- Many people think weeds live year-round in their lawn. Nope—most weeds are annuals, meaning they complete their life cycles in 1 year and then die. However, they do leave behind their seeds, waiting to germinate when they are treated to moisture and sunshine. (But once again, they won't get any sunshine, because your properly mown grass will crowd them out, right?)

- Understand this: Anytime you use an herbicide against weeds in your grass, you're just struggling to make up for mistakes you have made in managing your lawn. Herbicides don't qualify as positive "cheating" in the way this book uses the term. Cheat-at-gardening enthusiasts use simple, low-effort maintenance procedures to prevent large and messy problems (like a weed jungle) from developing in the first place.

- Yes, there are organic herbicides on the market: Corn gluten meal, applied in early spring, is one. But here's a reality check. Organic herbicides are only effective when used in conjunction with—guess what?—proper mowing, fertilizing, and watering. Synthetic herbicides are designed for worst-case scenarios. Are you really that desperate?

Freshen up your fuel. Gasoline can deteriorate within 30 days, says Sawchuk. So don't leave gasoline in your mower long-term or over the winter. If you're going to put your mower away for winter and there's still a little gas in the tank, start the mower and run it dry instead. Or you can add some fuel stabilizer, available at home improvement stores and gas stations. One bottle of fuel stabilizer will last you several years. Park it next to your gasoline can in the shed—it will keep your fuel supply fresh for 2 years. Some models of mower now include a tiny container of fuel stabilizer in the cap of the gas tank. Vibration of the mower causes the stabilizer to dribble into the tank.

Fill up with a no-spill can. Fill your mower's gasoline tank from a no-spill can. Such gas cans are designed to prevent the inevitable overflow when you're filling your mower. The can's nozzle cuts off the flow when it senses that the tank is nearly full. By preventing fuel waste, the can easily pays for itself, Sawchuk says. No-spill cans are good for the environment, too. In the United States, no-spill cans are required in California, and at this writing other states are soon to follow.

For trimming and blowing, go electric. Tired of your fuel-driven string trimmer and leaf blower—the finicky engines, the fuel, the pollution, and the noise? Then convert to the electric versions of those tools. Models now available perform as well as their gassy counterparts, says Sawchuk. But there's one important caveat: Skip the cordless type—they aren't ready for prime time.

If the prospect of dragging a long extension cord around the yard gives you pause, here's Sawchuck's clever way to cheat: Take that 100-foot cord, make a loop in it, and drop the loop over the back of your belt, between the belt and your pants. Now your legs will do the work of hauling the cord around the yard, not your poor arms, which are busy enough.

Quit mowing in Margaritaville. Twenty-four percent of people polled by *Consumer Reports* magazine said they had been injured while mowing the lawn. Interestingly, 12 percent of the respondents said they drink beer while mowing. Hmm. Could the two statistics possibly be related?

"You can draw some conclusions from that," says Sawchuk.

Come on, folks. If you're too impaired to safely operate an automobile, shouldn't you leave the lawn mower alone, too? Cheating at yard work is all about simplicity—avoiding hassle, pain, and frustration. Injuring yourself is just the opposite. Besides, a cold brew will taste all the better when your lawn mowing is *done.*

FEEDING TIME FOR TURFGRASS

Fertilizing a lawn is not hard. But the granules packed in that heavy bag you bought at the garden store are powerful stuff—not to be taken lightly or applied casually. Here are some tips for doing it right.

Read the label—duh! Trey Rogers, the turfgrass professor, shakes his head when he thinks about it. So many home gardeners mess up their lawns by applying an inappropriate amount of fertilizer—often operating under the ill-conceived "more is better" philosophy. So they kill grass with a fertilizer overdose, or they create other horticultural havoc. "It ought to be easy," Rogers says. You'll find no-brainer directions right on the package, no matter which manufacturer you decide to buy from. Look at it this way, he says: The fertilizer makers will only stay in business if they get repeat customers. Only happy customers who find that a product works will become repeat customers. And that requires that the fertilizer makers provide easy-to-follow directions that are guaranteed to work. So you can see where this is going: Read the label, follow the directions precisely, and quit improvising.

Know your numbers. I know that cheat-at-gardening enthusiasts don't like to hold a lot of details in their heads. So here's a quick refresher course on what that series of numbers (like 7-3-2) means on the bag of fertilizer you're thinking of buying. There are three primary active ingredients in fertilizer, and each of those numbers indicates the percentage of content for each active ingredient. The first number represents the percentage of nitrogen (N), which helps your grass green up and grow. The second number represents the percentage of root-strengthening phosphorus (P). The third number represents the percentage of potassium (K), which bolsters your grass against disease and weather challenges. (The rest of the material in the package is inactive filler.)

This yellow sign means "Fertilize." If, like a zillion other homeowners, you have forsythia in your environs, let the arrival of those dangling strands of yellow blossoms serve as a reminder to fertilize your lawn, says John Mollick, a lawn care expert. This is possible because of an unhappy coincidence in nature.

Go Easy on the Phosphorus

Of the primary ingredients in lawn fertilizer, phosphorus is the most vexing, because it can run off into waterways, causing algae blooms and other ecological problems. So buy fertilizer with a very small amount of it, says Rogers.

For routine fertilizing of an established lawn, Rogers recommends fertilizer with a low phosphorus rating, such as 10-2-6, which means this product has only 2 percent phosphorus. If you're starting up a lawn from scratch, you'll need a starter fertilizer, which will contain more phosphorus.

Many communities across North America have, or are considering, restrictions on phosphorus use in lawn fertilizer. Most fertilizer makers have done a good job of lowering the phosphorus content in their products,

Rogers says. There are exceptions, however. For instance, you might run across a fertilizer that's nicknamed "Triple-19" and is labeled, as you might imagine, 19-19-19. This may be the stuff your grandpa used, but it's not a good idea for modern yard maintenance. For one thing, it's not organic. For another, it's got way too much phosphorus. (You'll notice that Triple-19 is not labeled for residential use.) Speaking of labeling, says Rogers, only apply to your lawn a fertilizer that's labeled for use on turfgrass—not gardens.

Furthermore, many lawn fertilizers contain fast-release forms of nitrogen, which will force excessive growth and can actually damage your grass. Instead look for an organic lawn fertilizer with slow-release nitrogen.

Your forsythia will begin pushing out blossoms when the ground temperature hits 55°F—which is also the wake-up call for a wide variety of weedy menaces in your lawn. So just think of forsythia as a brilliant yellow Post-it Note reminder to fertilize your grass.

Tighten up your spreading routine. There are scores of ways to mess up the distribution of fertilizer when you're using a spreader. This could burn your grass where the fertilizer is applied too heavily, or it could create odd streaking where bands of grass get too little nourishment. Here are some pointers for

MYTH-BUSTERS
Nurture New Growth

You probably envision the life cycle of a typical grass plant going something like this: It comes alive in spring, sucks up water and nutrients all summer as it pushes up stems and blades, and then dies back in late fall. Right? Well, actually, individual grass plants only live for a few weeks before they naturally die off, says Felder Rushing, horticulturist, garden author, and host of the radio show *"The Gestalt Gardener."* This means that fretting about cosmetic issues in your lawn is misspent energy. Your primary task in caring for a lawn is helping the grass to perpetually replace itself with new growth. And how do you do that? Easy: with consistent mowing, fertilizing, and watering.

• • • • • • • • • • • • • • • • • •

getting a better spread, from turf-grass professor Rogers.

- If you're not sure you can get an even distribution of fertilizer, try this: Apply only half the prescribed amount of fertilizer, moving back and forth in strips across the yard. Then lay down the other half of the prescribed fertilizer by crisscrossing the yard in the opposite direction, perpendicular to the first spreading.

- When you're not moving, turn the spreader off. When you're ready to spread, start walking, then turn the spreader on. Turn the spreader off again before you stop walking. This avoids uneven application of fertilizer.

- Early morning is a great time to spread fertilizer. There's less wind to blow fertilizer where you don't want it to go, and the tracks of your spreader will show up in the dew, helping you remember where you have already applied the product.

TACKLING TROUBLE

Hey, I never promised you a rose garden. Now and then little problems and annoyances are going to crop up in your yard. Here are low-hassle ways to deal with some of the most common woes.

Give the worst weeds the shaft. So you've decided that a lot of the plants in your yard that you once called weeds are actually welcome little green guests. But your patience and hospitality don't extend to a certain one or two showy species that mock you by springing up with thick and obvious foliage. Perhaps they even have the gall to tarnish your green carpet with a bright flower. (Did the word *dandelion* come to mind?) No worry. This still doesn't call for a chemical solution—just a simple, straight-ahead mechanical one. Drop by your garden center and purchase a hand tool known as a fishtail weeder. It's a long, shaftlike digging tool with a forked (fishtail shaped) end on its bent tip. When you spot a weed in the lawn that you just can't tolerate, your mission is to excavate as much of its root system as you can—which you will never achieve just by pulling on the aboveground foliage. Instead, drive the shaft of your weeder into the ground alongside the weed's taproot. Pull the weeder to the side, prying the roots free of the surrounding soil. Then, using your other hand, ease the plant out of the ground, roots and all. Get in the habit of grabbing your fishtail weeder before you stroll around on your routine inspection of your yard and garden, and banish those occasional bona fide weeds that you just can't leave alone.

Watch where you step. When you walk across your lawn, take a quick look back at the spots where you placed your feet. If your footprints disappear very slowly, that's a sign that your grass is thirsty. The grass blades have lost their resilience and they need water.

Reseed in cooler weather. Got some bare spots in the lawn that you want to reseed? Many homeowners fail at reseeding because they do it at the wrong time, says Jon Feldman, founder of G. biloba Gardens in Nyack, New York. New grass seed responds best to cool nights, so save this duty for spring or fall. Also, prepare the soil by raking ½ inch deep before you sow your seeds, Feldman says. Don't rake vigorously. After scattering your seeds on the prepared soil, give them a thin protective covering of straw, hay, or peat moss.

If you're reseeding in spring, try this strategic trick, says Peter Sawchuk, home editor of *Consumer Reports* magazine: Use a cheap annual grass. It will green up quickly, helping you with that brown-spot problem. Then late in the growing season, you can toss in a perennial grass that's in keeping with the rest of your lawn. The slower-growing perennial grass will be coming into its own just as the annual grass you originally planted is dying back.

Screen out the birds. When you have reseeded a patch of lawn, how do you fend off the hungry birds who think you've just laid out a smorgasbord for them? Easy. Go to your garage, haul out an old window screen, and lay it over the reseeded patch for a couple of days. Sun and moisture will get through to the soil just fine. But the birds will learn that there's no such thing as a free lunch—not there, anyway. If you have a bigger area to reseed, look into a seed-starter mat made of weed-free wheat straw. After seeding, you just roll it out and wet it.

Protect your newly planted patch of grass from scavenging birds with an old window screen. Once the grass starts to poke up through it, you can take it away.

Dig up some troubled turf. If your lawn is ailing and you want a professional diagnosis, here's a simple way to go about it, says Feldman. Use your trowel to dig up a small cross section of your troubled turf, including both vegetation and soil, and drop it into a paper cup. Then take your sample to your garden center or to your Cooperative Extension office and ask their opinion.

Take the thatch test—step on it! Thatch seems to inspire fear and loathing in many homeowners. You see them out on their lawns flailing at the grass with

MYTH-BUSTERS
Sorting Out Thatch and Clippings

Many people fear they're contributing to thatch when they leave grass clippings on the lawn instead of bagging them up. Fear not, says turfgrass professor Trey Rogers of Michigan State University. Thatch is actually a buildup of the roots and stems of dead grass plants—an entirely unrelated problem. The clippings that your mower leaves behind on the lawn are very high in moisture content. That means they rot quickly and return their nutrients to the soil. Grass clippings don't contribute to thatch at all.

● ● ● ● ● ● ● ● ● ● ● ● ● ● ● ● ● ●

rigid rakes, trying to rip up that layer of dead plant material that underlies the living blades. The truth is, thatch is actually desirable in many cases, since the proper amount can keep your soil from drying out too quickly. So why torture your own lawn, when you could be out whacking divots into the fairway of your favorite golf course instead? Here's a quick way to test whether you have a thatch problem worth worrying about: Go out and walk on the grass. (That's it—pretty tough, huh?) If your lawn feels cushy, something like walking across a plush wall-to-wall carpet in your dining room, then you have a healthy amount of thatch. However, if it feels like you're walking across wall-to-wall bedroom pillows, you have too much thatch. That much thatch can actually prevent water from reaching the soil and hydrating the live grass. Here's another check to make: Use a shovel to cut a small cross section of soil out of your lawn. Thatch that's a half-inch to three-quarters of an inch thick is ideal.

If you decide that you really do have too much thatch, leave that rake in the shed anyway. There's an easier way to reduce the thatch and, besides, your rake will injure innocent little grass plants that were just minding their own business. Go to a lawn center and rent a lawn aerator, one of those rolling drums that punches holes in the soil to admit more moisture and air. This is great for the health of compacted soil (which happens when you get too much thatch). As more moisture penetrates the earth, the thatch on top of it will rot more readily and your problem will disappear on its own.

Rub out your grubs. Grubs, little beetle larvae that munch on your lawn's roots, are another common malady. They can turn blotches of your yard brown and make them easy to confuse with parched turf. Checking is simple: Kneel down, get a firm hold on some of the affected grass, and pull it up. If the surface sod peels away like a shred of carpet, you probably have a grub problem—look for the little white C-shaped critters in the soil.

Get ahead of these pests, says Sawchuck, or they'll do major damage to your lawn. The treatment is simple and direct. Pick up a can or bag of a product called milky spore and apply it according to the package directions. In colder climates, you'll need to apply milky spore once a year for several years to wipe out your grub problem, but it can work in as little as 1 year in warmer regions. Or you can use beneficial nematodes to kill grubs of Japanese beetles and chafer beetles. Nematodes come in the form of a powder that you mix with water and spray on the lawn. The effort will be worth it. Not only will your grass cease to be the salad course for baby beetles, but other creatures (including moles, raccoons, and skunks) will no longer tear up your yard trying to get to those tasty underground grubs.

Say goodbye to fungicides. Home improvement stores track the annual ebb and flow of lawn fungi. If fungi have made serious inroads near you, your home improvement store will be displaying huge pallets laden with bags of fungicide. But if you feed your lawn with compost and other organic soil

Sniffing Out the Culprit

Turfgrass professor Trey Rogers of Michigan State University was answering questions one day on the telephone hotline run by the lawn mower engine maker Briggs & Stratton. A Colorado woman called to ask what kind of malady could have killed her lawn. The problem started out with a small patch of brown, but it had spread over the entire yard.

Diagnosing such problems is better done in person, but Rogers did his best, asking a series of questions. He determined that the grass was truly dead, not just dormant or in need of water. He also found out that the yard was hemmed in on the sides by hard barriers such as a wall, sidewalks, and the street—an intriguing clue. Rogers had read about similar cases and told the caller that he suspected an underground gas leak had killed her lawn.

The woman called back 2 hours later, greatly relieved. The gas company had indeed found a leak under her yard and was repairing it. The caller had told her husband occasionally that she smelled gas, but he kept telling her she was crazy.

A factor to keep in mind, says Rogers: Nature doesn't kill entire lawns, and it doesn't kill off grass in straight lines. When you see that, some human influence is involved.

builders, you probably won't need those fungicides at all. If you top-dress your lawn with compost every year, and give it booster feedings of seaweed and fish fertilizers, the beneficial microbes in the soil should take care of any fungi that try to invade.

Solve hillside ups and downs. When you're watering grass, it's all too easy to deprive the vegetation on the side of a slope. If you're not careful, the water will trickle to the bottom of the slope, leaving the hillside grass still thirsty. The cure is just a little trick of timing, says Rogers. Water the slope for a few minutes, turn off your hose for a few minutes to let the water soak in, and continue that pattern as necessary.

If a slope in your yard is so steep that it makes mowing tricky, Felder Rushing has the sure cure: Plant the hillside with groundcover and quit mowing it altogether. Why risk a mowing accident as the result of a slip, fall, or tip-over on that hillside?

YOUR LAWN ON THE WILD SIDE

Animals and wildlife help us connect to the natural world. All that mowing and trimming, even using the cheating methods, create a manicured—and uninviting—appearance to insects, birds, and small animals. Maybe it's time to give up the cut and shave and get a little messy.

Get a little rough around the edges. A bare expanse of closely cropped grass decorated with a small tree and pruned shrubs isn't an open invitation to wildlife. Wildlife thrives along landscape edges, where grasses and flowers give way to the shelter of shrubs and trees. Be as orderly as you need to be around your house, but allow your yard's edges to grow beyond their trimmed sizes to make them more hospitable to wildlife. Wherever you live, your land was once home to a greater variety of animals than those that visit your yard today. Even though you can't revert to a landscape of yore, you can welcome in more of nature by letting things revert to more natural forms, meaning a lot less maintenance for you anyway.

Let your lawn be a welcome mat. Even though most wildlife, especially birds, love a forest of trees, it's not realistic for homeowners to let the yard grow into a thicketed field. You can, however, make the best use of your lawn for your wild visitors. First, look for ways to create pathways for wildlife to travel through your landscape. And second, work with your neighbors to form connected greenways for birds and animals.

Get lucky with a four-leaf clover. Just a few decades ago, a clover lawn was a sign of prestige. Clover's silky green leaves and pastel flowers make delightful lawns that are soft to walk on and pretty to look at. Clover also mows well and smothers other so-called weeds. Until the 1950s, clover was as common in home lawn mixes as bluegrass is today. So let the clover be and watch the rabbits enjoy a lucky feast.

By now, maybe you have changed your outlook on what it means to even have a lawn. Let's not be slaves to tradition and fanatical ideals that no longer apply to modern life. All you need is a simple routine that will produce a fairly green and orderly lawn. You know, *House Beautiful* has never asked to do a photo shoot at my house anyway.

CHAPTER 10

Trees *and* Shrubs:
TRIMMING DOWN
the MAINTENANCE

||||||||||||||||||||||||||||||||||||||||||||||||||||||||||||||||||||||||||||||||||||||||||||||

P lanting a tree is like setting off the world's slowest fireworks show. Your tree will soar above the landscape, unfurling all of its glorious color and drawing appreciative *oohs* and *ahhs* all the while (of course, "all the while" being spread over 20 years or more).

The life span of a tree requires quite a commitment on your part. A little tomato plant that's poorly chosen or poorly maintained will fail miserably in one season and will be forgotten the next. But a poorly chosen or poorly maintained tree will heap misery, mess, and added maintenance into your life for decades to come.

Considering how large the stakes are, let's take a careful look at how to whittle complications out of your life as you choose, plant, and maintain your trees. We'll discuss shrubs a bit, too, since a lot of advice applies equally to woody plants both large and small.

DECIDING WHAT AND WHERE TO PLANT

Pop quiz: Which is the easier gardening assignment?

1.   Plant any tree or shrub you want.
2.   Find a tree that will naturally thrive on your plot of land as it is now.

Green thumb genius that you are, you chose option 2 as the easier assignment. Some homeowners have the attitude that they can grow any plant they desire—all they have to do is "fix" the soil to meet the needs of the plants they have chosen. Well, the terms of my How to Cheat license require that I point out how much work that is. For instance, to transform a heavily clay yard into ideal loam would require dump truck loads of sand and organic matter, says Master Arborist Bill Graham of Graham Tree Consulting in Doylestown, Pennsylvania. Even then it would be a temporary fix. The natural soil type will eventually reassert itself unless you constantly work on it, which runs diametrically opposed to the cheating lifestyle.

Sure, adding organic matter to your soil is going to help, but why not preserve your sanity and do that gradually over the years? As you add compost once or twice a year, the worms and microorganisms in the soil will start smiling, and their biological processes will improve the soil more and more—and you don't have to pay them for their labors! Meanwhile, you get to spend your weekends reading mystery novels and practicing your backhand on the tennis court. Once in a while, you'll decide to add a tree or shrub to your landscape, and when you do, you'll simply choose a variety that's native to your terrain or from a similar environment. If the surrounding acreage is naturally woodland, then bring in a woodland species that will immediately thrive there. If you live in a seacoast environment, stick to the menu of shore varieties. You can still have a striking, lush landscape—but forgo the fantasy of exotic species from foreign climes. That needlessly complicates your life.

Narrow your options with simple research. Don't think of research as a bother. It actually will accelerate your decision-making process immeasurably. How? Well, the number of tree varieties that are available to homeowners today is vast enough to boggle even the most orderly of minds. But not if you're methodical about your selection process. First, consider two factors that will guide your choices.

- The environmental conditions that your tree will be growing up with. These include the average lowest winter temperature, the average highest summer temperature, soil type, wetness or dryness, sun exposure, and the amount of space you have available.

- Your personal desires. You may have landscape plans that call for shade or a particular size or shape of tree, or you may have a hankering for a particular type of foliage, flowers, fall color, or bark. Or maybe you're looking for trees or shrubs to help block wind, or to help lower your household utility bills.

Gather more input. Now start building a list of candidate trees and shrubs that fit those criteria. Some places to start are your local Cooperative Extension office, a nearby arboretum or botanical garden, or a nearby college with a horticulture program (talk to the professors). Also consult any staff you trust at your local nursery, horticultural societies, and garden clubs. A good reference book to check: Michael Dirr's *Dirr's Hardy Trees and Shrubs*.

Once you have established the criteria above and eliminated the tree varieties that do not fit them, your range of options will be much narrower. And that's a good thing—a path to sanity—since choosing among a smaller number of candidates will be a much easier decision.

Go beyond the tag. Don't count on the tree tag that comes with the plant when you buy it from your nursery to tell you everything you need to know about the tree you're considering buying, says Barbara Arnold, horticultural designer for the Franklin Park Conservatory in Columbus, Ohio. With smaller plants, you often get complete planting and care information on the accompanying tag, but that's not necessarily the case with trees. Look up the tree on the Internet, read up on it at the library, and place a call to your agricultural extension office. Why would a cheat-at-gardening enthusiast go to all of that bother? Because this research will save you so much work, time, and anguish in the long run. Consider this: You wouldn't buy a car without checking out the model thoroughly, and you may only own it for 8 years or so. On the other hand, a tree could be part of your life for 50 years. Isn't finding a laborsaving variety worthwhile? "Do your homework, do your homework," Arnold says.

Know the code. You often can get clues to the shape that a young tree will grow into just from reading its botanical name (those Latin tongue twisters put in parentheses after the common names). For instance, *pendula* indicates a "weeping" form, with low-hanging branches all around. *Fastigiata* and *columnare* indicate a tall and narrow shape. *Pyramidalis* indicates, as you would

LOW-MAINTENANCE MARVELS
Easy-Care Trees and Shrubs

Some trees and shrubs are a lot less demanding than others. Here are some to consider if you want to save work. They're adaptable and tough and don't need much in the way of pruning, fertilizing, or supplemental watering.

Blue-mist shrub	Hackberry	Hedge maple
Bottlebrush buckeye	Hawthorns	Shantung maple
Box elder	Hornbeam	Trident maple
Cotoneaster	Peegee hydrangea	Redbud
Leyland cypress	Junipers	Shadblow (serviceberry)
Forsythia	Thornless honey locust	Spiraea
Golden rain tree	Amur maple	Japanese zelkova

Cheat Sheet

|||||||||||||||||||||||||||||||||||||||||||||||||||||||||||||||||||||||||||||||||||||||||||||||||||||||||||||||||||||||||

Colorful Words

Need a primer for botanical Latin? When you find the following in the botanical name for a plant, you can expect the indicated color.

Argentea: Silver

Aurea: Gold

Caerulea: Blue

Candidus or alba: White

Luteus: Yellow

Nigra or nigrum: Black

Purpureus: Purple

Roseus: Pink

Rubus: Red

Viridis: Green

---

imagine, a pyramid- or cone-shaped tree. *Globosus* means globe-shaped. And *nana* indicates a dwarf variety.

Get in the zone. You will inevitably come across a "hardiness zone" map system used by horticulturists to tell where trees, shrubs, and perennial flowers are likely to grow well. Hardiness zones are a useful tool for matching plants to climate. After all, what's the point in trying to nurture a sapling that will do nothing but struggle with your local winters and summers? A hardiness zone map divides the United States and Canada into numbered zones according to average winter minimum temperatures. The lowest number is the coldest zone in which the plant can be expected to thrive; the highest number is the warmest climate in which it will likely do well. There's now also a "heat zone" map that divides the territory into zones based on the average maximum summer temperatures. This map is especially helpful to warm-climate gardeners, for whose plants summer heat is a bigger problem than winter cold. Plant labels at nurseries are now starting to show heat zones as well as hardiness zones.

Look at the maps to find the zone numbers in your area, and use those numbers to help you choose plants suited to your climate. Your Cooperative Extension office can help you get a copy of the USDA's hardiness zone map. Or you can find the map on the Internet. The heat zone map was developed by the American Horticultural Society and is available at its Web site, www.ahs.org.

Choose a tree that fits the space. To assess the spot where you want to plant a tree, consider size and space issues as well as aesthetics, says Nick Covatta, co-owner and general manager of Eastern Shore Nursery in Keller, Virginia. Select a tree whose size will be in proportion to the surrounding space when it reaches maturity. In a wide-open area, a large tree will work best (perhaps a red maple or oak). However, let's say you want a new tree on the edge of your yard, but you don't want to totally block the view of a picturesque meadow beyond. Then a small tree is the better choice (say, American hornbeam or Allegheny serviceberry).

If your tree is going to outgrow its space in 3 or 4 years, you'll either have to move it (a big undertaking) or prune it to keep it in bounds (which takes time and work and can ruin the shape of the tree).

Plant your feet in the planting spot. Stand in the spot where you want to plant your new tree and look up, down, and all around for anything that might clash with a growing tree. Are there power lines overhead that will force you to keep your tree awkwardly trimmed back? "Nothing's worse than a chopped off tree," says Pam Geisel, coordinator of her state's Master Gardener program, based in Davis, California. Other points to consider: Is your chosen planting spot between two houses—and therefore limited in span? Are other plants or landscape features nearby, and if so, will your potential tree look good with them? Are other plants in the vicinity struggling (there could be a reason, such as stony soil)?

SLEIGHT *of* HAND

Needle Those Would-Be Thieves

Plant thorny shrubs under the windows of your home. Burglars will decide that getting in and out of somebody else's house would be a lot less painful.

Pyracantha, also known by the prickly name of firethorn, is one good choice. And it's a lot less noisy than a guard dog.

Look to the light. If the spot where you want to plant a tree or shrub gets full, direct sun, select a variety that's happy in the "spotlight." Some varieties get bleached out and struggle in full sun, says Covatta—for instance, dogwood and redbud.

Weigh the wetness issue. Finding trees and shrubs that are a good match for your soil conditions will play a big role in the health of your plantings, too, says Covatta. For instance, heavily clay soil that gets muddy and stays wet will annoy azaleas, rhododendron, and holly. On the other hand, birch, blueberry, and crab apple don't mind "wet feet" now and then.

Here's how to test how well your soil drains in the spot where you're thinking of planting. Dig a hole 1 foot wide and 1 foot deep, fill it with water, and come back in 6 hours. If there's water still left in the hole, the soil is probably heavily clay and not draining well. Either select a tree or shrub that likes these conditions, add organic matter to the soil (the labor-intensive option), or find another spot for your new plant.

Drop by a tree "showroom." You go to an automobile showroom to test-drive the model of car you're thinking of buying, right? For the same reason, drop by an arboretum when you're trying to decide what variety of tree to buy for your yard. At a local arboretum—not one you visit while traveling—you will be able to witness how well a broad range of trees thrives in your particular climate. Only by standing next to a mature specimen can you fully appreciate what it might be like to have that variety in your yard. No picture book, magazine, or Internet browsing can compare to the direct experience.

Use trees to save energy. Thoughtful selection and placement of your trees and shrubs will help you trim down your heating and cooling bills, says Master Gardener coordinator Pam Geisel. Trees that are positioned to shield your home from the prevailing wind will help your house retain heat in winter and cool air in summer. Place deciduous trees (the type that lose their leaves in fall) on the west and south sides of your house. On the west side, you want low branches that will block the low-angled rays of the sun. On the south side, you want trees with a broader-spreading canopy to block the higher-angled rays of the sun. How about the east side? Doesn't matter much, says Geisel, but remember that

Cheat Sheet

The Wet Set

Want to park a tree or shrub in that soggy corner of your yard? Here are some that don't mind such conditions.

Alder

Ash

Azalea

River birch

Blueberry

Box elder

Buttonbush

Chokeberry

Clethra (summersweet, sweet pepperbush)

Bald cypress

American elder

Fringe tree

Inkberry

American larch

Sweet bay magnolia

Red maple

Swamp white oak

Dawn redwood

Sycamore

Tupelo

Winterberry

---

smaller deciduous trees will allow more morning light into the house. The advantage of deciduous trees is that they are bare throughout the winter and allow more sun to warm the house. On the north side of your house, evergreen trees and shrubs will add a nice layer of insulation to your home.

If you want to be even sneakier in your selection of deciduous trees, pick varieties that leaf out precisely when you need their shade most. If your summers get oppressively hot early in the season, then you want early-leafing trees to provide quick cover. If summer doesn't really start cooking until late in the season, then late-leafing varieties make more sense. Now, information about the foliation period of a tree is not always easy to obtain from your nursery. You might have to watch in your neighborhood for trees that leaf out at the ideal time. A couple of hints: Ginkgos and sunburst locusts are known to leaf out late and to retain their foliage late as well.

Shade your compressor. Position trees and bushes so that they shade the compressor of your central air conditioner. Compressors that are kept out of direct sunlight are 10 percent more efficient at cooling.

Does your tree love to litter? Here's a revelation for you: Trees are not cats. They will never use a litter box—they just shamelessly dump their "business" right where they stand. So before you position a tree where it will overhang a patio, deck, walkway, driveway, pond, or roof, find out what kind of litter your chosen variety is known to drop, says Geisel. This information could save you countless hours of cleanup duty in the future—sweeping, raking, leaf blowing, pressure washing, car washing, scrubbing, gutter cleaning, and more. For instance, in Geisel's neck of the woods (ha-ha!) the Chinese hackberry was introduced. It's praised as a fast-growing, drought-tolerant shade tree, but unfortunately it attracts a species of aphid that prompts leaves to drip a sticky liquid all over the place—stuff you don't want on your deck or car.

So if you must have a famously messy tree (catalpa and evergreen magnolia are other examples), park it in a remote corner of your yard where its droppings will do no damage and will not add to your to-do list. While you're checking a tree's résumé, find out how pest resistant your chosen variety is, too. If a tree has known, persistent pest problems, that means nothing but work and misery for you in the future—so why plant it at all? A good nursery or your agricultural extension office can suggest plenty of pest-resistant (and therefore low-maintenance) varieties.

Let trees assume their natural forms. Pruning is work. If you let trees and shrubs grow to their natural shapes and sizes instead of clipping them into globes and pyramids, or pruning them every year to keep them small enough for a too-small space, you save many hours of labor.

Mix speedy growers and slow growers. Sure, we have a culture of instant gratification. So it's particularly tempting to select trees that are advertised as fast growers. You may think: "Wow, my landscape plans will come to fruition overnight!" Unfortunately, trees that grow quickly tend to have weaker wood and lose their branches more easily. They just generally don't last as long as slower growers. Here's a wiser approach that will accelerate your landscape development without inviting undue risk: Plant a mixture of fast-growing and slow-growing trees. This way, the stolid slow growers will ensure that your landscaping survives far into the future, while those fast

Cheat Sheet

Trees and Shrubs That Misbehave

The following trees and shrubs are renowned for the messy debris they drop in your yard.

Crab apple: Lots of small fruits

Catalpa: Long, leathery seedpods

Black cherry: Messy fruit

Chinese chestnut: Lots of flower catkins in summer and nuts encased in prickly burrs in fall

Ginkgo: Females' stinky fruit

Mimosa: Seedpods

Monkey puzzle tree: Loads of spiny seed cones

Mulberry: Messy fruit that stains

Pin oak: Lots of acorns

Osage orange: Females' many large, heavy, messy fruits

Paulownia (Princess tree): Little winged seeds released in huge quantities from fruit

Plane tree: Generally messy leaves, twigs, and fruits

Sweet gum: Spiky seed balls

Black walnut: Nut husks that stain black when opened or damaged

Willow: Lots of small leaves as well as branches

And these trees and shrubs are invasive, taking over and crowding out other more desirable plants.

Japanese barberry

Scotch broom

Buckthorn

Chinaberry

Chinese tallow tree

Blue gum eucalyptus

Bush honeysuckle

Black locust

Melaleuca (cajeput tree)

Paper mulberry

Autumn olive

Russian olive

Paulownia (princess tree)

Brazilian pepper

Australian pine

Chinese privet

Multiflora rose

Tamarisk

Tree of heaven

---

growers mixed in will bring your plans to maturity more quickly. You get the best of both worlds!

Avoid a formal hedge. Instead of a classic hedge that needs regular shearing and clipping to look its best, go for an informal screen of trees or shrubs to provide privacy or mark a property line. Leyland cypress, arborvitae, and others can be planted in a row and left to their own devices. See the Cheat Sheet below for more good screening plants.

Diversify your tree choices. A cultivar is a variety of a tree species that has been propagated by humans in order to preserve specific traits (the term *cultivar* derives from *cultivated variety*). These preserved traits often translate into less grief and maintenance for the owner—for instance, great branch structure, disease resistance, pest resistance, and tolerance of certain climatic conditions. The variety is copied again and again, each time creating a genetic duplicate, usually by means of an asexual propagation technique such as grafting or budding.

Careful selection of the right cultivar is clearly a good cheat-at-gardening-and-yard-work strategy. However, overreliance on the most popular cultivars could lead to trouble in the future, says Master Arborist Graham. If you fill up your landscape with one of the cultivars that's selling like hotcakes—say the Red Sunset red maple—then you could be exposing those trees to unnecessary risk of blight. If a disease eventually surfaces, it could wreak havoc on your favored cultivar, spreading quickly among your trees (as happened with

Cheat Sheet

Trees and Shrubs for Screening

All these trees and shrubs make good screens that give you privacy without the bother of clipping and shearing a formal hedge.

Abelia	Hollies	Oleander
Arborvitae	Box honeysuckle	Osmanthus
Leyland cypress	Hornbeam	Photinia
Slender deutzia	Junipers	Pittosporum
Evergreen euonymus	Cherry laurel	Bridal wreath spiraea
Forsythia	Hedge maple	Yew

Dutch elm disease). The commonsense solution: Mix up your tree choices. Protect your landscape with genetic diversity and don't rely too heavily on one cultivar.

Beware those unruly roots. Some shade trees have root systems that are infamous for damaging sidewalks, walls, drain fields, water lines, sewer lines, and foundations. So there's more to think about than aesthetics when you're selecting a variety and deciding where to plant it. Some common troublemakers: crab apple, willow, poplar, ash, elm, and maple. Plant them far from any structures that will tempt them to misbehave.

Plant a shrub that lights up a gray winter. For the earliest, easiest to grow flowering shrub, try witch hazel—it blooms in February or March, before even many bulbs, and lights up a dreary landscape. It's easy to take care of, too. And the flowers are fragrant!

Don't let shrubs get lonely. Planting a lone shrub by itself in the yard is a common mistake, says horticulturist Arnold. This treatment invites extra maintenance duties, because the shrub is an added obstacle for your lawn mower. Also, it's a pain when you have to mulch and weed multiple separate locations around your landscape. Instead, group shrubs together in beds so you don't have to mow around each one, and cover the soil with mulch so you don't have to pull a lot of weeds. Another great lower-maintenance way to use your shrubs: planting them together with "friends"—perennials—in a larger mixed bed or border.

NURSERY SCHOOL: PICKING A TREE 101

Caring for young trees is a lot like caring for young children, says Master Arborist Graham. When you catch problems early, you have time to correct many of them. If you let problems go, those problems magnify as the tree

Cheat Sheet

||||||||||||||||||||||||||||||||||||||||||||||||||||||||||||||||||||||||||||||||||||||||||||||||||||||||||||||

Shrubs and Small Trees for Beds and Borders

If you want to make a mixed bed or border that combines trees or shrubs with perennial flowers, here is a dozen of each you can consider.

SMALL TREES

Red buckeye	Japanese maple	Crape myrtle
Dwarf conifers	Paperbark maple	Serviceberry
Fringe tree	Three-flower maple	Carolina silver bell
Pineapple guava	Texas mountain laurel	Japanese snowbell

SHRUBS

Azaleas	Butterfly bush	Hollies
Beautyberry	Camellia	Japanese kerria
Blue-mist shrub	Clethra	California lilac
Boxwood	Gold-dust plant	Persian parrotia

grows and they become harder to fix. Having those problems in a mature tree will mean much more labor, expense, and anguish for you—and as cheaters at gardening and yard work, we certainly want to avoid that. So let's look at how to select a tree that will give you minimal trouble in the future, and how some simple care in a tree's early years will help it burgeon into the spectacular and trouble-free feature you were hoping for in your landscape.

You may be shocked to read this, but growing trees and selling them to homeowners is an industry. In a business, such concepts as efficiency and mass production often take priority over concepts like quality and the health of the trees being grown and sold. The young trees that you find on sale at a nursery may have suffered root, trunk, and branch damage in order to make them easier to harvest, ship, and package. This is not always the case, however, so you as an informed consumer get to vote with your wallet to encourage higher quality.

Graham's global advice for buying trees: Don't go to a nursery and buy problems. And if you do bring home a tree with problems, make sure the problems are correctable. So here are some points of quality to look for as you browse among trees at the nursery.

Check the quality of the cuts. On the tree you want to buy, take a look at the spots where branches have been trimmed. Right at the base of any branch, where it attaches to the trunk or to a preceding branch, you'll see a circular swelling called the collar. A cut made to prune off a branch should never damage the collar. If the collar is left intact, the tree will emit its own preservatives that prevent decay in the wound, Graham says. A damaged collar exposes the tree to rot and disease.

Another indication of a properly cut branch: A solid ring of closing tissue will grow around the perimeter of the cut. If a branch was cut flush to the trunk, damaging the collar, the closing tissue will grow in an incomplete ring, leaving vacant spots that can develop into cracks, decay, or disease.

Favor branches that truly spread out. Look for a tree with branches well dispersed about the trunk. When too many branches emerge from the same area of the trunk, subsequent cracking, dead spots, and weakness can develop as the branches get bigger. So look for two different kinds of spacing on the trunk—radial spacing (that is, the branches do not all point in the same direction) and vertical spacing (most branches do not attach to the trunk at the same height). Good spacing will create a balanced look for your tree, and it will also allow beneficial airflow among the branches, making life tougher for potential diseases. It's good to have 12 to 18 inches between branches on a young tree, says Geisel, coordinator of California's Master Gardener program.

On the other hand, if you happen to live where summers are dry and hot, too much moisture among the interior branches of a tree is not an issue. In that case, you and your tree will benefit from thicker foliage and the shade it provides.

Play the right angles. Look for a wide angle where branches meet trunk, too. Ideal branches shoot off at a 90-degree angle from the trunk (in other words, perpendicular to it). Nature's not always that precise, though, so a 45-degree or greater angle will do. Trees with branches too sharply angled, like many Bradford pears, are more likely to break in storms or under heavy snow or ice.

Keep an eye on thickness. Ideally, a branch should not be thicker than one-third the diameter of the branch it departs from. Otherwise, the spot where the branches join will grow weak.

Stick to a single stem. Many trees are strongest when they have a single, dominant trunk (which horticulture types call a leader or stem) from bottom to top. A tree that splits into two main trunks in a V shape is headed for big structural and health problems as it matures. This co-dominant stem, as it's called, can be corrected by pruning one of the trunks away while the tree is small. If you have a choice, it's even better to sidestep this problem by not buying such a tree in the first place.

Know your roots. Trees are sold to consumers in three different forms, depending on how their roots are packaged. Here are points you should know about each type.

- **Bareroot:** As the term implies, these trees (usually small ones) are sold with no growing soil encasing the roots. Just before planting, trim away any damaged sections of root, cutting straight across the root with sharp shears.

- **Rootballed or balled and burlapped:** Here, the rootball of the tree is wrapped in fabric (often burlap) and a wire basket. Understand that as much as 90 percent of this tree's roots were trimmed away in preparing it for sale. The tree will have to devote more time and resources to rebuilding its root structure.

- **Container-grown:** These trees are sold in plastic pots or tubs. While this is the more advantageous way to purchase a young tree, containers are not

A twin, or "co-dominant," trunk will develop into a serious weakness as the tree matures. Prune away one of the trunks early in the tree's life.

without problems. Roots that outgrow the confines of their pot will turn and start to grow in a spiraling pattern that can eventually strangle the plant. While it's rare to find a container tree that *isn't* potbound to some extent, Graham says, the condition is curable (more on that in a moment).

So it's a good idea to check the condition of a container tree's roots before you buy. To do this, press in enough on the sides of the container to loosen the soil. Then anchor the container between your feet, grasp the tree by the base of its trunk, and pull up gently to inspect the condition of the roots. This is a reasonable inspection for a buyer to make in a nursery, and if a clerk objects to the procedure, reply that you won't buy unless you can check the root system, says Graham. The same root inspection technique will work for smaller woody plants as well, though tangling roots is less of a problem among shrubs sold in containers.

Make sure trees show their flare. At the very base of any tree's trunk you will find a spot where the trunk spreads as it meets the root system. This sensitive part of the tree, called the root flare, should not be covered by dirt, mulch, or fabric. If a nursery tree you want to buy has its root flare covered, gently remove the covering and check the flare for injury or insect damage.

Buy good trees and shrubs in small packages. If you want a tree that will mature more quickly in your yard, you would want to give it a head start on growth, right? So would you invest in the largest tree of your chosen variety that you can find at the nursery? Unfortunately, too many homeowners make this mistake—the "bigger is better" kind of thinking, says Geisel. In truth, the larger a tree or shrub is when you buy it, the more likely it is to be rootbound or to have other root structure issues, and the harder a time it will have adapting to its new home in your yard. Besides, once they are planted, the trees and

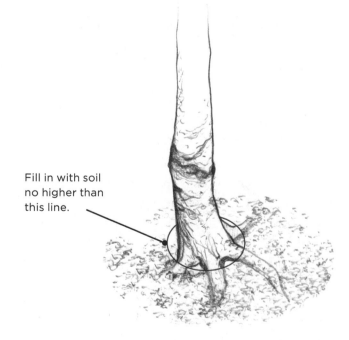

Fill in with soil no higher than this line.

The sensitive widening where trunk meets roots, the root flare, should be free and clear of mulch, burlap, and any other covering.

shrubs that come in smaller containers will quickly catch up with plants that come in larger containers. All of the larger trees' struggle and expense will have been for naught.

INTRODUCING TREES AND SHRUBS TO THEIR NEW DIGS

Perhaps this is how you were taught to plant a tree: Dig an enormous hole, line the bottom with a few inches of gravel, place the tree in the hole, and fill the rest of the hole with a mixture of compost and dirt. That approach is just rife with misconceptions, unnecessary work, and counterproductive measures, says Geisel. Here's how to start your new tree out on the right foot—er, root.

- Dig your planting hole two to three times the width of your new tree's rootball. This creates a broad area of loosened earth that your tree's roots can easily penetrate horizontally.

- Don't dig your planting hole any deeper than the height of the rootball. This will give the rootball a nice base to sit on, and it ensures that the rootball won't sink below the surface after planting.

- One caveat to the note above: If you discover that there's a hard, compacted layer of clay within 2 feet of the ground's surface, use a pick or shovel to dig through that tough layer. Don't return that clay to the planting hole. Instead, backfill the hole with the "native soil" (the original, looser dirt) that you removed, so that the top of the rootball when planted will be flush with the surface of the ground. Water this soil to let it settle before you place the rootball on it. Now the new tree's roots will be able to penetrate downward as well as laterally.

- Once the tree is in position, fill in the rest of the hole with the native soil. Contrary to common practice, there's no need to blend compost or other organic matter with the native soil. Research shows that the organic matter contributes nothing to the development of the new tree, says Geisel, although it's fine for planting new shrubs.

Here are more tricks for planting trees and shrubs that will save you time, energy, and money in the long run.

Plant in fall. It's human nature to start thinking about gardening and yard work in spring, when the weather warms up and the outdoors comes alive again. That's why most people plant trees and shrubs in spring. And human nature kicks in again when summer rolls around. That's when people start to neglect their watering duties, dealing their new trees and shrubs a serious blow. There are a couple of solutions to such episodes of Brown Thumb Syndrome, says Virginia nurseryman Nick Covatta. First, make fall your official tree- and shrub-planting season. In fall, the aboveground parts of woody plants are starting to shut down for winter and their water needs are less acute—so your neglect will have less of an impact. Furthermore, fall is prime time for tree and shrub root growth. In the cooling weather, these plants go about building a bigger "pantry" in their root system, socking away food generated aboveground as well as nutrients absorbed from the soil.

A second tactic for combating neglect of your watering duties: Provide any new trees and shrubs with a good, automated irrigation system, which will

MYTH-BUSTERS
When Everyday Dirt Needs No Help

You've made a significant investment in your new tree and you want to do everything possible to ensure its health and vitality. So surely a dose of fertilizer in that planting hole will help your newcomer along, right? No, save yourself the money and effort, says Pam Geisel, coordinator of California's Master Gardener program based in Davis, California. Research shows that everyday lawn or garden soil is perfectly fine for a new tree. The only time you might need fertilizer, she says, is when your soil has some definite nutritional deficiency—say if it's mostly sand.

whittle your watering chore down to nothing. An inground system of soaker hoses or drip lines that allows water to soak right down to the root zone is better (and a more efficient user of water) than a system of pop-up overhead sprinklers.

Untangle those twisting roots. If you take a container tree home and find that it's potbound, all is not lost. (Perhaps you were surprised by the condition of the tree's roots once you removed them from the container, or perhaps you were aware of the problem when you bought an otherwise perfect tree—knowing, as you do now, that potbound roots are correctable with a little effort.) Here is Master Arborist Graham's technique for fixing potbound tree roots.

Remove the tree's rootball from the container and set the tree on your lawn. Turn on the garden hose and with a gentle spray wash all of the dirt out of the rootball so nothing is left but bare roots. With your fingers, gently unwrap the roots and spread them out in a circle. Dig a wide, shallow planting hole for your tree—wide enough to contain the spread-out roots and deep enough (a few inches) to allow the roots to lie just under ground level. You also want the tree's root flare (the expanding part of the trunk where it meets the roots) to sit just aboveground. Set the tree in the middle of the hole and spread the roots out in a circle (you'll need a helper to steady the tree while you do this). Anchor the roots by placing rocks on top of them. Then cover the roots with 2 inches of native soil (the stuff you originally dug out of the hole). If the tree is unstable, use stakes and guylines to support it briefly (3 months ought to do it), until the ground is firm and the plant is anchoring itself. When staking the tree, allow some give in the guylines so the tree's trunk can flex a bit in the wind—it'll get stronger that way.

This technique puts the roots of your new tree into contact with the native soil immediately. The tree would have to struggle for at least several months to accomplish that on its own, so this trick puts your new tree off to a good start in its new environment. Understand that removing all of the dirt from a tree's rootball is extremely stressful for the plant. Once planted, it will need to be babied and watched carefully for at least a few months.

A landscape contractor planting a potbound tree in your yard would likely consider this technique to be too much work and would just plop the rootball into the ground, strangling roots and all. Visionary that you are, you realize that you're able to salvage just the tree you wanted for a small amount of effort—and you didn't have to settle for the wrong tree.

When digging, make one dirt pile. When you're digging a hole in which to plant your new tree, here's a trick that will save you some aggravation, says horticulturist Arnold. Shovel the dirt you dig up into only one pile, rather than spreading it around the hole in a circle or dumping it in several piles. Why does that matter? Because if the loose dirt is spread around the hole, you will inevitably walk on it and grind the dirt into the lawn. If the dirt is in one pile, you have lots of room to maneuver as you plant the tree. The other option, and one that landscapers use, is to shovel the dirt onto a plastic tarp. Then you can pull the tarp around to wherever you need the dirt.

Good landscapers know these tricks, Arnold says. Watch a group of them planting trees sometime—you can easily distinguish the experienced landscapers from the interns, who pile the dirt willy-nilly around the planting holes.

Trim half the wire and burlap. Here's Arnold's trick for planting trees that come with the rootball wrapped in wire and burlap: Set the rootball into your planting hole. Mix a little compost with the soil you removed from the hole, and start returning that dirt to the hole—filling only one-third of the way up. Use wire cutters and shears to remove the wire and burlap from the rootball only from the halfway point up—leave the rest in place to hold the rootball together. Then fill in the rest of the hole with the remaining dirt, and add just ½ inch of soil across the top of the rootball (but not touching the trunk). Note two exceptions to this technique: Some "burlap" is actually made of plastic. If you get a tree or shrub wrapped with that, you need to remove it as much as possible before you plant—it will not decay in soil and can keep roots from expanding. And while it's rare these days, if you happen to get blue-green burlap, remove this stuff entirely. Such burlap is treated against decay, and roots have trouble penetrating it.

Have an assistant hold the trunk. As you're filling the planting hole around the rootball of your new tree, make sure the tree is straight. (Yup, some people neglect this "fine point.") You can probably eyeball "straight" for yourself, but it will help if an assistant is holding the tree still. This allows you to step back and look at the orientation of the trunk from a distance. It also keeps the tree from tilting as you work to push the dirt around it.

Keep mulch away from the trunk. You often will see a new tree planted with an enormous mound of mulch heaped against its trunk. The owner's heart is in the right place, since properly placed mulch will help the tree. But neither soil, mulch, nor anything else should cover the base of a new tree's trunk, Graham says. You could actually be mulching your tree to death. A tree's root flare—the widened spot where the trunk meets the ground—is a particularly sensitive part of the tree. Mulching over the flare or burying the flare in soil will hold moisture against the tree and make it vulnerable to rot and disease. Also, mulch placed directly against the trunk of a tree will provide a hiding spot for mice and bugs. Mulching around your tree is okay, but a uniform circle of mulch 2 inches deep and 10 feet wide is plenty.

Graham bemoans a practice called "volcano mulching"—piling up a huge cone of mulch directly against the trunk of a newly planted tree. "Very bad," Graham says, "and not particularly attractive anyway." One theory holds that the practice is encouraged by mulch suppliers who want to sell more of their product. (So cynical!)

Find the ground-level marker. Any new tree or shrub should be planted at exactly the same depth it was growing in the nursery. You usually can tell which part of the tree or shrub was underground in the nursery pot. The underground part will be darker—that's your ground-level marker.

Keep competing plants at bay. When you plant a new tree, keep the ground free of other plants 2 to 3 feet out from the trunk. This includes lawn grass, bedding plants, groundcover, and, of course, weeds. Newly planted trees are in a delicate state as they try to get their roots established, and other plants—grass in particular—can be tough competitors for water and nutri-

Taking a Peek at Underground Water

Master Arborist Bill Graham, of Doylestown, Pennsylvania, recalls the time his son planted a dogwood tree in clay soil, which it's not perfectly suited to. When the tree started to wilt, there were two most likely problems: Either the tree was getting too *little* water, or it was getting too *much* water. Naturally, with the rootball beneath the surface, it was impossible to tell which was the case.

Graham instructed his son to take a posthole digger and dig a hole directly outside the dogwood's rootball. The hole went deeper than the rootball itself, down to the sandy layer of soil several inches below. Excess water that had collected around the tree's rootball promptly drained into the hole—evidence that the tree was getting too much water rather than too little. He was then able to scoop some of the excess water out of the hole and toss it elsewhere in the yard. Graham's son left the hole open for a few days so he could monitor the tree's water needs while it returned to health.

If you want to monitor the needs of a new tree in your landscape, here's another easy way to do it. When you place your new tree's rootball into its hole, before you fill in dirt around it, stick a narrow section of PVC pipe into the hole. The pipe should be tall enough to touch the bottom of the hole and extend a few inches above ground. (A 14- or 18-inch pipe will probably do it.) Then fill in the rest of the hole with dirt. When the tree's soil is saturated with water, some will collect in the bottom of your PVC pipe. When you want to assess your tree's water needs, slide a dowel or bamboo stick down to the bottom of the pipe. Then pull your "dipstick" back up. If the stick shows water on its end, the tree has plenty of moisture. If it's dry, give the tree a drink.

ents. Grasses, many of which originated in a tough prairie environment, can emit chemicals that interfere with competitors' development. (Talk about a turf war!) The mulching method described above will help discourage competing plants and will help hold moisture in the soil at the same time.

If possible, skip the stakes. You see it so frequently around the neighborhood—newly planted trees held rigidly in place by two or more guylines staked into the ground. You would be forgiven for thinking that staking trees is advisable—heck, it looks so thoughtful, caring, and protective. People are even careful to pad the guylines so they won't damage the tree bark. But staking new trees is rarely necessary and often will damage the tree, says Master Arborist and tree consultant Graham. Here's why: A growing tree will develop in response to the forces it's subjected to—in much the same way that your biceps will swell when you lift dumbbells regularly. So when a tree sways in the occasional breeze, it develops a larger supportive root flare at the base of the trunk. If you attach guylines to the tree halfway up the trunk, that's the spot where the flare will develop—not at the bottom, where the support will be needed long-term.

In most cases, your new tree will come with a firm enough grip on its soil that you can forgo staking altogether. There are a few circumstances when staking will help, but in such cases only leave the stakes in place for a short time—say, a few months. A bareroot tree (one that comes with no soil in the rootball) might be unstable enough in its new home that temporary support is a good idea. Likewise, a tree planted in muddy ground in the winter might need stake support until the ground has firmed up (probably by midsummer).

If you must stake a tree, don't install guylines that hold the tree rigidly in place—provide some slack that allows the tree to move some. Instead of the conventional guyline (wire covered with sections of hose for padding), use a straplike material for guylines instead. Attach the lines loosely, not tightly. If at all possible, use only one stake and guyline to prevent the tree from falling in the direction that it's leaning or in the direction of the prevailing wind. After the supports have been in place for a few months, remove them and test the tree's stability. If the tree still needs support, re-install the stakes for a few more months.

Sometimes a landscaping company will plant a new tree with stakes in place, but it will fail to tell the homeowner when to remove the supports—so they stay in place indefinitely, stunting the tree's development, Graham says.

THE KINDEST CUTS: PRUNING, PROTECTING, AND MAINTAINING

Plopping your new tree or shrub's rootball into the ground and watering it isn't enough. There's a bit more to maintaining your new plant—pruning in particular. Pruning is not just an aesthetic matter (getting the tree to grow into the shape you happen to like best). More important, proper pruning trains your tree to grow in the most healthful pattern and heads off future structural problems. Most of this pruning should take place during the first 7 years that you have your new tree—the first 3 years in particular, Geisel says. If you allow your trees and shrubs to grow into their natural forms rather than trying to force them into other shapes, you'll have less pruning to do than if you choose to shape them every year. The end goal, if you want to minimize pruning chores, is to prune well-established trees and shrubs only to remove dead and damaged wood and to get rid of suckers and water sprouts.

But left to their own devices, young trees sprout branches and shoots in all sorts of weird places and at inadvisable angles, destined to grow weak and damage-prone. Your job as the new tree's owner is to develop a strong "scaffold" system for it (think of it as a skeleton), Graham says. Ideally, you will make most of your corrective cuts during the time it takes your new tree to get established in its new location—and possibly for several years afterward. During the establishment period, your young tree is replacing the roots it lost when it was dug up at the tree farm and transplanted—it's reaching into the soil that lies beyond its original rootball. The basic form and structure of the tree emerges during this time. The length of this establishment period depends upon the size of the tree at the time of planting—the smaller it was, the more quickly it will recover. So here's a rule of thumb: For every inch of trunk diameter at the time of planting, it will take your tree 1 year to establish itself. So a new tree with a 1-inch-thick trunk (called a 1-inch caliper in the nursery trade) will take 1 year to establish itself.

After this establishment period, your tree-pruning duties become even lighter (unless you have decided that you enjoy shaping your tree every year). From that point on, all you need to do is assess your trees once a year for maintenance trims and to watch for damage or disease. Better yet, make quick inspections part of your normal routine as you walk about your landscape—"part of the whole gardening thing that you do," Graham says.

Don't just start clipping and snipping at your tree willy-nilly. Rule No. 1 is that you should have a reason for every pruning cut that you make. Here are some core pruning guidelines that will save you wheelbarrow loads of grief as your trees mature.

Reduce pruning duties by buying the right tree. As it often happens, your first opportunity to save a huge amount of work comes very early in the process—when you decide what kind of tree to plant. As discussed previously, the wise way to buy a tree is to first analyze your landscape and establish what role your new tree will play and where it will be planted. (You know—does the tree need to provide shade, color, privacy, and such? What shape are you looking for? How big should it be at maturity? And what soil conditions and climate will your tree have to cope with? Many homeowners fall in love with a particular variety of tree—perhaps a tree they discovered on vacation or saw in a magazine—and buy it for their own yards, determined to make the plant work in their landscape no matter what. These homeowners, apparently, enjoy long hours of work, struggle, anguish, and eventual failure.

But here's the sane path: Choose a tree that will fill your predetermined role precisely when it matures. If your landscape plan calls for a pyramid-shaped shade

MYTH-BUSTERS
Don't Be So Eager to Prune

Many people prune trees as soon as they are planted, on the theory that this helps the tree cope with root loss. That's a misconception, says the International Society of Arboriculture. Young trees need their leaves and shoot tips, so don't start corrective pruning until the second or third year in your yard. One kind of pruning you *can* do right after planting is the removal of any damaged limbs.

Sending Trees to an Early Grave

Pam Geisel, who coordinates California's Master Gardener program, was once called to a cemetery in her state to try to figure out what was ailing some of its prized trees. The cemetery had invested a considerable amount of money in 600 Chinese pistache trees, a beautiful ornamental shade variety that's known for great color and pest resistance. Some were planted in turf and others were placed in flowerbeds. Each was fitted with a heavy plastic collar around its base to protect its trunk. The groundskeepers tried giving the trees more water, but that didn't help the ailing trees. So they tried giving them *less* water—still no good. They tested the soil and checked for herbicide damage, and found nothing amiss. The cemetery operators were stumped, so to speak.

At the cemetery, one clue quickly emerged. The failing trees were the ones that had been planted in the midst of grass. (Geisel recommends leaving a plant-free zone around the base of young trees.) Investigating further, Geisel lifted up one of the protective collars around the base of a tree to inspect the trunk. She was shocked to find that the failing tree had been "girdled"—that is, stripped of bark around its trunk. Such damage often kills a tree. It turns out that workers cutting the cemetery's lawn had been lifting the protective collars and cutting the surrounding grass with string trimmers—which also stripped the tree bark. So the mystery was solved, but the cemetery lost about half of its cherished trees.

tree that's no more than 20 feet tall, then choose a variety that will grow into that exactly. A zillion varieties are available, and some of them are precisely what you want. Buying a tree that will grow larger than you want, or into a different shape than you want, means that you will spend hours *every year* pruning to re-shape that tree. You see, a tree will keep trying to grow into its genetically determined size and shape. If you tell yourself, "That's okay—I can shape it into the form that I want," well, that's no easier to do with trees than it is to do with spouses. The more you interfere with a tree's shape and size, the more work you will have to put into maintaining that shape and size in the future. Here's an illustration: Graham lets most of the trees in his own yard "do their own thing" with minimal pruning. However, he did decide to prune a crab apple tree to control its size. He calculated that over 14 years, he spent an entire day each year pruning that tree—2 full weeks spent maintaining the shape of one tree! Graham is a tree professional and didn't mind coddling his own baby. On the other hand, *you* can probably think of better ways to spend 2 weeks of your life.

If you do need to prune to establish a good branch structure for your young tree, look back at the tips starting on page 285 for guidance.

ZERO-MAINTENANCE MARVELS

A Cut Above: First-Class Pruners

If you're going to work with trees and shrubs in your yard, keep a pair of sturdy, high-quality pruners on hand at all times. With pruners at your fingertips, you will always be ready to make those impromptu trims that would otherwise be forgotten. You can't go wrong with a pair of Felco 2's, the standard of the landscaping industry, says tree consultant Bill Graham, Master Arborist and former consulting arborist and educator for the University of Pennsylvania's Morris Arboretum. The blades of Swiss-made Felco pruners work with a scissoring action (this type of pruner is called a bypass model). Avoid the type of pruners that cuts anvil-style: That is, the blade cuts the branch from one side toward the flat surface (the "anvil") that provides support from the pruner's other side. Felco 2's blades are contoured to allow easier access to awkwardly placed branches. The spring-loaded handle opens automatically.

Make sure your pruners come with a carrying sheath that protects both you and the tool. (Sheaths typically have belt loops or a clip for securing the sheath to the rim of a pocket or your waistband.)

Pruning is an instance when it really pays to invest in a good gardening tool. Cheap pruners are worthless: They're hard to use, they won't last, and they make ragged cuts that invite diseases and pests. High-quality pruners will need no maintenance other than occasional oiling and the changing of a dull blade.

Skirt the collar. When you're pruning a branch from the trunk, make your cut just outside of the collar, the swelling at the base of the branch against the trunk. If you are trimming away just part of a branch, make the cut just above a bud or just above a subsidiary branch that emerges in another direction. For small branches no more than 1 inch in diameter, sharp, clean, scissor-type hand pruners will do a nice cutting job. For branches from 1 to 2 inches thick, you'll need to use loppers, and for bigger branches you'll need a pruning saw.

Know your buds. Many trees and bushes have buds that alternate positions—one bud is on one side of a branch, and then the next bud is on the other side of the branch. When you are pruning a branch down to a bud, which bud

MYTH-BUSTERS
Lop "Topping" Off Your To-Do List

Many homeowners and landscape services still follow the practice of "topping" mature trees—that is, drastically trimming back the trees' large limbs. The theory used to be that topping invigorated the tree, prevented storm damage, and (strangely) looked better. Tree experts now recognize that topping, also known as stubbing or lopping, is a damaging and disfiguring procedure. Topping encourages the rapid growth of slender shoots that are weak and prone to breaking. This practice opens multiple large wounds that expose the tree to disease, insects, and rot. Also, because topping deprives the tree of much of its foliage, the tree is deprived of food, and its root system is weakened.

Hmm. You don't mind crossing one more maintenance procedure off your list, do you?

• • • • • • • • • • • • • • • • • • •

you choose is significant. A bud will create a new branch growing in the direction that the bud points, so make your cut just above a bud that's pointing toward the outside of the tree. If your variety of tree or shrub has double buds—one on each side of the branch—cut just above the double bud and then snip off the interior bud as well. This practice will train your tree or shrub to develop outward-growing limbs, which allow plenty of light and air into the interior of the tree. Crowded branches don't grow as well and can invite pest and disease problems.

When you make a pruning cut in mid-branch, make the trim just ¼ inch above a bud. Also, make your cut at an angle—say, a 45-degree angle, not perpendicular to the branch. With this technique, you will not leave a dead stub that will rot and perhaps harm the tree.

Keep an eye on head clearance. In some cases, you will want to prune one or more of a tree's lowest branches when the tree matures. For large-growing trees in your yard, allowing 8 feet of head clearance is standard. You will need twice that clearance for vehicles if your tree overhangs a street. Within your yard, keep lower branches intact if they're needed for privacy or to serve as a windbreak.

Keep ahead of the sprouts. There are two kinds of sprouts that you can automatically prune from your trees: suckers, which grow out of the ground or from low on the trunk, and water sprouts, vigorous, fast-growing shoots that originate on the upper trunk or limbs. These sprouts grow straight up and often cross and rub against other limbs. Aside from interfering with the tree's branch structure, water sprouts and suckers also deprive the plant of energy it would otherwise use for more productive growth. The easiest way to deal with sprouts: Snap them off by hand in spring, before they get woody, says Graham. If you leave them until later in the growing season, trimming those sprouts will be more of a chore, requiring hand pruners and disposal of the clipped branches.

Make a winter inspection. Winter is a great time to evaluate a tree for corrective pruning. Of course, with the foliage gone, you have a clearer view of the tree's structure and are in a better position to spot crisscrossing branches, upstart shoots, and imbalances. Besides, with your trees dormant in the winter, they'll lose less sap when you find cuts to make. So if you're getting cabin fever on some sunny winter day, pull on a jacket and go outside to evaluate the "scaffolding" (branch structure) of your trees. With a little corrective shaping already accomplished before spring growth hits—why, you'll feel all warm inside!

Go easy on shrubs. Just as for trees, you want to focus on removing dead and damaged growth from your shrubs, but not a whole lot else, unless you are sculpting formal shrubs or topiaries (which, as a cheater, you probably don't want to bother with).

Rejuvenate old shrubs. When shrubs like lilacs and butterfly bushes get old and woody and don't bloom as well as they used to, you can reinvigorate them without replacing them. What you do is prune one-third of the oldest, woodiest stems back close to the ground once a year for 3 years. After that your shrub will have all young, vital stems.

Get lazy with azaleas. Here's the typical maintenance routine that traditional gardeners slave through for their azaleas: Twice a year, they prune the bushes down into a formal dome shape. Considering all of the snipping involved, I'll bet you're not feeling very traditional. So you'll be glad to know that a modern trend favors a less formal, natural look for azaleas, says Virginia nurseryman Nick Covatta. That is, quit pruning them and let them do what they will. They'll bloom better, too, when left unpruned. I'm sold!

If you can't resist exerting some control over your azaleas, try this: When you spot a renegade shoot emerging from the bush, one that lends a sloppy appearance, follow that one shoot down into the bush and snip it off beside the next branch. Then call it a day.

Another key to keeping your azaleas looking good: planting a variety that's

MYTH-BUSTERS
Let Trees Heal Their Own Wounds

The time-honored practice of "dressing" a tree's wounds (caused by pruning cuts or damage) is unnecessary, according to the International Society of Arboriculture (ISA). A wound dressing for trees was a sealer that was brushed or sprayed onto wood that had been laid bare by pruning, branch breaks, or woefully misdirected vehicles. The theory was that painting over this exposed wood prevented decay, disease, and insect damage, and also encouraged healing of the wound. However, research has shown that this provides little benefit, says the ISA.

Many people cling to the idea that wound dressing provides a "finished" look to a tree that has had limbs removed. If you're going to use dressing for such cosmetic purposes, apply only a thin coating and double-check first that the dressing isn't toxic to your tree.

appropriate for the space in the first place. Some azaleas can easily bush up to 10 feet in height, so choose a variety that will be in correct proportion to its space at mature size—without all of that whittling and pruning.

Attack problems promptly. Don't let problems fester in your tree or shrub. Prune away dead limbs and any branches with disease or invading insects. Don't leave such branches lying around where the disease or insects can spread—bag them up for disposal and get them out of the yard.

Give your tree a clean break. If you need to prune a large limb from a tree, make your first cut up from the underside of the branch, about 6 inches out from the trunk. Saw toward the top side of the branch, about a third of the way through. Next, complete the cut from the top down and let the branch fall. Finally, saw off the remaining stump. But remember: To make healing easier for the tree, don't cut flush with the trunk. Cut outside the branch collar, the swelling at the base of the branch against the trunk. This three-step process will ensure a clean break when the limb drops off, instead of possibly splintering or stripping bark, which might expose the tree to disease.

Lower a heavy branch safely. If there are healthy branches directly below a large limb that you are pruning out of a tree, devise a way to lower the dead branch slowly and safely, so it doesn't damage other branches as it falls. For instance, you might tie one end of a rope to the dead branch, toss the other end of the rope over a strong branch above you, and secure the rope until your cut is done. Then you'll be able to lower the dead branch pulley-style. Another approach: Lop off a large dead branch in sections, so the smaller pieces will be less likely to cause damage as they fall. Naturally, make sure people and pets keep a safe distance.

Rub out stubs. Don't leave dead branch stubs on your tree—say, the few inches remaining where a branch snapped off. Such stubs will rot, and that rot could reach the trunk and do serious damage. Stubs also offer an entry point for pests and disease organisms. Prune off the stub as you would any problematic branch, making your cut close to the trunk or originating branch, but just outside the branch collar.

Let the leaves emerge first. When's the best time to prune a tree? The old-time conventional wisdom was to prune trees while they were dormant—in winter. However, "My Dad used to say prune anytime the shears are sharp," says Master Arborist Graham, who grew up in the nursery business. He's still flexible about when to prune, although he prefers to wait until the tree's leaves are fully expanded and its shoots are out—which means late in spring.

Choose pruning time for shrubs. On the other hand, if you're trying to regulate the growth of a shrub, you can take two approaches: If you're trying to invigorate your shrub, prune it down in winter. In spring, shoots will grow vigorously to replace the trimmed branches. Conversely, pruning your shrub in summer will slow the shrub's growth.

The timing of shrub pruning also varies depending on when the shrub blooms. If you want flowers, a good rule of thumb is to prune shrubs that bloom on old wood—spring bloomers like lilacs and some summer bloomers like macrophylla hydrangeas (the blue ones)—right after they finish blooming, so that you don't cut off next year's flower buds. These shrubs set next year's flower buds after they bloom. Shrubs that bloom on new wood, the current season's growth—mostly later bloomers, like peegee and arborescens hydrangeas (the white ones, mostly) and butterfly bushes—can be pruned in spring.

Sanitize your cutting tools. Pruning tools can transfer disease from one tree to another. So to prevent spreading misery all around your landscape, sanitize your pruning shears and saws when you're done with one tree before you're ready to work on another. It's not hard. Pour 1 cup of chlorine bleach into a pail and add 9 cups of water. Dip your tools into the solution for at least 1 minute, then rinse them off and dry with a clean cloth. If the tree you are working on is already diseased, dip the pruners in the bleach solution after each pruning cut you make.

Get some training. If you want to really sharpen your pruning skills, take a local class, says Geisel of California's Master Gardener program. Your agricultural extension office should be able to refer you to one. Or consult your local arboretum or a college that teaches horticulture. Books and videos on pruning are also easy to find.

Look in a book. One of the fastest ways to learn proper tree-pruning technique is to pick up a book of quick-reference illustrations, says Virginia nurseryman Covatta. Such books are commonly sold at garden centers.

Watering—give them an inch. Two of the most common errors that home gardeners make with their new trees and shrubs are watering them too much and watering them too little. So here's a rule of thumb that will keep your watering on target in most circumstances, says Covatta: In general, you want to simulate a nice 1-inch rainfall once a week for a newly planted tree or shrub. To do this, lay your garden hose by the plant's roots and set it on a mere trickle for 3 to 5 hours. If your soil is heavy clay, your new plant may need less than an inch of water each week, because the soil will retain moisture longer. If your soil is sandy, your tree or shrub will likely need more than an inch of water. Stick your finger down into the soil to check, and use your best judgment.

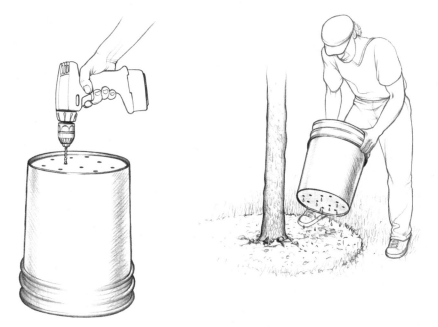

When your hose won't reach a newly planted tree or shrub, create a leaky bucket to help with watering chores. Drill small holes in the bottom of an old pail or bucket, fill with water, place it close to the tree trunk, and let the water drip out.

Water with a leaky bag. Got a newly planted tree or shrub in a remote corner of your property—say, a new dogwood in the woodland at the far end of your backyard? Even if you had enough hose to reach the new planting, it would be quite a chore to drag the hose out there every time that watering was required. That's when watering by drip bag comes in handy, says nurseryman Covatta. A drip bag is a special type of sack that you can fill at your outdoor spigot and just lay down around the base of your new planting. Its water leaks out very slowly, irrigating your plant. One brand of drip bag is a pillowlike, C-shaped sack that fits around the base of your tree or shrub. There are 14- and 20-gallon versions that release their water over several hours. You can buy drip bags at garden supply stores and over the Internet.

Or try Covatta's "poor man's version:" Find a 5-gallon plastic bucket (recycle an old spackle bucket—cleaned out thoroughly first!—or buy an inexpensive one at your hardware store). Drill a few tiny holes in the bottom of the bucket, fill it with water, and set it beside the tree or shrub that needs watering.

Water when it's most critical. If you've had a dry summer, late summer is the most important time to water trees and shrubs, because many of them are setting buds for next spring's flowers and leaves.

Pick the right hedge plant. How much labor you have to put into maintaining a hedge depends a lot on what variety of plant you choose for the hedge in the first place. If you like a precise look, a typical hedge may require pruning several times during the year, starting in the growing season—particularly if you plant a notoriously fast- and wild-growing hedge such as privet. To trim a lot of hedge-clipping duty out of your life, plant your hedge with a dwarf cultivar that will grow to precisely the size you want in a hedge. You'll be able to clip your hedge into shape with one simple annual trim, rather than battling nature four or five times a year (always an unfair fight). For a hedge plant that trims easily, choose a cultivar that's an upright variety with thin branches and small foliage (as opposed to a spreading variety with heavy branches and large leaves). For an even easier time, skip a clipped hedge altogether and plant an informal screen of plants instead (see the Cheat Sheet on "Trees and Shrubs for Screening" on page 271).

Leave the sides slanted. Homeowners often trim the sides of evergreen hedges straight up and down—perpendicular to the ground. That's a mistake, says Ohio horticulturist Barbara Arnold. Such hedges are healthier when their sides are trimmed to be wider at the bottom than they are at the top. Otherwise, the lower branches can't get enough sunlight and thus die off. So instead, trim the sides of your evergreen hedges at an angle, she says.

Make your trims early. Many homeowners make the mistake of waiting to prune a hedge until it grows larger than the intended size. This makes your hedge-trimming sessions a much bigger job than they need to be. Try this approach instead: Even when your hedge is young, shape it with at least one pruning during the growing season. This will redirect some of the plants' energy into healthful bushiness rather than into increasing size. This way, your hedge will only slowly reach its intended size over the years, and meantime your maintenance duties will be kept to a minimum.

When's the best time to give a hedge a trim? Anytime you glance at the hedge and think it's starting to look ragged. If you wait until a hedge is truly out of control, you're only inviting extra labor and mess. This is much the same way that you should decide when to mow the lawn.

Let that stump remove itself. Got a tree stump intruding on your lawn like a party guest who just won't go home? Sure, you can pay a tree service hundreds of dollars to grind it away. But if you're patient and inventive, you can make use of a stump in your landscape at the same time that you speed up its deterioration. My backyard had a crab apple stump with a soft core, making it an excellent little planter for flowers (after several years of rotting, there's nothing but a mild depression left in the grass now). If you need to carve a little wood out of the center of a stump to turn it into a planter, use a drill and wood chisel. Alternatively, just park a plant container on the stump and let it drain straight onto the wood when you water it. Or surround the stump with a small planting bed (you already had an obstacle for your mower there anyway), and toss some dirt and mulch over the offending wood to hide it and help it rot.

Deter deer with soap on a rope. If you have veggie-munching deer rampaging in your neighborhood, you probably have learned that nothing short of a castle wall will keep them away from your backyard garden. What's more, in late summer the bucks love to rub their itchy antlers against the trunks of your trees. They can easily destroy a small tree by stripping its bark. Sure, you can buy all manner of predator scents to scare deer away, but the most effective deer deterrent may be hidden under your bathroom sink, says nurseryman Covatta: a bar of heavily perfumed soap. Irish Spring and Cashmere Bouquet are the two brands that work best, he says. To protect a tree or another area of your garden, drill a hole in the bar of soap, loop some twine through the hole, and hang the bar from a branch. The scent will annoy any foraging deer and send them over to your neighbor's garden. A bar suspended outdoors this way will last about a year. To protect a cluster of trees, hang several bars of soap sentry-fashion around the perimeter. Be prepared to change soap brands on a regular basis—deer get used to them. Similarly, if you use a commercial deer repellent (containing garlic, hot pepper, rotten egg, and other unpleasant stuff), change brands periodically—Bambi gets used to them, too.

Fighting Mother Nature is one thing when it means pulling 3-inch weeds out of a garden bed. It's quite another thing when you're confronting a tree towering 100 feet above your head. With a force that powerful and enduring, the simplest strategy is clear: Make wise choices at the outset, plant and maintain sensibly, *and get out of Mother Nature's way!*

CHAPTER 11

The HANDIEST TOOLS and SNEAKIEST STORAGE

||||||||||||||||||||||||||||||||||||||||||||||||||||||||||||||||||||||||||||||||||||||||

I f you love corner-cutting solutions to everyday problems, then it's just about a given that you also love tools and clever uses for tools. To me, a good garden supply store, or a good hardware store, or a good home improvement store is more entertaining than an amusement park. Left to my own devices, I will prowl such stores with my eyes wide, marveling at the ingenious, laborsaving devices to be found—solutions to problems I often didn't even realize I had.

In that same spirit, I developed a tool-related habit while researching this book: I asked just about all the gardening and yard work experts I could find what their favorite tools were and what their favorite tool-related tips and shortcuts were. Their responses make for a wondrous grab bag of tool advice, and I know you're hooked already. So let's see what they said.

FAVORITE TOOLS

It's lovely to see a highly experienced gardener who gets really passionate about a hand tool. So let's find out which implements experienced gardeners pull out of their sheds when they start raving about their faves.

Solve a wrenching problem: woody weeds. Suppose you have a nice woodland on the edge of your property and you'd like to keep the jungly growth under control. But perhaps a maple tree has thrown thousands of seeds all over the area, and thick woody stems are popping up everywhere. Or perhaps an exotic or invasive shrub is threatening to take over with new suckers. Even the heartiest gardeners with bulging biceps are stymied now and then with that kind of weed-pulling duty. Sure, you could snip those stems off at the bottom with a large pair of pruning shears—but that leaves the root systems intact, meaning the offending plants will return for an encore. Master Arborist Bill Graham of Graham Tree Consulting in Doylestown, Pennsylvania, has the easy answer: the weed wrench, also known as a woody-plant puller, available on the Internet.

The weed wrench is an L-shaped device made of heavy-duty steel. Its handle stands about 5 feet high. At the bottom end, a grasping jaw fits around the base of the woody stem that you're trying to pull up. When you push down on the long handle, the levering action pulls up the small tree, roots and all. The weed wrench, which comes in different sizes, will extract plants that have trunks up to 1½ to 2 inches thick. The jaws will fit around shrubby, multistemmed plants. You can also use the weed wrench to pull up the stump of a small tree cut previously. You're guaranteed to feel like you're cheating!

Scuffle weeds away. If you've got loads of little weeds that would take forever to pull, try using a scuffle, or action, hoe to get rid of them in a fraction of the time (and with no bending over). This hoe has a head made of three flat, narrow blades formed into a triangle, which pivots where it is attached to the

The hefty jaw grip at the base of the weed wrench seizes the woody trunk or multistemmed base of an unwanted tree or shrub. A downward push on the handle lifts the intruder out by the roots.

handle. You just push the hoe back and forth over the ground to cut off the weeds—it's easy and fast.

Circle in on weeds. For weeding close to veggies, herbs, or flowers, a circle hoe can save you time and effort. It is, simply, a sharp-edged metal circle attached to a wooden handle. You'll have to get down on your knees to use it, but it lets you work close to plants without damaging them. It's a lot faster than hand-pulling. Searching the Internet will find you a source if you can't get one locally.

Choose a prudent pruner. It's hard to imagine getting passionate about hand pruners, but the Swiss-made Felco 2's are widely admired among professional gardeners and landscapers. These branch-and-stem snippers are pretty much the standard in the industry.

The blades of this model work by scissoring action, technology that's far superior to the kind of pruners with a cutting blade on one side and a flat "anvil" surface on the other side. Avoid the anvil design, Graham says. The blades of Felco 2 pruners are contoured to allow easier access to awkwardly placed branches, and the blades are replaceable, too—so you don't have to put up with the hassle of sharpening them. Felcos also come with a handy little tool you can use to change the blade. The protective sheath that comes with the tool can hang from your belt or can clip to a pocket or waistband. Don't just slip pruners into your pocket, says Graham. The sheath will protect you from accidents and protect the pruners as well. If you trip and fall, pruners left open in your pocket can cause dire consequences when rammed against your sensitive body parts.

Try hand-friendly pruners. Landscape designer Covner recommends two brands of hand pruner, particularly if you don't have much hand strength, if you have arthritis, or if you're susceptible to repetitive-motion injuries.

Fiskars pruner: When you squeeze the handles together, leverage rotates the head of the pruner to make the cut. This lightweight, low-effort pruner has an "ease-of-use commendation" from the Arthritis Foundation.

Florian ratchet pruner: This pruner delivers powerful cutting action through ratcheting technology (building incremental power that works something like a car jack). Follow the directions that come with the tool, Covner says. Don't get impatient and twist and turn the pruner. "It's really easy, and not a lot of force is required," she says.

Take a cobra to work with you. Garden author Clea Danaan's favorite digging-in-the-garden hand tool is called the Cobrahead. It has a comfortable plastic handle and a hook-shaped steel extension that ends in a flat blade. The blade is pointed on the tip and sharp on the sides. The multitalented tool is handy for uprooting weeds, trenching, turning soil, and digging holes for seeds, transplants, and bulbs. Referred to variously as a "steel fingernail" and a "miniature plow," the Cobrahead is available in short-handled and long-handled versions. You can find it at garden supply stores and on the Internet.

The sturdy Cobrahead's distinctive hook-shaped handle and "steel fingernail" earns points as a multitalented digging tool in garden beds.

Try a well-traveled weeder. One of Pennsylvania landscape designer Ellen Covner's favorite digging-in-the-garden tools may be a genetic cousin to the Cobrahead. Known variously as the Cape Cod weeder, the Japanese weeder, and the skritcher, this tool consists of a handle, an L-shaped steel rod, and a triangular tip. Covner says it's superior to any other hand cultivator she has used. You can run it back and forth through the surface of your garden soil and then use your hands to pick out the uprooted weeds. It's also great for weeding in narrow spaces, such as the gap between bricks or pavers.

Two-tool trick: Make trees and shrubs an inviting new home. Using a combination of a pick and a shovel is a great way to dig a hole for planting a tree or shrub. Start with the shovel, digging down to the desired depth. Then use the pick to loosen the dirt on the sides of the hole, says Charlie Nardozzi, spokesman for the Burlington, Vermont-based National Gardening Association.

Quick Bed-Making

Establishing a new garden bed is no small task when you consider the chore of marking off its borders and then removing the sod that's currently occupying that territory. That is, it's no small task unless you know the technique used by Master Arborist Bill Graham. First, let's get familiar with a couple of tools that simplify the process.

Nursery spade. As you might imagine, this looks much like a shovel, except that it has a rectangular blade with a flat, sharp cutting end. The heavy handle, which can bear lots of stress without breaking, is reinforced by a steel strap.

Grape hoe. Also called a vineyard hoe, this sturdy device looks like a cross between a conventional garden hoe and a pickax. It has a heavy-duty handle and a wide, flat cutting blade.

Now here's how Graham marks off a new garden bed and strips off the sod: First take a garden hose (use one that has warmed up in the sun, so it will be flexible) and lay it out on the lawn to delineate the edge of your new garden bed. You can stand back, reassess the shape of the bed, and nudge the hose to your heart's content. You can leave the hose in place for the next step, or mark the final border of the bed with spray paint (or special landscape paint, which won't harm plants and will wash away in time) or a sprinkle of lime. Then walk the perimeter of the bed, cutting the turf with the edge of the nursery spade. This kind of edging with the nursery spade takes some practice, but you'll soon develop a rhythm that will allow you to move quickly. (If you left the hose in place, this assumes you have good control of the nursery spade and won't chop the hose in two.)

Now use a combination of the nursery spade and the grape hoe to dig up sod. Standing just outside the edge of the bed, stab sideways with the nursery spade just under the edge of the sod to strip it up. You can also stand just inside the perimeter of the bed to chop the blade of the grape hoe under the sod to pull it up.

And there's one more laborsaving trick to Graham's technique. Once you have cleared a 1-foot-wide section of sod all around the perimeter of your new garden bed, stop stripping up sod. Yes, leave the rest of the grass in the new bed in place. Then cover it all over with a thick layer of mulch, newspaper, or black plastic. Deprived of sun, the remaining sod will die and decompose. (Since the sod will take some time to die off, consider doing this one season for use the next season.) Hmm, sounds like cheating, doesn't it?

A hoe would probably work for this, too. Leave that loosened side dirt in place. Then slide the rootball into the hole and fill in with more loose dirt. When the new plant's roots reach out, they will find it easier to penetrate the soil there.

Cut corners with electric saws. Covner says two of her favorite yard work tools are saws—no, not the kind powered by muscle and sweat, and not the gasoline-driven ones either. Go electric, she says. These tools offer substantial advantages over their gassy counterparts: in general, no special fuels to fiddle with and lighter weight. Some details:

Reciprocating saw: Also known as a sawsall, this is the kind of powered saw whose blade slides back and forth. Fast and lightweight, the electric reciprocating saw provides good, clean cuts when you're pruning thick limbs. It's powered through an electric cord, which means you'll need access to an outdoor outlet or need to run a long extension cord out a door or window.

Chain saw: Covner likes a lightweight, battery-powered chain saw. It's superb for cutting down yard waste (like downed tree branches) into short lengths for bundling with twine or bagging up. Before you buy one, says Covner, search online and read the consumer magazine reviews as well as customer assessments. Also, before you commit to ownership of an electric chain saw, test-drive one by renting one for a day from a tool rental company. And naturally, you will want to read up on all of the precautions that come with any power tool.

Look for portability. Garden and yard tools serve you best when you have easy access to them right where you're doing the work. Here are some laborsaving tools recommended by Lori Hayes, manager of the Horticultural Center in Philadelphia's Fairmount Park.

Work table: When you have easy access to a work table in the yard, you don't have to bend over every time you want to accomplish something. A small table with folding legs will easily slide into your shed or garage for storage. Your back muscles will thank you.

Milk crate: A milk crate is a multipurpose garden tool. It's handy for hauling myriad small objects around the yard. It's also handy to use as an impromptu stool when you need to pause for some low-down work in the garden or when you want to spend some time tending to your container plants. Another back-saver!

Toolbox: Keep a small toolbox stocked with all of your small, need-it-quick hand tools such as hand pruners and weed diggers. Take it with you every time you work in the garden. This way, you will always be ready for those impromptu garden tasks the second you think of them. (Otherwise, they'll never get done.) Similarly, some pros swear by a garden bag with lots of pockets on the outside, or an apron with multiple tool pockets.

Make like a camel. A pump-up sprayer is a very handy tool for distributing all manner of liquid concoctions on garden beds, shrub or tree foliage, or lawn. The official *How to Cheat at Gardening and Yard Work* model? It's the backpack variety. It holds 2 to 3 gallons of liquid on your back, and you can pump up the pressure in the tank without taking the pack off.

Be ready for a quick cleanup. What do you do when you hear the telephone ringing in the house—and your hands are smeared with garden soil? Shrug your shoulders and start spreading that dirt all through the house for the sake of a phone call? No, says Hayes. The simple solution is this: Stash a bottle of liquid hand sanitizer right with your easy-to-grab garden tools (your trowel and garden gloves, for instance). With a quick rubbing-off of dirt and a squirt of sanitizer, your hands will be clean and germ-free in no time and ready to open doors, pick up telephones, and shake hands with surprise guests. Hayes says using hand sanitizer is a great message for children who work in the garden with you: Sure you can have fun digging in the dirt, but you need to pay attention to sanitation, too.

Reach for a really big fork. Barbara Arnold, horticultural designer for the Franklin Park Conservatory in Columbus, Ohio, adores her garden fork. This heavy-duty tool has a D-shaped handle, fat and flat tines, and stands waist high. It's multitalented, too—excellent for digging, dividing perennials, and turning soil. It's passable for turning and spreading compost. There's another benefit as well: "It looks tough," Arnold says, so observers will know at a glance that you're a really serious gardener.

Try a trowel with a twist. When Arnold digs in the garden, she likes to use an innovative kind of trowel, one with a curved handle that makes her dirt-working easier. An ergonomic curve to the trowel's handle allows Arnold to do her favorite kind of digging: Rather than holding the trowel the conventional way (handle in hand, with the business end pointing away from her), she holds the curving trowel handle backwards (with the business end pointing toward her). Then she pokes the trowel tip into the soil and pulls toward her. This easier, faster way of digging a transplant hole will shave 30 seconds off of the job—which adds up to quite a bit of time if you have lots of plants to put into the ground, she says. Her trowel's heavier blade helps all the more. Padding on the handle isn't required, Arnold says, but it does help a bit.

Believe good things come in threes. Charlie Nardozzi in Vermont says his favorite garden tool has to be the three-pronged cultivator. For the uninitiated, this gizmo looks like a rigid garden rake (not a flexible lawn rake), but it has only three tines arching in a claw shape. It easily fulfills the functions

ZERO-MAINTENANCE MARVELS
Buy a Knife, Toss Your Weeder

Ellen Covner, a landscape designer in Wynnewood, Pennsylvania, likes to keep a garden knife on hand when she's working in the soil. The tool is versatile enough that it makes a number of other hand tools obsolete. Look for one with a padded handle, a V-shaped trench along the blade, a serrated edge, and measurement markings along the blade to help you determine planting depths. The garden knife is great for planting bulbs and digging holes for transplants. The knife is a superb digger and also can be used as a scoop to move dirt or little plants around. The forked tip helps with deep-down uprooting of weeds such as onion grass and dandelion.

of three or four other common garden tools (hoe, trowel, and weeder, for instance). Nardozzi uses it for digging small holes for transplants, making furrows for seeds, mounding up soil for potatoes, and weeding. He prefers the long-handled version of this tool (not the short three-pronged hand tool), which makes it easy to reach into his vegetable and flower beds. "Simple and multifunctional," he says.

Pull on these work gloves. Ask Pam Geisel, coordinator of California's Master Gardener program, what her favorite gardening tool is and she will point to her work gloves—a kind she never sees in garden supply stores. She bought her Atlas work gloves at a hardware store, where they were marketed to people who work with concrete. What makes Atlas work gloves so great for gardening? They have a rubbery sure-grip surface on the fingers and palms. They have a snug fit and stretchy back. They have a tough-but-flexible exterior that protects your hands from scratches, yet still leaves you with plenty of finger dexterity. Inside, Atlas gloves have a seamless nylon liner. They're also machine-washable and come in different weights, appropriate for spring and winter.

"I *love* them!" Geisel says.

Keep a saw in your pocket. Nardozzi is never at a loss when he stumbles across a limb that needs pruning or an errant root that needs to be cut back. That's because he carries one of his favorite tools right in his pocket—a folding handsaw. These handy tools have a sharp blade that cuts in both directions, fold closed against a protective sheath, and include a safety switch to keep locked when shut. Nardozzi likes versions made by Felco and Corona. The typical model is about 14 inches long when folded, has a 6-inch blade, and weighs less than 5 ounces.

Keep them simple. Gardening experts do love their handiest hand tools. However, sometimes inventors and manufacturers get carried away with "convenience" features that don't work as well as might be hoped. Two examples:

■ Bulb planters, those conical tools made for gouging a deep bulb-planting hole in the soil, supposedly perfect for plopping a bulb into. The problem is, says Covner, such tools rarely cut down into the soil satisfactorily, particularly in firm soil. They don't go deep enough for a lot of bulbs, either. Using a good garden knife or a sharp trowel is so much easier.

■ Multiheaded hand tools—a single handle on which you swap out the tool heads. For instance, with one set you might get a cultivator, a hoe, and an edger. That's a nice idea, says Nardozzi, but in general you don't get the tool quality that you would find if you had bought good tools individually.

Recruit an assistant. One of Covner's favorite gardening tools is not really a tool at all but a human assistant. For a professional landscaper like Covner, this means a hired crewmember. For you and me, this means a spouse or a teenager who would like to earn his or her allowance. Just having a warm body on hand to help in the garden isn't enough, says Covner. Look for someone who makes up for some of your physical shortcomings. If you're barely 5 feet tall, a 6-foot assistant will be an enormous asset—longer reach, more brawn for heavy lifting, and more body weight to make digging easier. A modicum of training is essential, too—your helper should know how to deadhead and cut back dying foliage without killing the plant, for instance, and how to edge in a straight line. When you're working in the garden with a sidekick, go overboard with your communication. Provide lots of detail about the work you expect, check that your assistant understands, and then watch as your helper starts the work. An hour of garden work done incorrectly is a sure formula for misery on both sides.

Tool Tips and Tricks

Landscape designer Covner wants us to remember the old lesson from the animated sequence *The Sorcerer's Apprentice* in Disney's *Fantasia*. The wayward apprentice may have conjured up scores of mops and buckets to do his bidding, but left to their own devices, the tools failed miserably and mayhem ensued. "That's the biggest thing—tools don't work by themselves," Covner says. Caring for and storing garden and yard tools is not hard, but if you want them to perform well for you, a little effort and organization are required. This means oiling hinges, wiping off occasional dirt, and protecting them from the elements (don't leave them lying outside). "No matter what incantation you use, it [the tool] won't work on its own," Covner says. So let's look at some favorite tips and tricks for storage of garden tools that will keep things from getting a little too Mickey Mouse around the garden.

Pop for a good hose and hanger. Spend the extra few bucks to buy a high-quality garden hose. Otherwise, you'll be trekking to the home store for a new one every couple of years. Here's a quick-and-easy test of a hose's quality: Bend a section of the hose in your hands. If it quickly regains its shape, that's good. Brass fittings are a good idea if your hose gets lots of use. Look for a hose that boasts a high UV rating, another indicator of longevity. An arc-shaped hose hanger is a must-have to store the hose in the proper shape and out of the way of your lawn mower and other destructive forces. (An old car tire rim makes an excellent hose hanger, too—spray paint it and mount it on a fence, on a post, or on the side of your house.) Position your hanger out of the sunlight, which will damage your hose over time. (Note: If you find one of those crank-style hose storage reels that *doesn't* turn into a rickety hassle over time, we'd like to hear about it. In the meantime, buyer beware.)

Revive your clogged lawn sprinkler. If your sprinkler heads get clogged up with mineral deposits, immerse them in white vinegar. Just pour vinegar into a plastic bucket or bin and place the stopped-up device head-down into it. Leave it for at least a few hours, or even overnight. When you pull it out, brush off any remaining mineral deposit with a stiff brush and rinse it with water. Vinegar is a wonderful, cheap household tool. A gallon jug will cost you less than $3 at the supermarket or a discount store.

Throw down the gauntlet. Hands in peril? Manufacturers haven't yet made an all-purpose garden glove that will protect your hands in all situations. So the sneaky trick is to buy a few sets of gloves to cover you—or your hands,

The Pruners' New Hiding Place

Charlie Nardozzi is usually pretty methodical about where he stores his handy garden pruners so they will be easy to find the next time he needs them. But one day the senior horticulturist and spokesman for the National Gardening Association in Burlington, Vermont, could not find his pruners anywhere. Eventually he gave up. At the end of the day, he went into the kitchen and started putting dishes away in the dishwasher. And that's where he found his pruners—sitting in the silverware bin, where they may have been for a couple of days. His best guess is that he was in the kitchen with his pruners, someone called and distracted him, and he put the pruners in there absentmindedly.

"It could have been a senior moment," says the 50-year-old. Eventually, it all comes out in the wash.

anyway—for all common situations. Go to your home store and pick up one pair of each of the gloves described below. Drop them all into a mesh bag—the kind they sell onions or oranges in—and hang the bag on a nail in the shed so your gloves will be easy to find and will dry out after a day's work. Or nail a row of mousetraps or clothespins to the wall of your shed and use them as clasps for holding your gloves.

Before buying, try on your garden gloves to make sure they're neither too tight nor too loose—either way will hurt your hands in the long run. Put both gloves on in the store and squeeze your hands into fists to test the fit. (If the gloves are clipped together, test them one at a time.) If you detect any annoying seams inside the gloves, pass them by. Test your finger dexterity with the gloves on (can you pick up a nail—or even tie your shoes, for instance?). To test the feel of the gloves in action, grasp the handle of a tool in the store and simulate a common gardening motion.

General-purpose leather gloves: Good for preventing blisters during routine tool handling. They provide modest protection from thorns and other pokes.

Waterproof gloves: Look for rubber-coated cotton gloves with an elastic wristband to keep dirt from dribbling inside. They give great protection when you're digging in soggy soil. If you're a serious gardener, you'll need more than one pair. Expect them to get saturated when you're working in a wet garden. They're machine washable and dryable on low heat.

Thorn gauntlets: These are thorn-proof gloves for handling roses, hawthorns, cacti, and other prickly plants. They're great for working with irksome shrubs and hauling piles of lawn debris that leave those red scratches on your arms, too. They typically offer protection right up to the elbow.

Stretchy composites: These are form-fitting gloves with extra padding on the palms and fingers. They're water resistant, but not waterproof, and they don't provide perfect thorn protection. The biggest advantage: They're snug enough that you can do precision work with your fingers.

Wrap your handles for comfort. Do your poor hands a favor. Wrap the handles of your most-used garden tools in adhesive sports tape, the stuff that ballplayers wrap around the handles of baseball bats. Sports tape contains a fine layer of cushioning foam, which will help to prevent blisters on your hands. The foam also will absorb shock when your shovel, hoe, or trowel strikes stones or firm dirt.

Get tools that match your body type. When you're selecting a large garden tool, make sure you get a model that's a good match for your size and weight, says landscape designer Ellen Covner. For instance, as a person on the small side, she prefers the lighter and shorter D-handled shovel. On the other hand, the larger men she works with tend to prefer long-handled shovels in the garden.

Try a little footwork. Lots of people perform shoveling and edging tasks using just the strength of their arms, says Covner. Big mistake. Your legs are stronger than your arms and your back, she says. Also, you are missing the opportunity to let your body weight play to your advantage. So whenever you can, get your feet involved—push down on the shovel with your legs to get more power in each stroke.

Brand your wood-handled tools. Now and then you haul your garden tools to another location—to help a sick friend, or when you pitch in with your church's landscaping, for instance. To prevent any confusion when your tools get mixed with other people's tools, make sure your initials are burned into the wooden handles. No, you don't need a wood-burner's kit. Just brush your initials onto the wood with nail polish and touch a lit match to it before it dries. If the letters don't burn in dark enough, repeat the process.

Baby those handles. The wooden handles of your garden tools will get dry and splintery after years of exposure to the elements. To prolong their life, treat them to an application of boiled linseed oil once a year. First, clean the handle with a stiff brush. If the handle has any rough spots, smooth them out with medium-grit sandpaper. Then moisten part of a rag with boiled linseed oil and rub it into the wood.

Brighten up your tool handles. You're doing your hand tools a disservice if you leave them lying overnight in the grass or garden bed (the exposure will damage both wood handles and metal). Perhaps the problem is that you're forgetful, and you fail to notice some of the tools lying amid that lush foliage before you call it quits for the day. So here's a trick that will remind you to return all of your hand tools to the shed: Paint their handles a bright red, orange, or yellow. Not even the most inattentive gardener would fail to notice such tools lying about the yard or garden.

Turn your wheelbarrow into a tricycle. With a simple modification to your one-wheeled wheelbarrow, you can turn it into a carrying device that can roll along more easily when you want to give your back a rest. At your hardware

SLEIGHT *of* HAND

Soften the Bed First

If you're planning to dig up sod to create a new garden bed or to do a big edging job, give that patch of ground a thorough watering overnight, says Pennsylvania landscape designer Ellen Covner. You'll be so much happier digging through soft, moist soil than trying to penetrate rock-hard earth. Don't go overboard with the water, however, since working very wet soil could compact it and create a sloppy, muddy mess.

store or home store, buy a 2-foot rod with threading on each end, two washers and a nut to fit each end, a couple of small wheels, and U-shaped brackets or other mounting hardware (the exact specs are going to depend upon the design of your wheelbarrow's back legs). Mount the rod across the back legs of your wheelbarrow, slide on the wheels with washers on either sides of them, and secure with the nuts. Now you're on a roll!

For cleanup, get a bigger hand. When you're raking leaves or cleaning up other tree debris on the driveway, here's a clever way Arnold knows to do the job faster. Find an old license plate (or cut a piece of sturdy plastic about that size—6 inches by 18 inches). When you're scooping up raked leaves, hold the plate in one hand and your rake in the other. Essentially, you're making your rake-free hand bigger—and able to scoop up much more debris. So you will remember where to find it each time, store the license plate (or sheet of plastic) in the same place where you keep your lawn rake.

Spare your garden a scalding. If you have a garden hose that's been baking in the summer sun, remember that any water left in the hose will be scalding hot, says Arnold. When you use the hose, let the water in it dribble onto the lawn first before you water your garden. Unless you're hankering for steamed vegetables right then and there!

Get the hang of tool storage. Your gardening and yard work will go faster when your tools are easy to find and easy to identify. So any time you have a tool with a handle, find a way to hang it up, says Arnold. Cluster all of your related tools together—either in the garage, in the shed, or wherever else your outdoor tools congregate. Arnold's added trick: Hang tools with the "business end" at the top, rather than dangling down below. This way, you can instantly figure out which tool is which. (You can find wall-mounted tool brackets or spring-loaded clips that will make this method of hanging easy.) A safety precaution: Don't hang tools any higher than your head. Arnold knows from direct experience that tools that hang high will eventually drop down onto your skull.

For cleanup, hang some "indoor" tools in the shed. You probably think of screwdrivers and putty knives as indoor tools that you would store in the basement. But it's a good idea to keep an old screwdriver and an old putty knife hanging on nails where you store your garden tools. That's because it's always better to put garden tools away clean. Dirt on your tools will accelerate their deterioration. But now and then a shovel or hoe will make it back to the shed with a seemingly impenetrable coating of dried mud that no garden hose can remove. That's when you whip out your screwdriver or putty knife and scrape that tenacious mud off and onto the ground. Both tools are also handy for removing caked-on grass trimmings from the underside of your lawn mower, by the way.

Let your tape measure tag along, too. You probably stash your tape measure with your household tools in the pantry or the basement. Landscape designer Covner's tape measure goes to work in the garden every day. It's an essential tool for precision planting, she says. Don't just "eyeball" how many plants will fit in your garden bed. Measure the space, find out the spacing requirements of the plants you're working with, and get the positioning right the first time. This way you will avoid waste and mistakes like overcrowding.

Get an edge on your digging. The more you use your shovel, hoe, or other cutting tool, the harder the work seems to get. But what you don't notice is that over time your tool has gotten duller and duller, making your work less and less efficient. Sharpening digging tools is super-easy, and you'll be amazed at how easy it is to use them afterward. Here's what to do: Get a file (be sure to use one meant for metal, not wood). Hold your shovel face up on a sturdy work surface or clamp it in a vise. The part you need to sharpen is the rounded edge on the tip of the shovel, and you're trying to restore its original angle (bevel). Hold your file against the shovel's edge at the same angle as the bevel. Push the file across the tip several times, thrusting across and away from the shovel's edge. When you're done, spritz both sides of the refurbished tip with a lubricating spray such as WD-40 and then buff both sides with steel wool.

Take out the "trash." A plain ol' bucket may be less than exotic, but it makes a great companion when you're working in a garden bed, says Covner.

Instant Garden Caddy

Tie a tool belt around an old 5-gallon paint bucket to make a handy garden caddy. Slip small tools, twine, and such into the pockets on the outside and use the inside to lug around bulky items—or the garden vegetables you pick. The handle, of course, makes it easy to grab and go.

As a container, of course, it's handy for transporting the miscellaneous tools you'll need from the shed to the garden. But a bucket also will help you keep the garden bed neat and tidy. As you deadhead, prune, weed, and turn up the occasional stone, drop the resulting debris in the bucket and dispose of it all at the end of the day. An alternative: A small tarp spread out near your garden bed can serve the same purpose, she says—toss your debris onto the tarp and drag it all away when you're finished.

Give excess soil a magic carpet ride. Tarps are an invaluable accessory when you're digging planting holes for trees or shrubs, says horticulturist and radio's *The Garden Guys* personality Sam Jeffries. Before you start digging, spread out your tarp near the digging site. As you dig, rather than tossing the dirt all about, shovel it onto the tarp. When the new plant is in the ground and the hole is filled in, you can grasp the edge of the tarp and drag the excess dirt off to a garden bed or some other disposal site. This way, you contain the soil and you prevent stones from sinking into your lawn, where they will hide until your mower finds them.

Save money with storage. If you have some extra storage space in your shed, why not devote a few square feet to saving money? In fall, your garden supply store will put its spring-oriented stock on sale, meaning you get a great deal on such items as fertilizer, mulch, and potting soil, as well as landscaping materials like pavers, other stones, and fencing. So if you know you're going to need these items the coming spring, save a wad of cash by stocking up early. Most nurseries also put their perennials, grasses, trees, and shrubs on sale in early fall—and that's also a good time to buy and plant.

Store tools between the studs. A lot of potential storage space goes unused inside a shed or an unfinished garage. The spaces between vertical 2-by-4 studs are a great place to stash long-handled tools such as rakes, hoes, pruners, and hedge trimmers. All you have to do is nail a thin strip of wood across the studs, about 3 feet above the floor. This creates a pocket that will hold your tools between the studs and out of the way. Use the same strategy to create storage between those rafters above your head. Strips of wood nailed across the rafters will create a handy storage spot for long items like spare wood trim and pipes, as well as yard tools like saws and loppers.

Put your *own* tools away. When you have helpers working in the garden with you, resist the temptation to have them put your tools away for you at the end of the day, says landscape designer Covner. Why? "Their idea of order isn't the same as yours," she says. If you put your own tools away following your own sense of organization, you will be able to find each one again in a split second. If someone else puts your garden tools away, it might be months before you find some of them again.

Cluster your tools by function. When you store garden tools, put the tools that have similar or related functions together, says Covner. For instance, when she travels to a job, Covner puts the digging implements in one bag, cutting tools in another bag, and in a tool chest she puts the pliers, twine, oil, and safety glasses. Even among a lot of tools, she can instantly find precisely the one she needs.

Avoid deep, dark mysteries. If you want functional storage, you're going to need to throw some light on the subject, says Covner. In her case that just means leaving her shed door wide open when she's selecting her implements. If you have any choice in the matter, windows in a shed are a great advantage for the same reason, and so is electric illumination. Even the most orderly shed will hide your tools from you if you have to paw around in the dark for them. If your shed isn't blessed with a window or wired for electricity, buy one of those battery-operated lights that stick on a wall.

Recycle your old inner tube. You can convert a worn-out bicycle inner tube into a simple-but-clever storage device for your garden hose. Drive a nail into

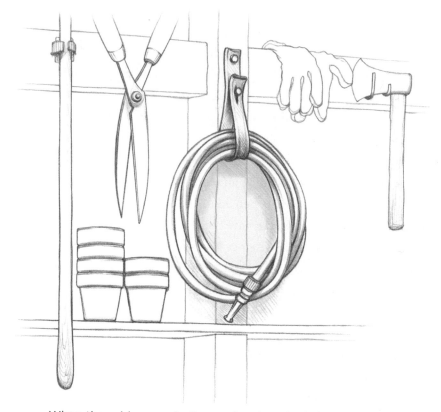

When the rubber meets the road and you're left with a worn bicycle inner tube, put it to good use in your garden shed. Cut a rectangular strip from the tube and use it as a hanger for garden hoses, tomato cages, and watering cans.

a stud in your shed, hook the inner tube over the nail, and let the rubbery circle hang down. When it's time to store away your garden hose, coil the hose up and take it to the shed. Draw the bottom of the inner tube through the center of the coiled hose, and then hook the inner tube over the nail so it holds the hose against the wall and off the floor.

Make blowing a breeze. Using a leaf blower on a breezy day? Don't try blowing leaves or debris against the wind—you'll have a hard time getting anywhere, says Jon Feldman, landscape designer and founder of G. biloba

Gardens in Nyack, New York. Always blow with the wind or at least perpendicular to the wind, Jeffries says.

Ooh, there's something satisfying in being able to tap some of the most experienced gardening minds about what tools work the best, feel the best in hand, and save you the most time, effort, and hassle. Often it comes down to basic simplicity: sturdy construction, science, ergonomic design—and ignoring the fiddly details that are created purely for marketing purposes. Sure, some impressions about which tools work best are highly personal. But in our How to Cheat tradition, you are totally in charge of your choices and preferences. Embrace the ones that work best for you, and if you have some favorite tool tips and tricks to pass along, feel free to do so at www.howtocheatbooks.com.

CHAPTER 12

Seasonal Challenges:
WEEDS, LEAVES, SNOW, ICE, HEAT, DROUGHT, *and* DELUGE

‖‖

W hen you plant a garden bed, you're bravely jumping with both boots into a blur of seasonal changes: Before you know it, flowers are blooming, tomatoes are plump, bees are buzzing, weeds are edging in, the sun is baking your broccoli like a vegetable casserole, your foliage is turning brown at the edges, the trees dump their leaves, in northern climes frost turns tender plants to mush, and then you get killer cold and branch-snapping snow and ice—unless you live in the Southwest, where it's baking hot and dry most of the year, with rain in spring. No matter what climate you stake your claim in, you're going to have a tailor-made set of seasonal challenges to contend with. What gardeners are going to get through these torments? The gardeners equipped with these sneaky shortcuts.

AS SUMMER APPROACHES

Irrigate your garden with recycled milk jugs. Want to give a flowerbed or shrub a deep soaking—without having to fiddle with a sprinkler hose? Just take a gallon milk or water jug and poke a hole in the bottom. Fill it with water from your garden hose and set it on the ground you want to water. The slow drip-drip will give your plant a healthful deep watering. You can easily store several of these zero-cost watering jugs in your shed. Tie one end of 3 feet of rope to the handle of one of the jugs, and then thread the loose end through the handles of the other jugs. Tie a loop on that free end and hang it on a nail in your shed.

In heat and dry wind, cool your grass down. If the summer temperature reaches 100°F or more and dry winds are crisping your lawn into a stretch of toast, give your grass some stress relief with a cooling sprinkle, says Trey Rogers, turfgrass professor at Michigan State University. Give your lawn a quick, light sprinkle—just enough to wet down the grass blades and cool them off. (The intent is not to have more water soak into the soil.) This cooling sprinkle will help your grass weather the heat without long-term damage. It's also a great relief for young seedlings that aren't yet fully established, says Rogers.

Alien attack? Check your watering pattern. Are you finding little brown "crop circles" in your lawn? Hmm, by any chance would your lawn be planted with St. Augustine grass, bent grass, or Kentucky bluegrass? And might you live in the southern United States, the East, or the Midwest? Likely as not, your problem is not attributable to aliens' mysterious crop circles after all. More likely, your culprits are insidious Earth-bound creatures called chinch bugs, which are partial to drought-stressed lawns and to the varieties of grass and the regions just mentioned. Chinch bugs relish lawns that have a thatch problem and are drought-stressed because of hot weather and a poor or uneven watering pattern.

Chinch bugs love hot, sun-exposed sections of your lawn. The bugs may congregate in grass bordering sidewalks, driveways, foundations, and other heat-producing landscape features. They have black bodies with white wings, and are as small as a tenth of an inch long. They do their damage by sucking the juices out of grass plants and emitting toxins in their saliva that turn that grass yellow or brown.

One way to tell for sure if you have an infestation: The bugs smell bad when crushed. If you walk across a lawn that's got a lot of them, they emit quite a stench.

To lay out the "unwelcome" mat for chinch bugs, says Dr. Stephanie Bledsoe, technical and training director for the pest prevention company Massey Services (serving Florida, Georgia, and Louisiana), first check over your system for lawn watering. If there are sections of grass that are routinely missed by your watering system, make corrections to achieve completely even watering. Also, assess your lawn for an excessive thatch buildup—that is, an unhealthy accumulation of dead plant material under the living grass blades. (For advice on thatch, see Chapter 9.) Attack chinch bugs as soon as you detect them. You might need to drench your lawn with insecticidal soap, or you can apply neem oil or spread diatomaceous earth. The latter is a white powder that will form a slug-resistant barrier when you pour a ring of it around the garden plants you want to protect. It is made from the silicon skeletons of algae, which will slice into the slugs' soft bodies when the hungry little critters try to cross over it. Follow package directions for use. Or you can even vacuum the lawn with a shop vac to suck up the bugs.

Alternatively, try this trick (from a Canadian health department Web site): Flood the infested part of the lawn with soapy water (use dishwashing soap) to bring the bugs to the surface. Lay a flannel sheet over the area and wait 15 minutes. The bugs will climb onto the sheet and their feet will get trapped in

Cheat Sheet

||||||||||||||||||||||||||||||||||||||||||||||||||||||||||||||||||||||||||||||||||||||||||||||||||||||||||

Your Beat-the-Heat Checklist

It's springtime, so naturally you are looking ahead and wondering how well your garden will weather the heat of the coming summer. Quite well, actually, with the following checklist.

☐ In the best How to Cheat tradition, we're going to tell you *not* to perform work you used to do. Lots of gardeners believe they have to till their soil 12 inches deep in spring. Stop that! Too much tilling turns your soil into airless powder and destroys the soil structure. That speeds evaporation of moisture from the soil, meaning your garden will be harmed more quickly by hot weather. So keep tilling to a minimum.

☐ Treat your plants to plenty of moisture-preserving mulch to help get them through dry spells.

☐ Add organic matter to your soil. Regular doses of compost will keep your soil loose, nutritious, absorbent, and pleasing to roots and worms alike.

☐ Have an easy-to-use irrigation system already in place, whether it's your garden hose or an automated drip system (which is about as easy and cheatin' as you can get).

☐ Mow your lawn at a high setting. The taller grass will shade your turf, keeping it cooler, and it will also crowd out weeds.

☐ By late summer—August for many of us—many gardeners start letting their routine maintenance duties lapse. Don't forget to stay on top of the following chores, however, as they all help to heat-proof your garden: Keep your weeds under control, because invading plants will sap moisture away from your garden plants. (Besides, letting them linger gives them a chance to reseed, which will compound your weed problem later on.) Keep current with your watering—often all that's required is an inch of water a week for vegetables and flowers, and daily watering for containers. Also, keep picking your vegetables every day (otherwise many of your plants will stop producing).

the flannel. Vacuum them off or drown them in a bucket of water. Because chinch bug infestations are not usually widely spread, you may need to apply these remedies only on the damaged grass, plus the surrounding 5 feet or so.

Another tactic for fighting chinch bugs is to plant shrubs and trees to create more shade. If you have to remove the grass and start over in an area, amend the soil with fine gravel and diatomaceous earth, and/or mix some white clover into the grass seed.

Storm alert? Check gutters and downspouts. As soon as you get word that a rainstorm or a snowstorm is on the way, drag the ladder out of the shed and conduct a quick inspection of your home's gutters and downspouts—particularly if you have a chronic problem of water leaking into your basement. The primary reason that you have that problem is that you have water building up in the soil that's next to your foundation, and that water naturally searches for a pathway inside. This means that your gutters and downspouts aren't doing their job, which is to direct rainwater well away from your foundation. So here's what you are going to do with that ladder: Set the ladder against your gutter near a downspout, and climb up there with a wooden paint stirrer or a putty knife stuck in your back pocket. Look left and right in the gutter to find any leaves or debris that could be clogging it and use your scraping tools (paint stirrer or putty knife) to lift up any debris and toss it onto the lawn. If there's a cylindrical wire filter fitted into the top of the downspout, and you have fine, seedy stuff collecting around it, clear that dirt away. Otherwise, it will form a dam. Repeat this inspection procedure for all of your downspouts and gutters, moving your ladder around as necessary. Then when the storm hits, you can take a tour around the house (inside looking out the windows, or outside in a slicker, braving the torrent). Smugly observe your gutters that aren't spilling their water against your foundation. This procedure is a good idea even when a snowstorm is coming, since the water from melting snow can overwhelm gutters and collect against your foundation just as surely as water from a rainstorm can. Under certain conditions, the melting snow freezes at night, creating ice dams that can force water under the roof, wreaking havoc with the home's interior.

Check those heat zone ratings. If you live in a hot climate, check the heat zone rating for every ornamental plant that you bring home to your garden. You will find this information on the label of the plant at the nursery. When you choose plants that are rated for your heat zone, rest assured that they will be a low-maintenance feature in the yard—saving you the extra work of additional waterings or rigging up shade tents for them.

Down South, avoid the worst heat. If you garden in the South, do yourself a favor and adopt a low-stress rhythm for your toil-in-the-soil duties—for instance, try working in the early morning or evening. Avoid that furnacelike afternoon.

AS FALL APPROACHES

Protect containers from cold. If you live where winters are cold, empty and upend your pots and containers in fall. If you have urns or other decorative, container-like fixtures in your garden, empty and turn them upside down too, before freezing nights arrive. Otherwise, they'll collect water, freeze, and break. (The hard way to protect them would require you to store such items in your garage or basement instead.)

Put trees and shrubs under wraps for winter. If the weight of winter's snow and ice have been known to leave your small evergreen trees and shrubs with snapped limbs, here's a simple way to prevent that damage, says horticulturist Sam Jeffries, radio cohost of *The Garden Guys*. Take a ball of garden twine (hemp will do) and tie its end at the base of a branch inside the tree or shrub you want to protect. This branch should be a sturdy one about halfway up the trunk. Hold the ball of twine against your stomach, and back up against the shrub to gently compress its branches inward. Letting the twine play out, hold in the branches as you walk around the shrub, still pressing them in with your back. Stop when you have wrapped half to three-quarters of the height of the shrub, snip the twine, and find a sturdy place to tie off the end. This will remind you of the way that some sellers of Christmas trees wrap up their ever-

Voila! Green, Where There Once Was Brown

Your boss is going to drop by your house this evening for your big backyard barbecue. But as you survey the condition of your lawn, you're ashamed to find several brown spots—where the hammock frame covered the grass, where a dog urinated, and that area that never seems to get enough water. Don't you wish you could "retouch" your lawn on special occasions just as some photographers doctor pictures to fix blemishes or inadequate color? The fact is, you *can* retouch your lawn from brown to green on special occasions. The product you're looking for is called lawn paint, available at garden stores and over the Internet.

Okay, okay . . . once you have picked yourself up off the floor from your laughing fit, allow me to review how lawn paint works. When you think about it, painting a brown lawn green is pretty much the definition of cheating. Lawn paint is a concentrated grass-green dye that you mix with water and apply with a garden sprayer. It dyes your brown grass green, a coloring that lasts until the grass gets high enough to be clipped off by the lawn mower. Manufacturers say lawn paint dries in about 30 minutes, is nontoxic, and won't rub off on your shoes (or, let's hope, on your boss's shoes), on your kids, or on your pets.

Some pointers:

- Apply lawn paint when the grass is dry.
- Paint a small area of your lawn first, to make sure the product and your spraying equipment is working as you had expected.
- If you're going to spray near concrete, wet the concrete with plain water first and hose away any dye immediately. Otherwise, you may color your sidewalk a permanent grass green.
- Spray from different directions, so the paint hits the grass blades from different angles.
- Use cardboard, planks, plastic, or other materials to shield such fixtures as the shed, the patio, and the garden wall from the green spray.
- Don't spray into the wind, or a green mist may waft next door and color your neighbor's car. Or spouse.
- When you're done painting your lawn, don't forget to sign your name down in the corner, as *les artistes* do.

greens. When you find that some branches pop out of place, go back and do a little doctoring to tuck loose limbs under the twine. This technique is especially beneficial for the kind of evergreens you would use in a hedge or along the house, particularly the column-shaped varieties. Do this shrub- and tree-wrapping before the first threat of snow and ice for the winter season. Remove the bindings once the threat of heavy snow and other frozen precipitation has passed. Old Man Winter will go stomping off, feeling cheated out of one of his favorite acts of cruelty.

Mow up your leaves. The very bravest cheaters I know find the gumption to walk away from years of tradition. That's because they realize that sentimentality can be a home-wrecking emotion that leads to an enormous waste of time and effort, merely because people think, "We've always done it this way." The traditional methods for fall leaf cleanup are a good example. The problem with raking or even blowing your yard's leaves into a pile is that after all of that effort, you still need to coax them into a bag for disposal. What's more, tree leaves are terrible space hogs. No matter how you push and stomp them into a lawn bag, they eat up tons of space. (In my neighborhood, it's not uncommon to see a dozen leaf bags at the curb of a quarter-acre lot.) The sneakiest solution to this dilemma is to quit raking and leaf blowing altogether. Just hook the grass clipping bag onto your lawn mower and give your lawn an autumn once-over whether the grass needs cutting or not. You'll have to empty the leaf-filled collection bag frequently, but those ground-up leaves pour easily. They make great mulch, so if you like, just tote the bag over to a garden bed, pour them on, and spread them with a rake. Or you could pour them onto a compost pile. Or pour the shredded leaves into a leaf bag—you'll save a lot of bags, since shredded leaves are so much more compact.

Give your leaves a trim. If mowing up leaves isn't practical for you, it's still easy to shred them for use as mulch or for easier handling in lawn bags. Instead of dragging a lawn bag around the yard and stuffing full-size leaves into it, take an empty trash can over to your leaf pile. The trash can will stand up on its own, of course, so it's a much more cooperative container for you to drop armloads of leaves into. When the trash can gets full, turn on your string trimmer and lower its head into the trash can to shred the leaves. Then pour them onto a garden bed as mulch, onto your compost pile, or into a lawn bag for disposal.

Keep your hydrangeas hydrated. Hydrangeas need special protection from severe winter weather. Otherwise, wind and cold air will dry out their branches and cripple their buds, and your hydrangeas won't be able to bloom well the next year, says Jeffries. Use his three tricks to keep your hydrangeas comfy and hydrated through the winter.

- Build up a few inches of mulch around the base of your hydrangeas (but not directly against the main stems).
- Then wrap each plant with twine (as described above for small evergreens) until they're bundled up and looking like Hershey's Kisses.
- Pick up an antidesiccant spray at your garden store. This is a liquid wax that you can apply with a pump-up garden sprayer, or right from the spray bottle if you don't have masses of hydrangeas. Apply it to your hydrangeas in December when the temperature is above 40°F and let it dry. Apply it again when temperatures climb above 50°F. By the way, antidesiccant spray will also help prevent winter moisture loss from your roses, rhododendrons, and azaleas.

Usher pests out the door. When you clean up your dying garden foliage in fall, make sure that no disease- or pest-carrying plant matter makes it back into your garden. Pull up your spent annuals—both flowers and vegetables—and drop those leaves and stems onto your compost pile. However, if those plants carried pests or diseases, bag up the debris and put it out with the trash. Cut your perennials down to within a few inches of the ground and dispose of those trimmings the same way. After all, your compost is headed right back to your garden beds eventually, and even a hot compost pile won't get hot enough to kill off all the bad guys. There's no sense in giving those old bugs and diseases another shot at your garden for the next growing season.

Make up for a dry fall. If you have had a particularly dry fall, give your small trees and shrubs a generous watering in late fall, before the ground freezes and the coldest winter weather arrives. The moisture will protect them from damage when those blasts of cold, dry wind hit.

Where winter's mild, plant for the season. In fall, warm-climate gardeners can start a whole new round of gardening. Vegetable gardeners can plant cool-weather veggies like lettuce and peas. Flower gardeners can fill their beds with cool-weather annuals such as pansies, spicy-sweet stocks, and honey-scented sweet alyssum.

Deflect the winter wind. To protect vulnerable shrubs and trees from a drying, limb-snapping winter wind, set up this simple windbreak on their wind-prone side (typically to the west or north). Drive three garden stakes into the ground, several inches apart. Then wrap burlap or some other windbreaking material around the stakes, and secure it with a few wraps of twine.

Pile that snow onto the lawn, not the garden. You're out on the driveway one winter's day with an enormous scoop of snow and ice on your snow shovel. Let's see: Where to dump this, where to dump this? Why, here's a nice open spot on the flowerbed . . . "Stop!" says John Marshall, a garden products expert in Ohio. The layer of snow and ice that accumulates naturally on a garden bed during winter is actually a benefit, because it insulates the ground. But shoveling more onto a garden bed can damage your plantings. That's because the weight of that ice and compacted snow will snap limbs and smash plants down. Also, if someone used salt or other deicer on your driveway, you will be passing along chemicals that could harm your plants and garden soil. So where's the best place to pile up that driveway snow and ice? Pick a convenient spot on your lawn, Marshall says, and give your landscape plants a break. Or just heap the worst of the driveway slush down at the curb.

Make the wind work for you. Many gardeners don't appreciate what a powerful ally the wind can be. A piercing winter blow or even a gentle summer breeze can complicate your work outside—or it can make your work easier if you know how to use it to your advantage. If you're sweeping the driveway, raking leaves, or using a leaf blower, always move along with the direction of the wind, says Barbara Arnold, horticultural designer at the Franklin Park Conservatory in Columbus, Ohio. Working against the wind is a losing battle. You will just find yourself sweeping or raking again and again. "Don't fight it," Arnold says.

Warm up a cool spring and summer. If you live in a region that gets a cool spring and summer, protect your garden plants and extend the growing season with these two simple tactics.

■ **Use the angle of the sun.** Lay out your garden rows running east-west, so all of your plants get a southern exposure, and thus maximum sun. Position taller plants behind shorter ones, and make sure that the rows are spaced enough apart so that the plants in one row are not throwing too much shade onto the next row. Also, try building soil-and-compost planting mounds, and position your transplants and seeds on the south side of the mounds for maximum sun exposure and protection.

■ **Capture reflected heat.** Planting near a white or light-colored wall, fence, or foundation ensures that heat reflected by these structures will spill onto your garden plants throughout the growing season. (In fact, this works so well that you'll need to check that your garden doesn't get too dried out on warmer days—nobody likes overcooked vegetables, after all.) A stone or brick wall will also absorb heat from the sun during the day and radiate it back outward to plants at night. In the absence of such preexisting structures that will bounce sunlight onto your garden, you can accomplish the same thing with a homemade reflector. Paint a piece of cardboard or plywood in a light color, and prop it up to the south of your garden rows—or wherever else it will cast sunlight back onto your plantings. For even more "solar power," cover your homemade reflector in aluminum foil.

Well, it sounds something like the famous Postman's Creed, doesn't it? "Neither drought, nor rain, nor snow, nor gloom of weather shall stay these clippers from the swift completion of their appointed rounds."

CHAPTER 13

At Peace with Mother Nature:
BUGS, BUNNIES, BAMBI, GROUNDHOGS, *and* MORE

|||||||||||||||||||||||||||||||||||||||||||||||||||||||||||||||||||||||||||||||||||||||||||||||||||

We share the great outdoors with Mother Nature. Our garden beds and landscape plants are outside, of course. As are the wild woods, streambeds, hills, shorelines, open skies, and an entire planet's worth of creatures. None of those creatures cares one whit about property lines, garden borders—or which garden vegetables you had intended for your own dinner plate. Nonetheless, we don't want to share our garden bounty with the animals roaming the outdoors quite as much as Mother Nature wants us to.

How exactly can you "cheat" at controlling the pests that routinely attack your garden produce and flowers? Time and again, the answer lies with Mother Nature herself. Any pest you can name is an animal that comes with its own set of powerful instincts and behaviors that are essential for its survival. Often, those very traits are keys to confounding the pests that invade our prized plantings. Let's take a look.

SLUGS, BUGS, AND OTHER THUGS

They creep and crawl and leave slime trails. They eat huge holes in foliage. They mar our fruits and vegetables, making them less than appetizing, and shred our flowers and their leaves into unsightly scraps. Bugs. Ugh. Let's go get 'em.

Go light on mulch and rotting debris. Slugs like to hunker down in the cool, dark, moist organic material on your soil's surface in spring and summer, so with a little discipline you can deprive them of conditions that help them thrive.

- Where slugs are a problem, keep the mulch down to an inch or so in depth, so this layer does not hold an inordinate amount of slug-coddling moisture against the soil.

- Resist the temptation to add rotting garden trimmings, fallen leaves, or grass clippings to your garden bed. Slugs love such food sources, so use them to make compost instead of putting them right into the garden.

- Keep your garden plants well spaced and well trimmed so there's plenty of air circulation to prevent the jungly steam bath that slugs adore.

- Attack your slugs the moment you realize they are staking out your garden. They multiply quickly, so a quick response is essential.

Offer slugs a comfy hiding place. Slugs are suckers for the shelter of flat, moist material lying against the ground. So dampen about a square foot of old newspaper or carpet and lay it on the ground near the plants that your slugs are having their slugfest on. (A melon rind turned fruit-side down will serve the same purpose.) After 2 days, turn your traps over, pluck up the slimy critters, and drop them into a container of soapy water to put them to rest permanently.

Draw a line in the dirt. Diatomaceous earth will form a slug-resistant barrier around garden plants when you pour a ring of it around the plant you want to protect. This stuff is made from the silicon skeletons of algae, which will slice into the slugs' soft bodies when the hungry little critters try to cross over it. Replenish the barrier when it gets wet. Pick up a bag of diatomaceous earth at your garden supply store (avoid the version intended for use in swimming pool filters). For safety, wear a dust mask when you're working with the powder.

Try a copper slug stopper. Slugs hate to cross a surface made of copper. That's because their mucus chemically reacts with the copper to deliver a small electrical charge. So put this knowledge to work the next time you browse your garden store, and look for such products as copper rings you can lay around cherished plants, and copper tape you can wrap around plant containers to keep slugs from crawling up the sides. You also can find plant stands made with copper feet.

Deliver a morning paper to earwigs. If earwigs are annoying your prized flowers, keep these bugs under control with the "morning newspaper" gambit, which works much like the slug traps described above. At night, take several separate sections of newspaper and roll them up individually. Dampen these rolls under the faucet and lay them on the ground where earwigs are damaging your flowers. Earwigs like to take cover in moist, narrow crevices, and they will happily crawl between the pages. Early the next morning, gather your earwig-infested newspaper sections and drop them into a plastic trash bag. Tie the bag off, making sure the bugs don't escape, and drop the bag into your outdoor trash can.

Make slugs "walk" on eggshells. Rampaging slugs in your vegetable or flower garden can be a horrifying sight. But Annette Pelliccio, founder of The Happy Gardener organic garden products company, has a clever way to keep the little slime monsters at bay. Crush up the eggshells that you generate at breakfast and sprinkle them around the bases of the plants that slugs seem attracted to. Slugs can't crawl over the shells, because the sharp edges will cut them, she says. And there's a bonus: When you get into the eggshell habit, you're also adding beneficial calcium to the soil.

Ply slugs with alcohol. Much to the amusement of party enthusiasts, beer actually is very good bait for killing slugs in the garden. Here's the official cheat-at-gardening technique—with one surprising wrinkle. Pull from your recycling bin a shallow container, such as a yogurt cup or a tuna can. Bury the container, open side up, in the garden soil where your slugs congregate. The rim of your container should remain a half-inch above the soil. Fill the container with beer. If you're expecting rain, devise a loose cover that will deflect the excess water without preventing slugs from entering the container. Slugs will be drawn to the beer and drown in the container. And here's the promised twist: Slugs really, truly prefer one beer among others, says Master Gardener Rebecca Kolls of *Good Morning America*. It's Heineken. No kidding. Beer traps, however, are just one technique for reducing your slug population—not

SHADES OF GREEN
Slug Bait with Advantages

A quick browse through your garden store will reveal some chemical solutions to your slug problem—but one variety is a decidedly greener approach, says Master Gardener Rebecca Kolls. Iron phosphate slug bait (also known as ferric phosphate) is considered fine for use near edible garden crops and won't endanger pets, birds, and other wildlife.

In contrast, another common slug bait, metaldehyde, is stronger and could harm pets and wildlife, so do not use it in your garden.

a wide-ranging solution, says Kolls. The beer will only attract slugs in the immediate vicinity of the trap.

Invite ladybugs to dinner. Ladybugs love to munch on aphids, those sap-sucking insects that can torment your garden plants. One adult ladybug can eat 5,000 aphids in a year's time! You can order hundreds of ladybugs at a time from catalogs or over the Internet. The instructions for releasing them into your garden are simple, but don't be surprised if a lot of them turn fickle and fly off. If you're not using pesticides in your garden, you can attract ladybugs to the vicinity with flowering plants that provide the nectar and pollen they depend on to mature and lay eggs. Ladybugs particularly like yarrows and morning glories. Another famous bug-fighting bug you can order up for your garden: praying mantises. See the Cheat Sheet on page 59 for a list of plants that attract beneficial insects.

Welcome other bug eaters into your yard. A bird can eat hundreds of pesky bugs in a day, and that's hundreds of bugs that don't have a chance to munch on your garden. So make an inviting home for feathered friends in your yard by installing bird feeders, birdhouses, and birdbaths—and make sure they're out of the reach of cats and other predators. Tall trees for nesting help, too.

In fall, try a "brownout." When the foliage in your garden beds starts to brown and die off, give your garden a little fall cleaning, says gardening products expert John Marshall in Ohio. Don't leave stacks of leaves and stalks against the ground in your garden. "That's what diseases and insects will harbor in to last the winter," Marshall says. You'll just be recreating past problems come next spring. Lightly work little snippets of refuse into the surface of your garden soil but haul the bulkier material to your compost pile.

Insist on resistant varieties. No matter where you garden, every region has its own selection of notorious pests, notes Marshall. Many people who buy a new home just blindly accept the builder's "landscape package" without getting details about the plant varieties that the builder intends to use. In your own defense, insist on plant varieties that are resistant to your region's most common pests and plant diseases. For a briefing on these hardy varieties,

A New Insect Species?

Garden products expert John Marshall of Ohio spent 4 years answering questions on a company's consumer hotline. One New Year's Day, a panicking woman called from Syracuse, New York. She explained that "snow fleas" had invaded her front porch and were trying to enter her house. She demanded the name of a product to spray on them. A tad suspicious, Marshall confirmed with the caller that there was in fact snow cover in her town and that it was indeed cold outside. He asked whether she had a fireplace in her home. Yes, she did. And had she perhaps just lit a fire, using newspaper as fire starter material?

"Yes. How did you know that?" she replied.

Marshall offered his analysis: The very fine ash from the newspaper had blown up her chimney, and those minuscule white bits had swirled around and gathered on her porch. Not "snow fleas"—harmless ash, caught in the breeze. There was a prolonged silence on the phone and then a click as the caller hung up.

"I don't think I sold any product that day," Marshall says.

consult your local extension agent. This applies not only when you're buying a new home, but anytime you're adding to an existing landscape.

Plant a bug-annoying border. Marigolds are a renowned bug repellent, so plant them as a border for your garden beds, says Marshall. French marigolds (these are the smaller varieties, of the species *Tagetes patula*) offer the additional benefit of repelling harmful nematodes that can attack plant roots. Other plants with insect-repelling qualities include mints, catnip, rue (wear gloves when handling it; some people can get a rash from touching it), basil, and tansy.

Fire back at fire ants. Much to the dismay of gardeners in parts of the southern United States, fierce fire ants have invaded gardens, damaging plants and hurting people with their painful stings. The ants cannot tolerate cold weather, but as our climate warms, their range is expected to expand northward. However, there are some effective tools that you can use to fight fire ants, says pest control expert Stewart Clark of St. Louis. (Let it be said that other species of conventional, non-aggressive ants are not inherently bad in your garden, because they help to aerate your soil.) As often happens with garden pests, the cheating-est approach is to deal your fire ants a discouraging one-two punch that's more powerful than taking one single measure.

■ **Drench 'em.** Try a drench made with rotenone or pyrethrin that is poured directly into the ant mound. Rotenone is a crystalline insecticide obtained from the roots of several tropical plants. (Be careful not to use it around water as it is toxic to fish.) Pyrethrin is a compound found in chrysanthe-mum flowers that works as a pesticide. It is very widely available in garden centers and has always been fine for organic gardening. Rotenone is also available in garden centers.

■ **Then spread granules.** One week after using rotenone or pyrethrin against your fire ants, spread a granular contact insecticide over the territory where your fire ants roam. Such products kills fire ants as they're out and about, further discouraging the spread of the colony. Organic granular products are likely to contain diatomaceous earth, rotenone, pyrethrin, or spinosad. (Spinosad is derived from a naturally occurring soil bacterium; it controls pests without harming beneficial insects.) However, follow the package directions carefully and understand that the granules tend to kill only roaming workers and may not kill the queen and nest.

■ **Fight back with beneficial nematodes.** Nematodes are microscopic worms that live in soil. Some are bad guys that attack plants. Others are helpers that attack pests. Nematode products that fight fire ants come in the form of a drench that you pour into ant mounds or a spray that you use on the lawn.

Brush off fire ants—immediately! Fire ants will quickly climb and attack any gardener who blunders into their midst, stinging your hands and arms, your feet and legs, or any other part of you. A little knowledge of how these ferocious insects attack may save you a world of pain. When a fire ant decides

MYTH-BUSTERS
Fire Ants, How about Some Breakfast?

A purported natural cure for fire ant infestation is making the rounds of the southern United States. It calls for pouring dry grits, that Southern staple made of ground corn, onto the fire ants' mounds. The homespun theory is that fire ants will eat the grits, the grain in their stomachs will absorb moisture and expand, and then the fire ants will explode from internal pressure.

This is as good a use for grits as I have ever heard. However, scientists at Texas A&M University say their experiments show the approach does not work. Fire ants have too good a filtering system in their digestive tracts. Homemade solutions are always appealing, but for now we're stuck with the other ones described in this chapter.

● ● ● ● ● ● ● ● ● ● ● ● ● ● ● ● ●

to inflict pain, it does so with a frantic two-part procedure. First, it grabs your skin in its jaws, and then it uses its rear-end stinger to inject a nasty venom with several rapid-fire thrusts. So here's how to cheat a fire ant out of an effective attack: The moment you feel that initial pinch from its jaws, use your hand or some other object to brush the ant off of your skin right away, before it has a chance to start its stinging stage. Then check yourself thoroughly for any more fire ants. And give careful thought to the fact that you are probably standing in the wrong place at the moment!

Lay out the welcome mat for bats. Bats eat tons of bugs. No, you might not want bats living in your attic, but having them live *near* you is a big plus for your garden. One way to encourage bats to relocate from your attic is to provide a cozy alternative roosting spot—a bat house. Bat houses are easy to order over the Internet. And many garden centers, nurseries, and farm supply stores carry them. You'll find plans for making them there, too, if you're the handy sort. Position your bat house at least 15 feet off the ground. You can mount one on the side of a house or another building, on a pole, or in a tree. Position your bat house so it gets at least 6 hours of sun daily. If you're in the process of evicting bats from your attic, set up your bat house a few months in advance. That way, the bats will already be familiar with the bat house by the time they have to move.

Pass That Bug Zapper Right Next Door

At first, it might seem like a great idea: controlling the annoying bugs in your backyard (mosquitoes, for instance) with one of those devices that electronically zaps them right out of the air. However, if anyone gives you a bug zapper for a gift, here's the wisest thing you can do, says Stewart Clark, who does pest control research and development in St. Louis: Give it to your next-door neighbor.

Think about it: Such gizmos work by attracting bugs toward them. Wouldn't you prefer that annoying bugs be attracted next door rather than toward your home? Yes, this is cheating—but you needn't explain your generosity, right?

Tell mosquitoes to buzz off. Mosquitoes may not be a direct threat to your vegetables and flowers—unless they make you so miserable outside that you're reluctant to tend to your garden. But there's no sense in making life easy for these annoying, disease-carrying bugs. Here are some simple measures you can incorporate into your yard work routine.

- Identify low spots in your yard where water pools and improve drainage there to prevent long-lasting puddles that mosquitoes can use for breeding. Similarly, rearrange any outdoor containers so they do not hold standing water—this goes for old tires, buckets, pots, cans, and other vessels around the yard.

- If you have outdoor water bowls for pets, horse troughs, or birdbaths, change the water in them at least every few days (daily is better).

- Make your yard a friendly place for mosquito-eating creatures, such as frogs, lizards, birds, and fish. A fishpond helps, of course, as well as sheltered places (such as a flowerpot turned over with a piece knocked out of the rim) for toads, plus food sources (yummy plants and feeders) and bushy shrubs for birds to take cover and nest in. Keep a chemical-free garden, too.

- Keep your gutters and downspouts clear, so they don't collect standing water.
- Mosquito dunks are nontoxic disks that float in any open water in your yard (decorative pools and birdbaths, for instance). They kill mosquito larvae before they can turn into adults that munch on your skin.
- Deck and patio enthusiasts swear by citronella candles for their mosquito-repellent properties.

Bambi and Other Furry Critters

As we move on from bugs and up a few rungs in the animal kingdom, the stakes get higher—if for no other reason than because deer, groundhogs, and rabbits are capable of so much more garden destruction than a few insects are. So let's find out how to use the ingrained habits and instincts of furry critters to banish them from your landscape.

Keep switching to annoy those deer. Here's the No. 1 strategy for repelling deer from your garden, says Master Gardener Rebecca Kolls: Realize that there *is* no No. 1 strategy for repelling deer. That's right, during your gardening life you will encounter a wide variety of techniques for driving off those hoofed garden munchers—some of them quite effective and some of them earning marginal folklore status. But even the most effective approaches will not provide 100 percent protection against deer indefinitely. Eventually, deer will overcome their reluctance to enter your garden and their lust for garden plants will draw them back. Your surest defense is to rotate your deer-repelling tactics, Kolls says. So you may spread coyote urine for a month, switch to a "liquid fencing" product for another month, and then try garlic spray the next month. (Most garden centers have loads of these kinds of products.) Whatever you do, don't let down your guard, Kolls says—persistence counts.

Protect trees with barriers. A hungry deer can strip a young, newly planted tree of foliage and bark in no time. If you have set out saplings in a deer-prone area, protecting them with a couple of barrier techniques is a good bet, says garden product expert John Marshall. Either devise a cylinder of chicken wire and place it around your sapling, or cover the young tree with protective plastic netting from your garden store. Unfortunately, you won't find this approach practical if you have zillions of little trees to protect.

You can also use netting to enclose a veggie garden, or to fence the perimeter of your entire property. But hang strips of cloth or foil on the netting to alert passing birds to the fence—they don't always see it and can get trapped in it. If you are using netting for fencing, know that the fence has to be at least 8 feet high (10 is better) to keep out deer. They are amazing jumpers.

Feed 'em and you'll weep. Sure, you are a kindhearted person, but resist the temptation to take food out to deer when they venture into your backyard. Not only will they be more likely to return and nibble even more in your garden, but there's an added danger as well. It's not uncommon for deer to learn quickly that the interior of a house is the source of yummy food. As a result, they've been known to dive through glass doors and windows, cut themselves, and wreak havoc inside a home, bleeding all over and wrecking furnishings left and right. Deer don't understand that clear window glass is a barrier, so help them out by placing stickers, decorations, or blinds across your sliding doors or windows. And resist that temptation to feed Bambi at all.

For deer, use a trio of tactics. Keeping deer out of your garden requires use of three core tactics, says pest control expert Stewart Clark in St. Louis.

- ■ **Bad taste.** That is, plant the foods that deer don't like to eat and not the ones they lust after. See the Cheat Sheets on pages 344 and 345.

- ■ **Bad smell.** Provide odors that deer find offensive or frightening. Products that produce this effect might include dried blood, set out in containers or mixed with water and sprayed as a liquid, or predator urine (both sold in garden supply stores), which might persuade deer that a killer beast is lurking nearby.

- **Bad vibes.** Take advantage of the deer's fear response. Some people set out radios tuned to talk stations at night, some use gizmos that shoot a jet of water when deer step on them, and others let their dogs out at night.

Okay, if you exhaust the limits of those first three tactics, Clark might add a fourth: bad access. That is, use tall fences or netting (mentioned earlier) to create a physical barrier between the beasts and your bounty. Here are some more things you will want to know about repelling deer from your garden.

Mix it up. Clark says the "big cheat" in shooing deer from your yard is this: Switch frequently among products that repel deer through the tactics of taste, smell, and fear (or "vibes.") You'll notice that this is similar to the approach with moles in your lawn, discussed later in this chapter. The fact is, deer are adaptable and persistent creatures. While one repellent product may annoy them for a few weeks, the effect is likely to wear off. So keep introducing new deer-annoying products into your repertoire and rotate them.

Cheat Sheet

Plants Deer Love to Eat

Here are some plants that deer are known to favor and that, therefore, you may choose *not* to plant.

- Fruit trees, bushes, and vines, such as apple, peach, cherry, pear, and plum, as well as grapes, raspberries, strawberries, and blackberries
- Yews, eastern white pine, Atlantic white cedar, fir, redbud, and hollies
- Azaleas and rhododendrons, roses, and hydrangeas

- Sweet corn, lettuce, broccoli, cauliflower, beans, and peas
- Spring bulbs (except for daffodils and narcissus, grape hyacinth, snowdrops, and squills); tulips a particular favorite
- Pansies, daylilies, dahlias, hostas, trilliums, hollyhocks, sunflowers, impatiens, phlox, black-eyed Susan, and sedum

Avoid planting the plants that deer adore. Making a list of the plants that attract deer is problematic, but it makes sense that if you set out favorite deer munchies, that, unfortunately, is a sure way to attract the animals to your yard. Food preferences among deer will vary from season to season, according to location, deer species, the deer's nutritional condition, and the local weather conditions. Nevertheless, see the Cheat Sheet on the opposite page for information you can use in your garden and landscape planning.

Serve deer their "yucky" foods. As with any favorite-deer-food list, listing foods that will repel deer is tricky, too, because food preferences will vary according to multiple factors. Nevertheless, deer often will shy away from spiny, bristly plants; plants that have intense odor; plants with a milky juice in the stalks or leaves; and plants with a bitter taste. The bottom line is, when deer are hungry enough, they will eat just about anything. But the plants listed in the Cheat Sheet below will at least give you a fighting chance.

Test out your deer-repelling plant first. If you want to experiment with plants that might repel deer, first save yourself time, money, and anguish with

Cheat Sheet

Plants Deer Don't Usually Like

Try these in your backyard, observe how the deer react, and adjust accordingly.

- Ash, birch, cypress, oak, spruce, sycamore, ginkgo, maple, beech, Russian olive, hawthorn
- Witch hazel, juniper, lilac, barberry, smokebush, inkberry, jasmine, mountain laurel, Japanese kerria, leucothoe, bayberry, oleander
- Virginia creeper, Boston ivy, bugleweed (ajuga), periwinkle (vinca), wisteria

- Foxglove, lobelia, snapdragon, alyssum, bee balm, baby's breath, chrysanthemum, monkshood, agave, ageratum, allium, anemone, artemisia, butterfly weed, baptisia, calendula, ferns, ornamental grasses, heliotrope, lantana, catmint, evening primrose, Russian sage, marigolds, yucca, zinnias
- Yarrow, chives, dill, oregano, mint, rosemary, lavender, tarragon, thyme

this little corner-cutting tip: Without making a large investment in an untried plant, set a small version in a container positioned near the garden. Check the new plant a day or two after you set it out. If it has been seriously nibbled, keep looking for alternatives. If the deer pass it by, that's a great sign for garden cheaters—plant more!

Position deer-repelling plants strategically. As creatures of habit, deer are likely to keep entering your yard by the same route. When you have bought a selection of deer-repelling plants, position them along their routine entryway. Not sure where they come in? Look for their hoofprints in soft ground and muddy places after rain. Deer munch as they walk along, so they will get the message that your garden is a repugnant place. Also, intersperse your deer-resistant plants with any plants in your garden that need special protection. Deer will have trouble distinguishing the repellent food from the delicious and will head elsewhere for better grazing.

Remove their cover. Underbrush and deep grass around the outside edge of your property will give deer a comfortable feeling that cover is nearby. Deer are edgy, paranoid animals, so play on those insecurities. Keep all brushy, brambly areas well trimmed so your visitors won't feel at home. They'll be less likely to linger over your garden.

Pick up the fallen fruit. When your fruit trees drop fruit all over the yard, that's a resounding dinner bell to deer from all around. Quickly pick up any fruit that hits the ground and dispose of it. Otherwise, you're abetting another fruit-loving pest as well—yellow jackets!

Offend deer with a soapy smell. Some soaps serve as an effective deer repellent in your garden. Their action is a one-two punch: Highly scented soap will overwhelm a deer's protective sense of smell and give it a disturbing feeling of being vulnerable to danger. Also, there is animal-based fat in many kinds of soap that help to frighten deer as well.

So to scare deer out of your backyard, do this: Take a pair of old panty hose and cut it in half so you have two separate legs. Unwrap each bar of highly scented soap (Irish Spring is famously effective) and place it in the foot of one stretch of panty hose. Tie the top of the material onto a support so that the

Stop deer (and other critters) in their tracks by creating a planting bed barrier at the edge of your yard. Use deer-proof plants and plant them densely so deer won't bother traversing or exploring that area.

hanging soap is strategically placed—3 feet off the ground is ideal. The radius of the soap's effectiveness is about 3 feet, so you could hang multiple soap bars, each 6 feet apart. Hang soap bars this way around the outer perimeter of a fruit tree, or hang them from stakes around your garden. Replace the bars once they have dissolved in the rain.

Scare deer with a hairy experience. Lots of frustrated gardeners are in the habit of visiting barbershops, collecting human hair, and stuffing panty hose with it to frighten deer away. (Using a bag made from cheesecloth will work, too.) However, the effectiveness of this tactic depends upon how much your deer have been exposed to people in the past. Over long-term exposure, they might well come to consider humans harmless. So here's how to cheat your way out of that dilemma: Deer will be plenty afraid of the scent of dogs. So go to an animal grooming shop and ask for a bagful of trimmed puppy fuzz. Hang the dog hair in your garden using the cut-up panty hose trick described above. Replace the hair once the dog scent has faded—which takes about a month.

Scramble their sense of smell. The stench of rotting eggs is a famous deer repellent. Here's how to make your own concoction. Break two eggs into your food processor, add 2 cups of water, toss in a few garlic cloves, and add a few shakes of Tabasco sauce. Blend the ingredients until smooth and pour into a tight-sealing container. Close the container and let it sit at room temperature for a week. Sprinkle this stinky mixture on the plants that need protection from deer—and onto the ground around them as well. (From the Use-Your-Brain Department: Don't put this putrid stuff on garden produce that you intend to eat.)

Scare up some scary urine. When deer feasting in your backyard get the idea that a bobcat, mountain lion, wolf, or bear has staked out that territory, the grazers won't hang around for long. That's why selling predator urine has become an odd little micro-industry. (The cheater's philosophy is that it's better to buy mountain lion urine from distributors than to try collecting it yourself.) You can buy containers of your favorite predator's pee from garden supply stores or through the Internet. Special containers are sold for dispensing the odor in your backyard, or you can easily make your own: Take a lidded plastic tub—the kind cottage cheese comes in—and punch several holes high on the sides to release the scent. Pour predator urine into the tub, clap the lid on, and set your "pee pot" near backyard plants that need protection from deer. Not surprisingly, thanks to the stink, rabbits and squirrels will find better places to congregate, too.

Wow them with Bowser. A dog in the backyard is a sure way to repel deer and rabbits from your garden. What size or breed of dog scares them best? It doesn't matter! All you need in a dog is one that's alert, able to bark, and excited about furry, interloping creatures. Don't chain up your dog—that's tough on Fido. Don't forget that deer are quick learners and will quickly real-

Seeing Green and Brown Spots Before Your Eyes?

If you're finding odd little circles in your yard—brown spots and circles of bright green grass—that's a sure sign that your dog, or a neighbor's dog, is urinating on your yard. Salts in dog urine cause the browning, and nitrogen in the urine causes the excess greening, just as would happen with an overdose of fertilizer, says turfgrass expert Trey Rogers of Michigan State University. Here are some sneaky ways to keep "dog spots" to a minimum.

🌳 If your dog absolutely insists on urinating on a particular part of your yard, give the spot a good sopping-down with the garden hose the moment the deed is done. This will dilute the damaging chemicals in the urine and protect your grass.

🌳 Walk your dog in areas where there's no cultivated grass (yours or your neighbors'). Woods or an open field are both good bets.

🌳 Train your dog to urinate in part of your yard where there's a spread of mulch or pea gravel to absorb the liquid harmlessly.

🌳 Remember that smaller dog breeds mean smaller amounts of urine—and therefore smaller amounts of damaging chemicals. Many toy breeds can urinate indoors in litter boxes or on newspaper.

ize the limitations of a tied-up canine. Usually, a 4-foot-high backyard fence will do nicely to confine your dog. A fence that high will not deter a hungry deer from leaping into your yard, but a yappy creature inside it will.

Try a change of venue. If you're annoyed by the bunnies that saunter through your vegetable garden, cropping more lettuce down to the ground every day, consider an effective preventive strategy, says Kolls. Simply put: Make your garden hard for the rabbits to get to. Think about it: You don't really have to dig up part of your backyard to garden in a swath of green rows that rabbits view as an alluring smorgasbord. Instead, do your vegetable gardening in containers on your patio or deck. Elevated off the ground, your vegetables will be out of reach of marauding bunnies. "Every vegetable I know can be grown in a pot," says Kolls. Hmm, sounds like cheating. Exactly!

Spread used litter as a bunny barrier. If you have cats using litter boxes in your house, you have a steady supply of rabbit repellent. Once a week, sprinkle a new trail of used, urine-soaked cat litter around the outside of the garden bed that rabbits seem to visit frequently. The stench of cat urine will scare the rabbits. One would think it would make them lose their appetites as well.

Stink up your groundhog's hole. You and groundhogs have something in common: You both hate the stench of used cat litter. If you want to persuade a groundhog in your backyard to relocate, routinely dump your old cat litter down his hole to annoy him. (One fellow we know gave his little boys permission to urinate down a backyard groundhog hole, and they gleefully complied.) Once the groundhog has packed his bags and moved on, fill any old holes with rocks so that no other bothersome critters will set up housekeeping there. There's no sense in setting out a "Vacancy" sign for skunks.

Zap moles with a trap. There is no 100-percent-sure silver bullet against moles in your yard. However, here is your priority No. 1 approach, straight from Stewart Clark, who researches and develops pest control products in St. Louis. (By the way, that's a town he calls "The Mole Capital of the World," since the destructive little critters seem to revel in river country.) Go to your garden store and buy a spring-loaded mole trap, a device that drives a small stake into the pest as it tries to crawl through. As you might imagine, you're going to have to overcome the same kind of distaste you might have for working with spring-loaded mousetraps.

Where and how do you place your trap? First, locate a mole tunnel in your yard that you know is active. To test a tunnel, take a broomstick and poke it down through the top of a tunnel. Check that spot 12 or 24 hours later. If you can see that some busy little pest has done repair work where you intruded with the broomstick, you know that the tunnel is active with moles. And you have discovered a good spot to place your spring-loaded trap. There are various designs of mole traps, but generally you just slide the trap into the tunnel, and the trap sits there, waiting for a mole to pass through. Check the trap periodically and replace as necessary.

Here are a few more of Clark's mole-fighting pointers, which you can rotate into your battle plan to keep those little diggers away.

- Stomp down on a mole tunnel in your yard, grab a shovel, and sit back in a lawn chair to work on your MBO for a while. (No, you office jockeys, that stands for Maintenance By Observation). When you see signs that a mole is repairing a stomped tunnel, get to work with that shovel. Trap the mole with shovel cuts on either side of it, thrust the shovel under the mole, and flip it up to the surface. Then finish off the little beast in whichever way you wish.

- Reduce the population of grubs in your lawn, since moles relish these larvae. If you do, moles won't be as happy rooting around under your grass. Applying milky spore powder (available at garden stores) to your lawn will inoculate it with otherwise harmless, grub-killing bacteria. Grub reduction won't be your one-and-only solution, however, because there's plenty more yummy stuff in a lawn for moles to feed on.

- Alternate among these tactics the occasional use of the commercial mole baits and repellents, which include such ingredients as castor oil (yes, one widely available kind is clay granules impregnated with castor oil). Mole repellents are available at your garden store or over the Internet. Read the package to be sure the product contains only organic ingredients and follow application directions carefully, of course.

- Try annoying your moles with a "sonic repellent," a device that you stick into the ground to emit a whiny, whistling noise that's supposed to scare moles away.

- Above all, be persistent, says Clark. Try one of these tactics, and then try another. "The bottom line is that moles are a pain," he says.

Flood the mole out. Here's another way to capture moles that are ripping up your lawn: Flush them out. First, identify an active mole tunnel in your lawn, as described earlier. Then open up a hole in the tunnel, slide the end of your garden hose into it, and turn the hose on. Grab up a trowel and a small lidded jar or box. When a mole surfaces, sputtering, scoop him up with your trowel, drop him into the container, close it, and dispose of the wet and befuddled creature in whatever way leaves your good conscience untroubled.

Give armadillos a whiff of ammonia. You might have an image of armadillos as cartoon-cute little armored creatures. That is, unless you have a yard in southern North America or South America, and armadillos have shredded your turf in search of grubs and worms. Fortunately, armadillos have a sensitive spot—their noses. They particularly hate the odor of ammonia. So find a rag, soak it in an ammonia-based cleaner, and drop it into your armadillo's burrow. When it appears that your armadillo has grown tired of the stink and moved on, fill his burrow's entrance hole with loose dirt and check it daily for signs of new digging. Once the hole has been inactive for a week, pack it with rocks and dirt to discourage other creatures from moving in.

Resist the trap temptation. You know you've entertained the thought: You see a fat little groundhog belly-crawling across your backyard and you think, "I could catch that little guy in a 'humane' trap and release him somewhere else." Well, banish the thought, says garden products expert John Marshall. Yes, there are traps available that will capture furry critters without harming them. But if you play the catch-and-release game, there's a great chance that the beast you release will end up right in your backyard again. Besides, many

Give the Gas a Rest

Stewart Clark's pest control company in St. Louis once held a contest inviting customers to complete this sentence: "I hate moles because . . . " One finalist in the contest explained how he decided to asphyxiate the moles in his yard. Early one morning, he pulled his truck onto the front yard and removed the exhaust vent from his home's clothes dryer. He duct-taped one end of the vent to his truck's exhaust pipe and plunged the other end into a mole tunnel. Then some police cars roared up and officers jumped out, telling him to step away from the truck, reassuring him that whatever problem he had, "It's not all that bad!"

Turns out that his neighbors had reported an apparent suicide attempt in progress.

Need we add that this is a don't-try-this-at-home tactic? The carbon monoxide in automobile exhaust is deadly, of course, and you would have no idea by what unknown passages it might enter a nearby dwelling.

A Plant Pest Infiltrates

Years ago, Barbara Arnold, horticultural designer at the Franklin Park Conservatory in Columbus, Ohio, worked with an energetic, gung-ho intern. This nice woman was replanting her own entire yard. One day she mentioned that her 2-year-old had come down with a case of poison ivy so severe that the child had to go to the hospital—but she had no idea how the child could have been exposed.

Several days later, the intern was raving about a vine she had discovered near her porch, one with beautiful, shiny leaves. She had liked it so much that she had trained it up a trellis—and had her 2-year-old help. Arnold asked the intern to bring in a cutting, and sure enough, the vine was poison ivy.

"So know your plants," advises Arnold. A painful lesson learned.

local governments frown on do-it-yourself trapping. Instead, remember our official How to Cheat HIRE criteria for deciding when to call in a professional. If a job is Hard, Important, Rarely done, and Elaborate, then HIRE a pro who has all of that training and equipment that you don't have. This removes a considerable amount of danger from tangling with wild animals—not the least of which could include claws, teeth, possible rabies, and a surprise skunk spraying. So call your local government and ask who handles animal control and consult your local extension agent as well.

There you have it—finally, ways in which you can coexist with Mother Nature. That's what gardening and landscaping are all about, after all: Working with the gifts of the natural world to produce food and a pleasing environment. That's all the easier to accomplish when you know how to cheat the common pests out of a share of your efforts!

Recommended Reading

Here's a list of books, most of them mentioned in the text, for gardeners looking for more information.

Rosemary Alexander, *The Essential Garden Design Workbook* (Timber Press, 2004)

Mel Bartholomew, *Square Foot Gardening* (Rodale, 2005)

Mel Bartholomew, *All New Square Foot Gardening* (Cool Springs Press, 2006)

Christopher Brickell and Judith A. Zuk, Editors-in-Chief, *The American Horticultural Society A-Z Encyclopedia of Garden Plants* (DK Publishing, Inc., 1997)

Clea Danaan, *Sacred Land: Intuitive Gardening for Personal, Political, and Environmental Change* (Llewellyn Publications, 2007)

Michael A. Dirr, *Dirr's Hardy Trees and Shrubs* (Timber Press, 1997)

Anne Halpin, *Homescaping: Designing Your Landscape to Match Your Home* (Rodale, 2005)

Ann Lovejoy, *Ann Lovejoy's Organic Garden Design School* (Rodale, 2001)

Trey Rogers, *Lawn Geek: Tips and Tricks for the Ultimate Turf from the Guru of Grass* (NAL Trade, 2007)

Lin Wellford and Kristen Helams, *Painted Garden Art Anyone Can Do* (ArtStone Press, 2007)

Index

Boldface page numbers indicate illustrations. <u>Underscored</u> references indicate boxed text, tables or charts.

A

Animal pests
  armadillos, 352
  deer, 296, 342–49, <u>344</u>, <u>345</u>, **347**
  dogs and, 348
  groundhogs, 350
  moles, 350–51, <u>352</u>
  rabbits, 348–50
  trapping, 352–53
Annuals, 219–20
  cool-weather, 330
  deadheading, 228
  low-maintenance, <u>103</u>, <u>219</u>
  points to remember about, <u>225</u>
  watering, 228
Antidesiccants, 329
Aphids, inspecting plants for, 41
Armadillos, 352
Arugula
  flea beetles and, <u>61</u>
  growing, 74
Azaleas, pruning, 291–92

B

Basic gardening principles, 1–8
  Bartholomew's five truths, <u>4–5</u>
Bats, 340
Beans
  in children's garden, 139–40, **140, 141**
  pole, 75–76
  spacing for, <u>62</u>
  supports for, 55

  bean tepee, 139–40, **140**
  tunnel, 140, **141**
Beets, spacing for, <u>62</u>
Beneficial insects, 337
  beneficial nematodes, 339
  encouraging, 58–59, <u>59</u>
  ladybugs, 337
Birds, protecting reseeded lawn from, 254, **254**
Botanical Latin, 264
Broccoli
  growing, 76–77, **85**
  spacing for, <u>62</u>
Bulbs, 214–15
  deadheading, 229
  fertilizing, 229
  flowerbeds for, 222
  foliage of, 229
  planting, 227
  purchasing, 215
  separating, 214–15

C

Cabbage, <u>46</u>, <u>62</u>
Cantaloupe, growing, 77–79, **79**
Carrots
  growing, 80–81
  spacing for, <u>62</u>
Cauliflower, spacing for, <u>62</u>
Celery, spacing for, <u>62</u>
Cheating, basic principles of, 1–8
Chemicals
  herbicides, <u>248</u>
  insecticides, 339

Equipment *(cont.)*
  mowers
    blade height for, <u>240</u>, 241
    blade sharpness, 245–46
    gasing up, 244, 249
    maintenance of, 245, 247, 248–49

F

Fall garden cleanup, 328–29
  diseases and, 337
  insect pests and, 337
Fencing, materials for, <u>108</u>
Fertilizer, 61
  aquarium water as, 27, 69
  feeding soil with, 25
  grass clippings as, <u>243</u>, 247
  for lawns, 250–52, <u>251</u>
  nutrients in, 14
  organic, 14, <u>16</u>
  phosphorus in, <u>251</u>
  for seedlings, 45, 48–49
Fertilizing, 66, 69
  container plants, 154
  lawns, 241, 251–52
  newly planted trees, <u>279</u>
  rooftop gardens, 182
  of transplanted seedlings, 52
  via soaker hose, 60–61
Fire ants, 338–40, <u>340</u>
Flea beetles, trap crop for, <u>61</u>
Flowerbeds
  for bulbs, 222
  cool-weather annuals for, 330
  creating, 18–19, **20**, 21
  deer
    deterring in, 342–49, <u>345</u>, **347**
  disease prevention in, 226
  edgings, 223, 224
    temporary bridges for, 224–26
  foliage plants in, 218
  layout of, and mowing, 226, 242

mapping, 223
paths in, 24, 223
positioning plants in, 224
preparing new, 224, <u>313</u>
shrubs for, <u>273</u>
small trees for, <u>273</u>
staggering bloom season in, 216–18,
    <u>217</u>
using color in, 217–18
weed control in, 61–63, 218
Flowers
  annuals, <u>103</u>, 219–20, <u>219</u>, <u>225</u>, 330
  beneficial insects and, 58, <u>59</u>
  for children's gardens, 139, 141
  cut
    prolonging life of, 231–33
  deadheading, 228, 229, <u>229</u>
  humidity and, 227–28
  in landscape design, <u>118</u>
  low-maintenance, <u>219</u>
  perennials, <u>102</u>–3
    combinations to try, <u>130</u>
  planning for
    color and, 217–18, 221
    for cutting garden, 222
    fragrance and, 221
    height and, 221–22
    spacing, 220–21
  selecting which to grow, 210–16
    bulbs, 214–15
    checking plant labels, 211, 216
    choosing plants at nursery, 214
    growth patterns and, 211
    lifestyle and, 214
    maintenance and, 213–14, 216
    narrowing choices, 215–16
    native plants, 211–13
    site assessment and, 210–11
    starting from seed, 26–27
  shrubs and, 218, 219, <u>220</u>
  using in vegetable gardens, <u>5</u>, 56
  watering, 228

Foliage
of bulbs, 229
using plants featuring, in flowerbeds,
218
Fruit, growing in container gardens,
161
Fruit flies, 202–3

G

Garden design. *See* Landscape design
Gardening
basic principles of, 1–8
five truths of, 4–5
Garden maintenance. *See also*
Equipment; Supplies; Tools
beating "weekend warrior" syndrome,
143
cleanliness during, 66
fertilizing (*See* Fertilizing)
mulch (*See* Mulch)
observation and, 66
organic products and, 66–67
picking vegetables, 70
watering (*See* Watering)
Garden records
of flowerbeds, 223
maps as, 120–21
seed packets as, 37
Garlic, spacing for, 62
Gloves, 308, 310–12
Gourds, 143–44
Grass. *See also* Lawn care; Lawns
diagnosing problems, 255, 257
fungal diseases of
preventing, 256–57
grubs and, 256
lawn paint and, 327
life span of, 252
low-maintenance for lawns, 239
reseeding lawns, 253–54, **254**
thatch and, 255–56, 255

Grass clippings
as fertilizer, 243, 247
as mulch, 63
Green manure, improving soil with, 70
Groundcovers, 125–26, 125
using in place of grass, 236
Groundhogs, 350
Gutters, storms and, 325
Gypsum, 17–18

H

Hardiness zones, 265–66
Hardscaping
installing, 109–10, 116–17
selecting, 108
Heat zones, 326
Hedges, 270–71
maintenance and, 130–31
pruning, 295–96
Herbicides, lawns and, 248
Herbs
attractive to beneficial insects, 58, 59
freezing, 181
low-maintenance, 103
Hydrangeas, keeping hydrated in
winter, 329

I

Insecticides, 339
Insect pests. *See also* Beneficial insects
aphids, 41
bats and, 340
bug zappers and, 341
chinch bugs, 322–23
earwigs, 335
fall cleanup and, 337
fire ants, 338–40, 340
flea beetles, 61
fruit flies, 202–3
inspecting seedlings for, 41–42, **41**

Insect pests *(cont.)*
mosquitoes, 341–42
nematodes
French marigolds and, 338
plants repellant to, 338
resistant plant varieties and,
337–38
slugs, 334–35, 336–37, <u>336</u>
whiteflies, 41–42, **41**
Invasive plants, 131–32, <u>131</u>
compost piles and, 192
groundcovers as, <u>125</u>
growing in raised beds, 170–71
shrubs, <u>270</u>
trees, <u>270</u>
Irrigation. *See* Watering

J

Japanese beetles, lawns and, 256

K

Kale
growing, 82–83
spacing for, <u>62</u>

L

Ladybugs, 337
Landscape design. *See also* Flowerbeds;
Flowers; Plant selection
choosing plants by function, 116
color in, 217–18, 221
containers as part of, 162 (*See also*
Container gardens)
contractors
finding reliable, 112–13, <u>112</u>
key to working with, <u>112</u>
designers, 109–11, <u>109</u>, <u>110</u>
key to working with, 111
value of, 110–11

designing for easy mowing, 226,
242
disguising eyesores in winter, 149
flowers in (*See* Flowerbeds; Flowers)
garden map, 120–21
garden rooms, 115–16
gathering information about, 109,
110
hardscaping in, 116–17
house interiors and, 117
inspiration for
arboretum, 267
garden shows, <u>232</u>
reference books, 119
layering plants in, <u>128</u>
lighting in, 118–19
master plan for (*See* Master plan)
matching plants to conditions,
122–23
native plants in, 123
off-season interest in, 149
open space in, 122
ornaments in, 222–23
plant shadows in, <u>120</u>
pre-design tasks
considering airborne contaminants,
<u>114</u>
crucial questions, 101
determining public and private
areas in, 114, 115
property analysis, 113–14, 122–23
private areas in, 114
public space in, 114, 115
purchasing plants wisely, 117
reference books and, 119
rock painting in, 144–48, **145**
soil and, 119–20
trees in (*See* Trees)
varying vistas in, 115
wind and, 120
working with nature, 121–22
Zen of, 99–100

Landscape fabric, using, 61–63
Landscaping
    in children's area, 138–44 (*See also*
        Children's gardens)
    recycling in, 133
    rescuing plants for, 132–33
    scrounging materials for, 132
Lasagna gardening and, 21
Lawn care. *See also* Grass; Lawn care
    aerating, 256
    core activities, 240–41
        fertilizing, 241, 250–52, <u>251</u>
        mowing, 226, <u>240</u>, 241, 242–49,
            <u>243</u>, <u>244</u>, <u>248</u>
        watering, 241
    diagnosing problems, 255, <u>257</u>
    fungal diseases of
        preventing, 256–57
    on hillsides, 257
    insect pests of
        chinch bugs, 322–23, 325
        grubs in, 256
        Japanese beetles, 256
    low-maintenance
        grasses for, <u>239</u>
    moles and, 350–51
    reseeding, 253–54
        protecting from birds, **254**
    thatch and, 255–56, <u>255</u>
    trimming and blowing, 247, 249
    urine damage from dogs and, <u>349</u>
    watering, 253, 257, 322
    weeds and, 237–38
Lawns. *See also* Grass; Lawn care
    converting to garden, 18–19, **20**
        lasagna gardening and, 21
    dandelions in, 253
    grass in (*See also* Grass)
        life span of, <u>252</u>
    herbicides and, <u>248</u>
    inviting wildlife into, 258–59
    lawn paint and, <u>327</u>

trees and, 124
using groundcovers in, <u>236</u>
Leeks, <u>46</u>, <u>62</u>
Lettuce
    date to start from seed, <u>46</u>
    growing, 83–85, **85**
    spacing for, <u>62</u>
Light, seedling requirement for, 48
Lighting, in landscape design,
        118–19

M

Maintenance. *See* specific task
Manure, 17, 24
Marigolds, 59, 338
Master plan. *See also* Landscape design
    determining garden goals, 101,
        105–6
    garden map and, 120–21
    hardscaping in, <u>108</u>
    implementing, 107–9
    narrowing it down, 107
    property inventory and analysis
        creating drawing of, 104–5, <u>105</u>
        yard limitations and, 101
    sketching the plan, 106–9, <u>106</u>
Melons
    date to start from seeds, <u>46</u>
    supports for, 55
    typical yield per plant, <u>34</u>
Moles, 350–51, <u>352</u>
Mosquitoes, 341–42
Mowing, 242–49, <u>243</u>, <u>244</u>, <u>248</u>
    blade height for, <u>240</u>, 241, 243
    checking yard for litter, 244–45
    clothing for, 245
    equipment maintenance, 244, 247,
        248–49
        blade sharpness, 245–46
        gasing up, 244, 249
    flowerbeds and, 226, 242

Weeds
    as clue to soil type, 11–12, <u>13</u>
    controlling in flowerbeds, 218
    landscape fabric and, 61–63
    in lawns, 237–38
    soil solarizing and, 23
Whiteflies, inspecting plants for, 41–42,
        41
Wildlife, inviting into lawns, 258–59.
        See also Animal pests
Wind
    considering in landscape design, 120
    protecting trees and shrubs from in
        winter, 330
    rooftop gardens and, 182

Witch hazel, 272
Wood ashes, <u>26</u>
Worms. *See also* Vermicomposting
    attracting to garden, 20
    watering and, 20

Z

Zucchini
    growing, 95–97
    typical yield per plant, <u>34</u>